An Uncommon Tongue

This book explores the theme of language usage in its widest sense: usage as what we say or write; usage as a social question; usage as a literary convention; usage and creativity. Walter Nash reflects, with wit, precision and insight, on the practice and status of the English language in the modern world, and the demands it makes on its academic disciplines.

The argument develops from the notion of Standard English and the individual user, through technical questions of usage, to considerations of composition and literary creativity, with a concluding chapter on English as a world language.

Nash argues persuasively that the study of usage transcends both the 'prescriptive' and 'descriptive' and is ultimately 'constructive', displaying the resources of language, and exploring their use.

Walter Nash, who is Emeritus Professor of Modern English Language at the University of Nottingham, has had a wide experience of teaching at universities and colleges in Britain and Europe. His academic interests include English usage, composition, stylistics, rhetoric and the language of literature. Recent publications in these fields include *Rhetoric, The Wit of Persuasion* (1989), *Language in Popular Fiction* (1990) and (in collaboration with Ronald Carter) *Seeing Through Language* (1991).

An Uncommon Tongue

The uses and resources of English

Walter Nash

London and New York

First published in 1992 by
Routledge
11 New Fetter Lane, London EC4P 4EE

Simultaneously published in the USA and Canada
by Routledge
a division of Routledge, Chapman and Hall, Inc.
29 West 35th Street, New York, NY 10001

Typeset in 10/12pt Times by
Selectmove, London
Printed in Great Britain by
T J Press (Padstow) Ltd, Padstow, Cornwall

British Library Cataloguing in Publication Data
Nash, Walter
    An uncommon tongue: the uses and resources of English.
    I. Title
    428

Library of Congress Cataloging in Publication Data
Nash, Walter.
    An uncommon tongue: the uses and resources of English/Walter Nash.
    p. cm.
    Includes bibliographical references and index.
    1. English language–Social aspects. 2. English language–Usage.
I. Title.
PE1074.75.N37 1992
420–dc20

ISBN 0 415 06360 4
        0 415 06361 2 (pbk)

But I know not how it comes to pass, that Professors in most Arts and Sciences, are generally the worst qualified to explain their Meanings to those who are not of their Tribe.

Jonathan Swift, *A Letter to a Young Gentleman*

Contents

Preface

This book is a collection of lectures given by me in recent years at universities in Britain and Europe; inasmuch as they typify my activities and academic interests, they are collectively a sort of *apologia pro vita mea*, an explanation offered to anybody who might very properly wonder what a Professor of Modern English Language does while other people are working hard in less privileged occupations. The audiences consisted usually of undergraduates, but sometimes of conference participants or members of the general public. Since these were more or less formal occasions, I spoke from scripts which in a few instances (chapters 2, 5 and 9) were subsequently claimed by colleagues editing collections of papers or conference reports. Otherwise the text of my lectures is here published for the first time, with little or no re-working of the delivery script. I have occasionally deleted a no longer relevant paragraph, dropped an allusion to yesterday's news, or expanded a possibly obscure point; in general, however, I have tried to present these discourses in their original form and wording, not attempting to hide or neutralize the symptoms of a speaker intent on a personal engagement with his topic and his hearers. The resultant impression for some readers may be of odd vagaries of tone from one piece to the next; but while I would have to agree that the lectures reflect different moods, in adjustment to different audiences, I do not think that the continuity of address to a central theme is essentially impaired.

That theme is stated in my sub-title: the uses and resources of the English language. By 'resources' I understand those elements of form and organization on which we routinely draw, and which are codified in grammars, dictionaries and other descriptive or instructional texts. To such sources we look for assurance in matters of usage, that is, in the search for a standard or consensus of practice in vocabulary, idiom and grammatical construction. 'Usage', however, overlaps with 'use'; and by 'use', in this book, I mean the exercise of language in the communicative skills of interaction, of composition and of literary creativeness. The argument, that a sense of 'usage' accumulates in the 'uses' that establish more than one kind of standard, is implied in the sequence of the papers, which are presented here in psychological order (as perceived by me) rather than in actual order of composition. The last paper in the volume, the text of my inaugural lecture as Professor of Modern English Language, may appear to be extraneous to my general theme, but I do not by any means consider it so; for me it has the contextual relevance of a postscript, recalling themes touched upon in preceding chapters, and dwelling above all on the resources of the English language and the ingenuity of speakers who have carried it round the world and contributed to its growth and influence. As to that influence, I am not so far gone in foolish patriotism as to believe that English rules, OK? – and yet I am persuaded that it is an uncommon tongue.

WN
University of Nottingham

1 Standards and stuff

It is a gaudy scrap of paper, a page torn from the monthly catalogue of a book club to which I once belonged, and from which, as I recall, I had some difficulty in escaping. I see why I have kept this memento, for what it advertises – along with a diet and exercise programme specially designed for heavy hips and thighs – is a book on English usage. I do not really care about diet, and I am resigned to the proposition that most of my body's fat slumps irresistibly into its lower half, but I still live in hope of learning more about my native language, and do not easily resist anything that promises to increase my command of it.

My book club bargain appears to have promised to do just that. The blurb challenges potential readers to look into their hearts and discover their own inadequacies. **Do you know**, it demands – in bold type – **when to use which or that, your and you're, elder and eldest? Or even** – it continues, just in case we were lucky enough to clear these preliminary hurdles – **when to use the Present Perfect Continuous?** Here people who have been using the Present Perfect Continuous all their lives without thinking too much about it may perhaps wonder if they have been doing the right thing. But the advertisement speaks reassuringly. *Well, don't panic!* it cries, in italics. *This splendid book will help. It is a simple and practical guide to improving your written and spoken English.* Then the copywriter, faced with the challenge of describing marvels, delineates them in italics and bold print together. It appears that the book is furnished with hundreds of exercises, *covering everything from **the Indefinite Article** to **Adjectives, Prepositions** and **Reported or Indirect Speech***. Perhaps I am professionally jealous, but it seems to me that this grand offer amounts to rather little; to boast of 'covering everything from the Indefinite Article to Prepositions' is like shouting your intention to run the gamut of complexities from A to B.

That, however, is not my first and last objection to this puff for proper English. What raises my hackles is the cool commercial playing on the fears and faltering confidence of people who are bullied into thinking that their mother-tongue is their worst enemy, keeping them out of tea-rooms, boardrooms and the better sort of bedrooms, leaving them tongue-tied and manacled among the masses who will never achieve success. There is a kind of blackmail in this, all the more objectionable for being practised by someone who, on this showing, would hardly know the Present Perfect Continuous from a penny whistle. But what visions of insupportable anxiety it raises! I imagine the restless nights, the hot, moist pillows, the recurrent chagrin of worthily ambitious folk held down, as they see it, by their ignorance of Reported or Indirect Speech, their painful inability to sort out 'elder' from 'eldest'. 'Don't you worry, old chap', I want to tell them, 'never you mind, my dear, it's *your* language, you have a right to it, go ahead and use it and see how you get on. It's a bit like riding a bicycle, really. You only wobble when you worry about the theory of it'. I would perhaps not be wholly prudent in saying that, because I cannot believe that go-as-you-please and free-for-all work any better in language than they do in other forms of social activity; but I would a thousand times rather that people should discover things for themselves than that they should be obliged to suffer the apprehension and guilt of being shut out from ineffable secrets which only the chosen may disclose and share.

Let us agree that people in an English-speaking country need to know English. So much is self-evident – until we venture to ask what is meant by 'know'. The question raises the possibilities of at least three kinds of 'knowing'. In one very important sense, 'knowing' the language means having access to a primary source of power. The language we 'know', for the purposes of administrative convenience and social recognition, is a preferred dialect, variously enjoined upon us by hostesses, copy editors and the chairfolk of interviewing boards. It is a form of etiquette and safe conduct, and in certain situations becomes an instrument of social judgement. We may be allowed to make fun of it, but we neglect it at our peril. Candidates for positions of responsibility with suitable emoluments, applicants for membership of the most desirable clubs, aspirants to literary and academic honours, even politicians, do not say 'me and the wife', or 'we was', and they do not call two glasses of sherry 'a couple of bevvies'. Nor, for that matter, do they refer to 'my good lady and self'. They say 'my wife and I', and 'we were' and 'cocktails', not because such expressions are more lucid and forcible but because, as we all know, this is the way to get on in the world.

A second kind of knowing is knowing *about*: knowing about the structure of the language, about the forms it takes in speech or on the page, and consequently being able to talk about these forms. It is the metalanguage – the language in which we talk *about* language – that requires terms like Present Perfect Continuous, and it is with the suitability and consistent use of the metalanguage that many academic discussions are concerned, to the puzzlement and frequent exasperation of laypersons. Scholars, like other people, are wedded to their own customs. It happens that in describing constructions of the type 'We have been discussing the new proposals', I would not use the term Present Perfect Continuous, but would prefer Present Perfective Progressive. I have my reasons for this, notably a need, as I see it, to distinguish terminologically between *tense*, the reference to a point in time, and *aspect*, the way in which the action of the verb is interpreted with respect to time. In 'I kissed the redhead', 'kissed' is in the past tense; in 'I was kissing the redhead when this guy with the tattooed nose came into the bar', the construction 'was kissing' expresses an aspect of the action, called the progressive, as well as the time (past) of the event, and is accordingly labelled Past Progressive. In 'I had been thinking about kissing the redhead when this guy with the tattooed nose began behaving unsociably, like he had been reading my thoughts or something', 'had been thinking' and 'had been reading' express not only 'pastness' but also two kinds of aspect, the progressive and the perfective (meaning the aspect of an action completed over a stretch of time, or within a 'time zone'); they are therefore described as examples of the Past Perfective Progressive. The English constructions traditionally labelled 'Perfect' and 'Pluperfect', following the descriptive practice of Latin grammar, are not primarily expressive of *tense*; their function is rather to convey *aspect*, for which reason it is preferable to refer to them as 'Perfective'.[1] 'So what?' cries the average layperson, as well he or she might. The metalanguage is the grammarian's business, and expresses the grammarian's view of linguistic structure. Its only value for the laity must lie in its potential expediency in clarifying matters of usage. To ask a non-grammarian the question 'Do you know when to use the Present Perfect Continuous (or Present Perfective Progressive)?' is therefore to raise a pseudo-problem. It suggests that ordinary people of sound mind and sturdy mother-wit choose their constructions as they might choose neckties or petticoats, to fit the mood of some social occasion. It further suggests that these same people do not share the beatitude of Molière's comic hero, Monsieur

Jourdain, who discovered that he had been speaking prose all his life without knowing it. You do not have to know *when* to say 'I have been writing some letters', as opposed to 'I have written some letters' or 'I wrote some letters'. You have been making the right choice at the right moment for most of your life. Knowing *why* is perhaps a different matter; but that, too, can be left to the grammarian, until the knowledge is required to sort out a practical problem.

For it is certainly the need for knowledge of a pragmatic kind, alias skill, in the vulgar tongue called 'know-how', that sends the Ordinary User (somehow that category calls for capitals) on what is too often an unavailing search for bibliographical guidance. The relevant questions are not 'Do you know when to use which or that, your and you're, elder and eldest?'; but rather, 'Do you know how to write a letter? Make a speech? Frame an argument? Deliver a reproof? Rebut an accusation? Make a polite enquiry? Express condolences? Tell a benevolent lie? Soften a hurtful truth? Say a great deal without revealing anything much? Say the very little that says it all?' In short – 'Do you know how to make your native language reflect your thinking and feeling, conduct your interactions, define your social position, negotiate your difficulties and ambitions, day in, day out, as life goes by?' Books do not answer these questions, the replies to which, could they be set down and brought together in a single volume, would amount to a schooling in the most valuable knowledge: the knowledge of how to use language creatively, in its diverse functions.

Now we have proposed three ways of 'knowing' English: a knowledge of the power dialect, a knowledge of linguistic structures and descriptions, and a knowledge of language in creative action. The last of these is undoubtedly of the most general interest, and the second presents sharp challenges to minds that love the rigours of analysis and codification, but it is always the first that draws public attention, always this to which we refer when we speak of a Standard. Yet here we catch a glimpse of a notoriously elusive term. What does it mean, this 'Standard'? In my copy of the two-volume *Shorter Oxford English Dictionary*, Standard English is defined as 'that form of the English language which is spoken (with modifications) by the generality of cultured people in Great Britain'.[2] The definition begs the question of what 'cultured' means, and is in addition blatantly insular; 'Standard English' is a term not unknown to Americans, Australians and others who in using it care little enough about what goes on in Great Britain. Nevertheless, this dictionary definition manages to convey an essential feature of Standard, wherever the term is used: the notion of status.

That notion is present in some of the names that have been given during the present century to socially approved forms of British English: for example, 'Oxford English' and 'BBC English', names now somewhat out of date since the Oxford drawl came to a glottal stop, the 'wireless' gave place to radio and TV, and pomaded gentlemen in Portland Place were no longer obliged to don evening dress to read the news.[3] Labels like 'Oxford English' denoted a style of pronunciation, regarded with a mixture of envy and resentment by those who had not acquired it. You will doubtless remember D.H. Lawrence's poem on 'The Oxford Voice':

When you hear it languishing
and hooing and cooing and sidling through the front teeth
  the Oxford voice
    or worse still
  the would-be Oxford voice
you don't even laugh any more, you can't

For every blooming bird is an Oxford cuckoo nowadays.
You can't sit on the bus or in the tube
  but it breathes gently and languishingly in the back of your neck.

That typical piece of Lawrentian spleen is a response to a way of speech but not to a way of vocabulary or grammar. Lawrence may have detested Oxford English, but as a writer he sedulously observed the conventions, in lexicon and syntax, of Standard English – or, as he might very well have put it, the King's English.[4]

We still occasionally hear that expression, though you might have thought it would have died out by now; after all, a Queen has been reigning over us for the best part of forty years. If the phrase lives on, it is almost certainly because it is the title of a very well known book by H.W. and F.G. Fowler. It is worth reminding ourselves of the date of publication of this classic: 1906, three years after the accession of King Edward VII. The title thus adroitly served three purposes. It announced a book on the very latest condition of the English language; it recalled a centuries-old phrase, with its intimations of authority and prestige; and it made a patriotic obeisance in the direction of Buckingham Palace.[5] The Fowlers were, in their chosen field, men of great and lasting achievement. You can hardly discuss usage without mentioning the name Fowler. They were also, it has to be said, middle-class mandarins, whose examples of 'correct' usage often bear the credentials of a peculiar loftiness. Here they are, for example, illustrating the difference between 'one' used as a so-called 'indefinite pronoun' (as in 'One does one's job as well as one can') and as a 'numeral pronoun' (in, for instance, 'One [of them] did his job badly'). The Fowlers exemplify in a way that suggests the best people seen in the best settings – strolling, it may be, through the park:

> One does not forget *one's* own name: I saw one of them drop *his* cigar, *her* muff, *its* leaves.[6]

There is nothing at all wrong with this, except its comic conveyance of the notion that the Fowlers were writing for persons of the cigar-smoking, muff-carrying, promenading class, an impression not dispelled anywhere else in the book by exemplary reference to somewhat humbler personnel. These authors, indeed, refer explicitly and flatteringly to 'the ordinary man, of average intelligence and middle-class position', and rather less flatteringly to 'the masses' and 'the vast number of people who are incapable of appreciating finer shades of meaning'.[7] This arrogance would be insufferable if it were not just a little comic. Had the Fowlers bothered to take an attentive walk through a street market they might have learned something about finer shades of meaning among the masses, though they may not have seen anyone drop his cigar or her muff.

But the Fowlers evidently thought of themselves as representing Standard, or 'correct' English, the usage of the well-educated and the well-bred. Their views on language are in no way different from those concisely expressed nearly a century and a half earlier by Lord Chesterfield:

> The common people of every country speak their own language very ill; the people of fashion (as they are called) speak it better, but not always correctly, because they are not always people of letters. Those who speak their own language the most accurately are those who have learning and are at the same time in the polite world; at least their language will be reckoned the standard of the language of that country.[8]

This, incidentally, is an early occurrence of the term 'standard' in reference to language. Chesterfield's observation is most memorable, however, for its presentation of Standard as a practice with two complementary elements, the social and the literary.[9]

The idea of Standard is substantially based in the idea of social class; and the class-base is in its turn related to political and economic ideas which we can trace back to the Middle Ages. Here, for example, is a comment on the English language made in the fourteenth century by a West Countryman, John Trevisa:

> All the speech of the northerners, particularly at York, is so abrupt, piercing, harsh and outlandish, that we southerners can barely understand it. I believe this to be because they live near to strangers and foreigners with alien speech, and because the kings of England always live far away from that region. . . . The reason why they keep to the south rather than the north may be that the south has better arable land, more people, finer cities, and more profitable ports.[10]

Although this passage, well known to historians of the mother-tongue, does not explicitly use the phrase 'the King's English', it strongly implies the concept. It is striking, furthermore, as a piece of sociolinguistic explanation. The standard is where the king is; but the king is where he is for mainly economic reasons. Urban life, commerce and a high density of population, all have their influence on the location of the court, and the court has its influence on the shaping of a standard language. Trevisa's analysis is only one instance (though possibly the earliest in English) of a historic connection between socio-economic power and the evolution of Standard. Later ages tell their stories of power-shift and social change, with an implied redefinition of the governors of the language. H.C. Wyld writes excellently on this theme, alluding to 'the social, political, and economic events in our history which have resulted in bringing different classes of the population into positions of prominence and power in the State, and the consequent reduction in the influence of the older governing classes':

> Among these events . . . are the break-up of the feudal system, which upset temporarily the old social conditions and relations; the extinction of most of the ancient baronial families in the Wars of the Roses; the disendowment of the monasteries, and the enriching of the king's tools and agents, which produced an entirely new class of territorial magnates in Henry VIII's time; the rise of the great merchants in the towns in the late Middle Ages, and the further growth of this class, which under Henry and Elizabeth produced men of the type of Gresham; the Parliamentary Wars and the social upheaval of the Protectorate; the enormous growth of commerce and industry, and the rise of banking during the eighteenth and early nineteenth centuries; and especially, perhaps, the development of steam in manufactures, and the

building of railways. By these means many families, in the course of two generations, passed from the shop, the hand-loom, the plough-tail, or from trundling the wheelbarrow, into the great land-owning classes, and became endowed with political influence, and, occasionally, with political insight, one or both of which often rapidly led them into the peerage.[11]

Seventy years have lapsed since that passage was written, and an updating would find much to add in the way of social, political and technological change. Language reflects in its smallest details current shifts in social power and prestige. If we listen and read attentively, we can detect in our own time modifications in the power dialect brought about by the success of the young and upwardly mobile, not only among the brokers and so-called wealth creators, but also by the 'stars' in the world of entertainment, by the leaders in the various provinces of fashion and by the opinion formers in the domain of journalism.

But the story of Standard is not wholly concerned with the history of dominant classes and social groups. It also involves the companion history of writing for administrative, literary and scientific purposes. The advent of the printing house is of obvious importance in the evolution of a literary standard. One of the consequences of the circulation of increasingly large quantities of printed material is that conventions are developed, by writers reading the work of other writers, and hence by printers setting up what the writers produce. This is important; in an age when we are beset by print, from the moment the junk mail flops through the letter-box in the morning until the private hour when we take up our bedtime reading, we forget how deeply we are indebted to print for our notions of what language is. Even more important than the printing house are those institutions which have defined for us our ideas of propriety and efficiency in the style of the written language. Among those institutions (which include the Universities, the Church, the Civil Service and the Press) the most significant, historically, must be the Royal Society, founded by Charles II in 1662, for the advancement of science.

How odd it seems to reflect that the standards of expository prose, as we now commonly understand them, may have been evolved initially at the behest of scientists impatient with the fanciful language of literary men. Yet the reflection has its substance in historical fact. Part of the programme of the Royal Society in the 1660s was a proposal to bring the English language under rule: to purge it of its inconsistencies, ambiguities, confusions; to combine lucid expression with regular construction and thus to create a prose idiom at least approximately fit for the transactions of philosophy and science. A committee was actually appointed to discuss the regulation of the language, but in the fashion of academic committees it passed peacefully away, among good resolutions, after only a few meetings. The regulatory spirit, however, rose up to haunt the world of polite letters; and the regulator it most commonly offered to the aberrant and perplexed was Latin, a language gloriously dead, immutable, and therefore (unlike English) incorruptible. John Dryden said that when his English puzzled him, he would translate it into Latin and so back again into English, to be sure of saying what he meant to say.[12] This is often quoted as an oddity, eccentric to the point of silliness; but in fact there is a great deal to be said for using another language as a point of reference from which to criticize and more fully understand your own – especially if, as in Dryden's case, you have comparatively few native grammarians to help you out of your puzzlements. Latin is a language in which relationships between words are very precisely encoded in the written text (the popular assertion is that Latin is 'logical'). This cannot always be said of English, in which meanings sometimes have to be retrieved from utterance or text without the guidance of explicit formal clues to 'agreement', 'case' and so forth. For example:

Dick had his car insured

and

Dick had his car stolen.

In the first of these sentences, Dick is what is known as the 'agent'; he instructs someone to insure his car. The second sentence seems to be constructed in exactly the same way, but in this instance we can hardly suppose that Dick is an agent, instructing someone to steal his car. His role is no longer that of the doer, but rather, someone who is done by, done over, or simply *done*. His role now is that of the patient, or victim. We might say that in the two sentences Dick is in a different *case* – case being a formal grammatical feature, an explicit clue, as it were, which English generally lacks but which Latin regularly supplies.[13] Of course I do not mean to suggest that John Dryden was ever troubled by the problem of insuring his car or having it stolen. I use the example only to represent the kind of difficulty Dryden had in mind – the frequent 'opacity' of English by comparison with the apparent 'lucidity' of Latin.

Latin has had a great deal to do with the evolution of academic, expository or generally 'educated' prose in English. Deference to it as an arbiter has been in some ways useful, but it has also burdened us with notorious myths of prescription: for example, the appeal to etymological sense, which dictates that A is 'different *from*' B; the stylistic embargo on prepositions at the ends of sentences and coordinating conjunctions at the beginnings; the absurd dislike of putting the word 'however' first in a sentence because the models and masters of Latin prose do not put *autem* or *tamen* first; and so on and on, generating beliefs that nurture the fear that drives decent people into a panic over 'which' and 'that', 'elder' and 'eldest' – the fear of not being 'correct'.

And yet it is not an utterly disreputable idea, this notion of correctness, of a universal and exclusive standard which can be prescribed as a model of procedure for those who are in doubt. At least it is arguable that grammars and dictionaries, if they are to be made at all, require assumptions, possibly tacit, about what is usual, what will be most widely understood, what will pass muster in most places, between most persons, among most people. Looked at from one point of view, Standard presents a democratic aspect, as the outcome of a consensus. From another point of view, however, it can suggest an exclusiveness which is potentially harmful. The harm is not in snobbery, a vice from which few of us are wholly immune in every possible respect; it is the entrenchment of snobbery in positions of morality and rectitude that does the damage.

Because of its 'illogical' ways – that is, because it does not appear to keep a tidy textual surface of distinctly signalled verbal relationships – English readily breeds little problems of meaning for enthusiasts to bicker over. Take, for instance, this sentence: 'The parents objected to the teachers sending children home.' What would you suppose to be the 'correct' way of writing that down? Would you, or would you not, put an apostrophe after 'teachers'? If you choose to put in an apostrophe, you are suggesting a possessive relationship between 'teachers' and 'sending'; in other words, you mark 'sending' as a noun, even though it is derived from the verb 'to send'. This is what is meant by *gerund*, commonly defined as a 'verbal noun'. But if you write no apostrophe, you imply that 'sending' is to be read as a verb, specifically as a present participle. To make the issue a little clearer, let us rewrite the content of this sentence in two forms: 'They objected to *their* sending children home', and 'They objected to *them* sending children home'. There are people who would worry a great deal, and perhaps even quarrel a great deal about the 'correct' form.

But if meaning is the sole criterion, does the formal distinction matter very much? In the examples just quoted, surely not, and surely not in the following:

It is no use him (his) doing it.
Excuse me (my) interrupting you.
I was annoyed by Tom (Tom's) hesitating.
Without us (our) hearing the man, the facts cannot be got at.
Without the man (man's) telling us himself, we can never know.

Surely not, we say, and yet the originators of those examples, the mandarin brothers Fowler, find only the versions with a gerund – 'It is no use his doing it', 'Excuse my interrupting you' – acceptable as civilized English. They suggest that the alternatives would be considered 'ignorant vulgarisms' among 'those who, without being well versed in grammar, are habitually careful how they speak and write'.[14] Here they articulate a prejudice still quite commonly voiced. The question it implies is not 'What do you mean?' but 'What sort of person are you?'. H.W. Fowler invented a sin called the Fused Participle (represented by 'excuse me interrupting you', etc.), and went on deploring the morals of those who committed it, even after his views had been substantially criticized by the distinguished Danish linguist, Otto Jespersen. Jespersen was able to demonstrate not only that the so-called fused participle was a natural development in English syntax, but also that it had been used by generations of 'good' writers from Jonathan Swift down to George Bernard Shaw.[15] Fowler was unimpressed. 'I confess', he said, 'to attaching more importance to my instinctive repugnance for "without you being" than to Professor Jespersen's demonstration that it had been said by more respectable authors than I had supposed'. In other words, a gentleman may drop his cigar, but he will never fuse his participles.[16]

Anyone who feels imperilled by the judgements implied in the traditional representations of Standard has recourse to at least two psychological defences. One of these is to challenge that notion of Standard which requires our assent to a view of language as a social phenomenon organized simply and vertically: simply, because it assumes one language, or one 'best form', and vertically, because it implies the existence of the best people ('best authors', 'best speakers') whose practice judges that of others standing lower in the scale of social and intellectual excellence.

This may be the view that informs our textbooks, but it is not the only way of looking at language functioning in society. Against the image of a simple, 'vertical' organization, we may set that of a complex, 'horizontal' array of types or varieties of usage, each with its own demands and conventions. The conventions of academic prose, for example, differ from those of journalism. The same language is at work, but under different conditions, one of the relevant considerations being that the journalist has always to work to a word-count. That in itself is enough to promote the development and regular use of some types of construction that would not be considered appropriate to academic prose, but which could be regarded as 'standard' in journalistic composition. (An example of this is the preference for 'premodified' noun phrases, as in 'the Channel Tunnel planning controversy', over lengthier 'postmodifying' structures, as in 'the controversy over the planning of the Channel Tunnel'.) The evolution of standard practices within each variety of English is apparent to anyone who tries to observe the language tolerantly, without preconceptions about what must be 'vulgar', or 'inferior', or marginal or aberrant. Different types of English, particularly of written English, involve diverse features of language management: layout on the page; vocabulary; the preferred idiom of the particular register; the accepted forms of phrase and sentence-structure. There is 'correctness' within each type. Or rather say, that the governing requirement is not for 'correctness', but *acceptability*. Do you ask me to act as an arbiter of language? Then tell me what the occasion is, whether the medium is speech or writing, whether we have to do with an exposition or an interaction, if an interaction, who the interactants are, where the transaction takes place, when, and for what purpose – and perhaps I will then be able to assess the acceptability of words spoken or written.

The second defensive resort for those who feel themselves victimized by the potential tyranny of Standard is the consciousness of change and the futility of trying to bully language and its users. The history of English since the eighteenth century is full of vain attempts to prescribe some usages and damn others. Samuel Johnson struggled against the idiom 'to make money', which he said ought to be 'to get money'; Lady Holland, a contemporary of Sheridan, grumbled that she 'could not break him of saying "gentlemanly", though he allowed it was wrong' (she preferred 'gentlemanlike'); Coleridge disliked such forms as 'gifted' and 'monied', arguing that we might as well carry the analogy through and talk about people being 'shillinged' or 'pounded'; the Fowlers for various reasons deplored the impudence of words now considered wholly respectable, such as 'amoral', 'banal', 'bureaucracy', 'distinguished', 'femininity', 'meticulous' and 'racial'.[17]

The perception of change in old and trusted meanings is always likely to irk those of us who think we have the beauty and efficiency of the language at heart. I still grumble when 'refute' is used in the sense of 'to deny', but that change is now accomplished in British English, and what is more, 'rebut' is going the same way. I do not think that 'cohort' should mean 'follower', 'henchman', but it is increasingly used as though it did, by people who never had to spend Monday afternoons desperately trying to make sense of *De Bello Gallico*; and I am a little worried about 'compatriot', which I have seen used, in a reputable newspaper, in the sense of 'colleague'. It is perhaps destined to make a match with 'ex-patriot', which is one of the new journalistic spellings of 'expatriate', and which is often shortened to 'ex-pat'. About 'ex-pat' I feel much as Swift felt about 'mob' – which is to say, I feel a refined and humorous fury.[18] But this is to no avail; so many of our words are upstarts, bustling among usurped forms and meanings, and in most cases we do not know it, and are quite happy with our ignorance.

The vocabulary of English has never been 'fixed', as the reforming scholars of the eighteenth century would have wished; it is shifting all the time in its forms and references. No less inexorable, though perhaps less frequently noted, are changes in syntactic construction. A typical case, illustrating the influence of American usage on British English, is that of 'persuade' and 'convince'. Twenty years ago, right-thinking Britons construed 'persuade' with a following infinitive clause ('They persuaded him to release the hostages') and 'convince' with a 'that'-clause ('They convinced him that he should release the hostages'). Then, during the next decades, a blend-construction, already established in American English, began to creep in: 'They convinced him to release the hostages.' This is doubtless enough to set a decent fellow's teeth on edge, but it will have to be endured, like 'refute' and 'cohort', and even 'compatriot' – for by the time a usage becomes visible in the daily newspapers it is nearly always too late to attempt a suppression.[19]

Linguistic change is, in any case, a potential liberator; it frees us, if we are wise, from the bondage of *must* – though some changes may seem to deliver us from the stocks in order to put us into manacles. 'The question is, which is to be master – that's all', said Humpty Dumpty, usefully reminding us that we have some control over how we behave and how we use the facilities at our disposal. The facility of language may indeed benefit from the kind of idiomatic change that exploits a parallel or explores a vacancy in the system. A case in point is the establishment in English of 'hopefully' as a commentary disjunct, an innovation which, far from going unnoticed, has attracted a good deal of righteous odium. One American critic has cried out, in anguish, 'I have declared eternal war on this bastard adverb', and another, 'This is one that makes me physically ill'.[20] The history of this development is fairly simple. Compare these sentences:

To travel happily is better than to arrive.
Happily, to travel is better than to arrive.

In the first, 'happily' is a manner adverb ('to travel in a happy manner'), and nobody would dispute that this is a well-formed English sentence. Nor could any objection be raised to the second example, although 'happily' in that instance is not a manner adverb, and means something different. It functions as a commentary disjunct (a word disjoined from its companion statement, but making some kind of comment on it), and its meaning may be paraphrased as 'It is a happy circumstance that . . .'. A disjunct of this type, commenting on the content of what is asserted, may take up more than one position in the sentence, provided that it is always clearly disjoined by commas, e.g. 'Happily, to travel is better than to arrive'; 'To travel, happily, is better than to arrive' and 'To travel is better than to arrive, happily'.[21]
Now compare these:

To travel hopefully is better than to arrive.
Hopefully, to travel is better than to arrive.

The correspondence with the preceding pair of examples must be quite obvious; the case is in no way altered, for we have once again a manner adverb in the first sentence, and in the second a commentary disjunct paraphrasable as 'it is to be hoped that . . .' or 'we may hope that'. Long before the controversial use of 'hopefully' came along, it was possible to marshal words like 'happily', 'fortunately', 'foolishly', 'cleverly', in dual roles, as manner adverbs or disjuncts: 'He spent all his money foolishly' or 'Foolishly, he spent all his money'; 'He landed fortunately in a haystack' or 'He landed in a haystack, fortunately'; 'She did not weave all of the tapestry cleverly', 'Cleverly, she did not weave all of the tapestry'. All the howling about 'hopefully', all the moralizing and execration, ignored the fact that a pattern of usage already existed, and that the hated word was merely taking up an available position. Other words of the same kind are currently being treated in the same way. One of them is 'regretfully', which is now being used as a commentary disjunct with the meaning 'It is to be regretted that . . .' ('Regretfully, we cannot serve early morning tea'). This usage might be criticized on the grounds that we already have a perfectly adequate commentary disjunct in 'regrettably', and that there can be no good reason for pressing an impostor into service. Users, however, are stubbornly unanswerable to the gods of good reason.[22]

Although 'users' and 'usage' are words related in form and meaning, they diverge from each other in psychological and social implications. The implication of 'usage', when all is said and done, is normative and authoritarian. There are but two paces from 'what *may* be said or written', to 'what *ought to* be said or written', to 'what *must* be said or written'. 'User', on the other hand, implies choice – not utterly free choice, but choice through democratic consensus. Users make the usage, democratically; the usage tends to intimidate the users, autocratically. But Humpty Dumpty was right, and the question is which is to be master. Let us create a Standard – or better still, let us create *standards* which command our assent because we understand how and why they have come into being and because we realize that they are not immutable laws but conventions of human behaviour, subject to time and change. And let us never again be afraid of splitting our infinitives, fusing our participles, or even of not knowing when to use the Present Perfect Continuous, for a standard is one thing and stuff is another.

The text of a lecture delivered in March 1990 to the Nottingham University Graduates' Association.

2 Usage, users and the used

And out of the ground the Lord God formed every beast of the field, and every fowl of the air; and brought them unto Adam to see what he would call them; and whatsoever Adam called them, that was the name thereof.

Genesis, 2:19

There's a cool web of language winds us in,
Retreat from too much joy and too much fear;
We grow sea-green at last and coldly die
In brininess and volubility.

Robert Graves

I recall my pleasure, as a student, on coming across an old treatise, the author of which was ready to affirm that the language spoken in the Garden of Eden was English. The rhetorical possibilities of this charmed me. In imagination I reconstructed the intonations of Eve and the dialect of the serpent; I particularly liked to picture that momentous episode recorded in the book of Genesis, describing how God presented the beasts and birds for Adam to name. How jolly it was to think of that old rogue, our aboriginal abecedarian ancestor, reclining on some grassy knoll, clad only in his curls and his *insouciance*, calling out, in bell-bright Britannic tones, 'horse!', 'cow!', 'pussy-cat!', 'duck!', while the Almighty, smiling with the pleasure of a parent whose offspring is performing nicely, led in the livestock. It was, you might say, a green thought in the shade of a green time; for in that postwar year of our Lord, everything in the garden *was* lovely, and even if English was not to be considered literally as the language of Eden, there was at any rate a poetical rightness in the notion.

But now we are more than forty years on, with other expectations of the world, and other views of language. No longer ours the simple confidence of Adam's naked response to experience; no longer the happy supposition that words name things, and that proper words in proper places will name all things properly; no longer for us the conviction of being the user, the controller, the agent, but always the suspicion of being the used, the victim, swaddled in language, huddled in it, our realities of thought and feeling coddled in it. But I am not going to indulge in a jeremiad bewailing the decline of the English tongue. What I want to suggest is simply this: that if language purports in any way to mediate what we truly perceive, feel and think – and I know how many questions that raises – then in current usage there are features, almost mechanisms, that promote habitual flight *from* the direct perception, the unrehearsed feeling, the clear thought. I would add that I find these mechanisms most busily operative in a particular kind of English: not the English of poets and men of letters, not the English of the street and the workplace even, but the English of the weekly journals, of the better newspapers, of TV reports, of public debate on social and political matters. I said *a particular kind* of English, and I have promptly named several kinds. Then let us lump them together and call them collectively Public Transaction English, or PTE for short. The realm of PTE, I may say, is a long way from Eden; if Adam had been a PTE speaker, he would not have called a cow a cow. He would have called it a milk production facility.

ABSTRACTEDNESS

In language, I suppose, as in personality, there are virtues that entail vices. Two virtues of language that I now have in mind are the very sources of its growth: the power of abstraction, and the power of metaphor, or figurative extension and transference. It is hard to see how language could extend its authority over our experience if it were not possible to abstract, to generalize and to make the figurative analogies that inform perception. The language of science, for example, requires the naming of categories and concepts; often, the names it finds are in some way figurative, conveying perceptions of the scientist in terms that present analogies with common experience.[1] Without the abstract and the figurative all discourse would be gravely impaired. Yet these central virtues have their attendant vices. The power of abstraction is dogged by a failing which I shall call 'abstractedness'; and the power of metaphor is continually dwindling into 'tropery' (I have been obliged here to invent a word, a blend of 'trope' and 'frippery' or 'trumpery'). PTE is full of abstractedness, of tropery, and consequently its power to make clear, sensible propositions is impaired.

By 'abstractedness' I mean perhaps something more than *abstractitis* – the word employed in Fowler's *Modern English Usage*.[2] Abstractitis, as I understand it, is a malady of usage having its germ in the pretentiousness of the user; thus if I talk about 'maximizing my endeavours in the area of orthodontic hygiene' instead of 'cleaning my teeth as often as possible', I am suffering from abstractitis. Abstractedness is this, and also much that is not so obvious as this. Abstractedness is ingrained in the language itself, at all levels from the morpheme, the smallest meaningful particle, up to the complex sentence.[3] The elaborate and subtle resources which enable us to symbolize experience become, if we are not careful, the devices that set experience at an almost irretrievable remove.

What I am talking about is no doubt a condition deplored by all right-thinking citizens, from Amsterdam to the Antipodes, whatever their native tongues may be. It does seem to me, however, that each language, in its historical development, lays its own paths of abstractedness. As far as English is concerned, there is one major historical characteristic that always attracts attention, as a source of blessings and a well-spring of problems. I refer to the fact that our language has broad Germanic foundations, upon which time, literature and technology have erected a great superstructure, of French and Latin and Greek. This is of course very largely a superstructure of vocabulary, and it is an asset for which every writer of English must be profoundly grateful. I will not enlarge on this, and I will resist the temptation to develop the view that this asset is potentially treacherous, because much of the language has become opaque to its users. My present concern with the 'classical' element in English is its importance in word formation. Here indeed we have one of those 'paths of abstractedness' that I mentioned just now.

There is nothing an upwardly mobile Briton likes better than a Latin suffix, unless it be a Greek suffix. Of course we make fun of *-isms* and *-ologies* and *-istics* and *-ifics* and other such professorial pets. Yet we go on manufacturing '*isms*' – 'monetarism', 'confrontationism', 'interventionism' – as though the charm of the classics were impossible to withstand. If, with the help of the daily press, you study patterns of word formation in current English, you will soon discover that what linguists call the 'productive' suffixes are not the Germanic endings like *-ness*, *-hood*, *-ship*, *-ful*, *-dom* (as in 'kindness', 'childhood', 'hardship', 'thankful', 'kingdom') but rather the endings derived from Latin through French, or directly from Latin, or from Greek. An interesting, if rather obvious, example is the verb-ending *-ize*.

Now, *-ize* has been in English, naturalized and enfranchised, for a long time. 'Let them anatomize Regan', cried the distracted Lear – the stylistic point of Shakespeare's usage being that in his day the *-ize* formations were still comparatively new and strange; 'anatomize' was a good mouthful for a mad king to chew on. (The *Oxford English Dictionary* gives 1541 as the first recorded occurrence of the word.)[4] Since the sixteenth century, however, words of that kind have made their way into English in great and familiar numbers. Not a recent phenomenon, then; and yet it does seem that the jargon and journalism of the last hundred years have spawned more and more verbs in *-ize*: 'privatize', 'customize', 'motorize', 'transistorize', 'sanitize', 'homogenize', 'rubberize', 'plasticize', 'regionalize', 'pressurize', 'compartmentalize', 'prioritize' – and as a student of language dare I add 'nominalize', 'lexicalize'? Future scholars, tidying our vocabulary into the reference books, may amuse themselves by studying the distribution of the *-ize* words over different fields of usage. They may well find that increasingly during the twentieth century words of this kind have been the incidental products of commercial technology and administration.

They may also note that in our time most words coined with the *-ize* suffix have been transitive verbs implying human agency and goal-directed processes. Here I am obliged to make some sketchy allusion to the morphological and idiomatic history of these verbs. Historically, three types of word formation are evident. In one, the Greek suffix is attached to a Greek root – as in 'anatomize', 'anthropomorphize'; in another, the Greek suffix is attached to a Latin base, commonly an adjectival form, e.g. 'regularize', 'normalize'; and in a third type the ending is affixed to a non-classical base, even to a proper noun, e.g. 'womanize', 'rubberize', 'galvanize', 'Thatcherize'. The first type is, in philological terms, the purest; the second and third types are hybrids that obviously allow much greater freedom, even licence, to the word-maker. The fact that one can simply invent a word like 'Thatcherize' suggests that the suffix has at length shaken off constraints imposed by users with a sense of etymology, and can now be used almost randomly.

The semantic relationships between this suffix and its bases are complex. The *-ize* of 'rubberize' means something different from the *-ize* of 'authorize', which in its turn is different from the *-ize* of 'temporize', and, again, from the *-ize* of 'normalize'. One can spend a long time puzzling over the significance of the suffix in particular instances. Broadly, let me suggest that the *-ize* affix generates both transitive and intransitive verbs, embracing two general kinds of meaning. My two meanings are 'behaviour', as in 'attitudinize', and 'process', as in 'modernize'. The 'behaviour' group can be further subdivided into verbs of inward-tending, or 'intensional', behaviour, e.g. 'He fantasizes a great deal', and verbs of outward-tending, or 'extensional', behaviour, e.g. 'She socializes a great deal'. The 'process' group is generally divisible into (a) verbs with impersonal, non-human subjects, e.g. 'In the dry cupboard the jam crystallized', or 'Long residence acclimatized him to the cold and damp', and (b) verbs of personal (human) agency, or activity-and-object verbs, e.g. 'pressurize' as in 'The government pressurized the local authority', or 'customize' as in 'For a slight extra charge the salesman will customize your purchase'. Thus, verbs of the 'behaviour' type, whether 'intensional' or 'extensional', represent some form of role-playing, whereas those of the 'process' type express transitions from cause to effect.

Shifts of behavioural and process meanings are interestingly apparent in the histories of some well-established items. 'Womanize', for example, meant at first 'to make someone womanish' – a verb denoting a process with a personal agent; then, 'to behave like a woman' – a behaviour verb of the 'intensional' type; after which it shifted to its current meaning, 'to consort with women', as a behaviour verb of the 'extensional' type, like 'socialize', 'fraternize'. We must wait and see if it will make a further shift and become a process verb with non-personal agents – enabling us to say, for example, that 'drinking gin womanizes you' (= 'makes you womanish'), or that 'Jack's got womanized since he took up knitting'. Then compare the history of 'womanize' with that of 'brutalize'. This was originally a behaviour verb of the 'intensional' type, meaning 'to behave brutishly' (NB not 'brutally'), as in 'The human race has been brutalizing since we were thrown out of Eden'. The verb then developed to a 'process' type with impersonal subjects, as in 'Alcohol brutalizes people'; this being followed by the further development to a 'process' meaning with a human agent, as in 'The overseers brutalized their slaves' (= 'treated them brutally'). Currently the two 'process' meanings are in rivalry. We can say that 'Imprisonment only brutalizes a man' (= 'makes him brutish'), and we can say that 'Some warders brutalize their prisoners' (= 'treat them brutally'). Observation suggests that this latter meaning – of process governed by personal agency – will eventually supersede its rival.

What is evident from all this is a shiftiness of meaning, accompanied necessarily by a syntactic shiftiness, since the meaning of the word is accommodated in the grammar of the phrase and sentence. Thus, I stand before you and Groningenize (= behaviour, 'intensional', like 'attitudinize'); on my return to Britain, I may well boast how I have been Groningenizing with some eminent Netherlanders (= behaviour, 'extensional', like 'socialize'); I shall tell my colleagues how after a few hours in the place one feels thoroughly Groningenized (= process, 'impersonal', like 'acclimatize'); and they will probably assume that Nash, in that way of his, Groningenized his hearers till they could bear no more (= process, 'personal', like 'anathematize'). The frivolous example illustrates a serious point; that this small suffix, this mere morpheme, is one of the potential makers of what I have called 'paths of abstractedness'. It will take you a long way – and get you lost if you are not careful.

To see how some of the byways of the abstract are extended, note what happens when we join this affix to other affixes. Current usage is busily extending the established practice of forming nouns on the model of 'organization'; thus we have 'unionization', 'democratization', 'privatization' – a vogue-word which for political reasons has ousted the earlier 'denationalization'. All the verbs of agentive process are ready candidates for this; the idea of agency – one might say the 'myth of activity' – is extended to the noun. Take the case of a coinage now current in political jargon – 'prioritize'. The form is already double-suffixed. The adjective 'prior' has provided a base for the noun 'priority', then part of the noun suffix (*-ity*) has been deleted to accommodate the verb suffix, *-ize*. Thus emerges 'prioritize', which is now ready and waiting for the further step to 'prioritization'; then there will be nothing to prevent the formation of an adjective, 'prioritizational', and an adverb, 'prioritizationally'. We may then call in the aid of prefixes, to form 'deprioritization' and 'reprioritization', 'preprioritization' and – why not? – 'autoprioritization' (something carried out, perhaps, by computers). Next, letting one abstract noun enjoy the support of another, we can venture into phrasal compounds like 'prioritization process', 'prioritization debate', 'prioritization scheme'. And from phrases we may embark upon the wider wanderings of clause and sentence, declaring, perhaps, that 'the management of the consumer economy demands the reprioritization of Government options', or that 'a reappraisal of the strategies of monetarism is prioritizationally imperative'. And then, perhaps, we can pause and remember Adam, naming horses and cows and great big innocent lizards; and wonder what happened to the simple speech of Eden.

Let me dwell a little on this matter of phrase-making, and particularly on those constructions that hover between the status of noun phrase and compound noun. I invented one just now – 'prioritization process'. Look in any of the so-called 'quality' newspapers, and you will find abundant examples of such phrases. Here are a few, collected from one issue of the *Observer*: 'feasibility study; tax incentive; tax net; incentive scheme; growth area; package deal; pay deal; market confidence; market forces; wage freeze; key worker; key issue; currency fraud; fee fraud; fraud boom; commodity swindle; crime haven; inquiry team; race relations; peace movement; union power; power base; helicopter capability'. Are these constructions to be identified as noun phrases, or should some of them at least be interpreted as compound nouns? Our lexicographers are not altogether sure; the compiler of my desk dictionary (*The New Collins Concise English Dictionary*) lists 'feasibility study' as a noun, but not 'work study'; 'wage freeze' but not 'pay increase'; 'market research' but not 'market forces'.

These phrasal compounds – let us call them that – are binominal, and consist of a noun head, e.g. 'incentive', and a premodifying noun epithet, e.g. 'tax'. In the various examples I have just quoted, this common pattern superficially cloaks a variety of underlying syntactic relationships. Behind the two nouns lurk patterns of sentence-structure – subject and verb, verb and object, subject and complement, verb and adverbial, and so forth; so that 'power base', for example, might be interpreted as a subject–object relationship ('the power has a base'), whereas 'home help' is a verb–adverbial pattern ('someone helps in the home'). This is the kind of analysis that would be suggested by some modern grammarians.[5]

But allow me, for present purposes, a somewhat simpler line. These phrasal compounds, fostered by the headline language of journalists, now abound in the current language of politics and economics. In their syntax, they represent a switch from postmodification, when attributive expressions *follow* the noun head, to premodification, when they *precede* it. Thus, a 'packet' (noun head) 'containing pay' (postmodifying clause) is transformed into 'pay' (premodifying epithet) 'packet' (noun head). It seems simple enough, until you come upon an example like 'tax proposal'. How, in this instance, is the underlying postmodifier to be reconstructed? 'Proposal to increase tax'? 'Proposal to decrease tax'? 'Proposal to introduce a new tax'? 'Proposal to change an old tax'? We could judge only from a larger context. Evidently the simple syntactic conversion – superficially simple – involves a degree of semantic ellipsis. In the resultant phrasal compound, some element of meaning is not designated, is thought to be 'understood', or to be apparent from a context.

For the hard-pressed politician and the unscrupulous publicist, this is one of heaven's gifts; something unspoken is a loophole for evasion or even for downright falsehood. Take, for example, a fairly recent formation, the phrase 'helicopter capability'; it arose in connection with what was to become a bitter dispute over the fortunes of the Westland Helicopter Company. In the *Observer* for 15 December 1985, Mr James Prior, MP, was reported as saying that 'Every effort must be made to maintain helicopter capability in Great Britain'; and a subsequent issue of *The Times*, using a metaphor I find a little obscure, speaks of 'squeezing' the 'European helicopter capability'. Now what does 'helicopter capability' mean? The phrase presents two obstacles. One is that of realizing the underlying construction, which is presumably something like 'capability of producing helicopters'. The other is that of assigning a meaning to the word 'capability', a vague abstraction. What did Mr Prior have in mind? That we should have the technical knowledge that would enable us to produce helicopters? That we should have facilities for manufacturing them? That we should have money to finance their production? Is the assertion that we must maintain helicopter capability merely a polite way of saying that we ought to keep the Americans out? Does 'capability' *have* any meaning? Is its function that of a large, supportive, importantly empty word – so that the banal 'We need helicopters' can become the more impressive 'We must maintain helicopter capability'? Nobody really knows. But consider the value of such a phrase to the PTE speaker. Now we can 'mount a feasibility study for the restructuring of a Europeanized helicopter capability project'. And as this is patently a 'growth area', we should adopt 'an interventionist policy', which will facilitate 'the introduction of tax incentives in exchange for non-mandatory productivity agreements'. Well, you may object that this is merely parody, and so it is; but, I assure you, the parody is not so very far removed from sober everyday performance. And when language is allowed to occur in this way, we can hardly speak of *usage* – if usage implies something purposeful and controlled. I have been talking about some means by which language slips out of control, while speciously retaining the appearance of a purpose. Under such conditions, users are disqualified and become, in effect, the used. Our competence to exploit the underlying patterns of a linguistic system is exercised, but to no avail. We become the victims of our own inventiveness.

TROPERY

It is with the assumption that language should avail us in some way – should avail us as a form óf action, should avail our grasp of things, should avail our perceptions – that I turn to my second topic, metaphor. Metaphor is frequently an attempt to give substance to fugitive concepts; to enable us to perceive relationships between things that otherwise elude perception and definition. Figurative language has an exploratory and an explanatory value. The teacher knows this, the metaphysician knows it, above all the poet knows it, for it is in poetry that we can find the most elaborate organization of metaphor. I recall that when F.R. Leavis wished to praise a poem, he would use words like 'integrated' and 'organic' – employing metaphoric terms, indeed, to express his perception of figurative cohesion and unity.

This purposeful, planned use of metaphor is rather rare in PTE. There, instead of imagery, we find *tropery* – a haphazard, cliché-dominated, often absurdly ill-conceived use of figures with decorative or emphatic intent. Woefully mixed metaphor is surprisingly common, in the most respectable quarters. This, for example:

> Mr Poul Schluter, the Prime Minister, has had several things going for him (although Denmark's awesome foreign debt is not one of them), and he has kept his head above water with some nimble footwork.[6]

If that were from a tabloid paper one might suspect a joke, but it is from the *Daily Telegraph*, and the editors of that journal are not given to frivolity. One can only suppose that the writer's sense of metaphor has momentarily lapsed, and that he (or she) has lost sight of the fact that the expression 'to keep your head above water' connotes swimming, whereas 'nimble footwork' is properly applicable to sports like boxing or tennis. (The definition of 'footwork' in sporting activities will hardly extend to the process of treading water.[7]) This figurative mishmash tells us more about the writer than it does about Mr Schluter. But in PTE, as I have said, the purpose of metaphoric language is rarely to illuminate perception. If it has a purpose beyond mere decoration, it may be to *control*, for social and political purposes, the way in which things are perceived.

Metaphors of social control are probably as old as language itself. One fairly ancient specimen still in circulation is that of the 'ship of state'. Anacreon used it, Horace used it, Longfellow used it, and any day now the President of the United States is going to invent it.[8] The importance of the ship of state metaphor is that it implies two references: to disciplined security on the one hand, and to uncontrollable danger on the other. Thus the ship of state is at the mercy of the raging elements, but if we all pull together and trust our captain, we shall survive the tempest and come safe to port. It really is amazing to think how long this hoary figure has remained current. We still hear of the economy being 'blown off course', and I can recall, from not too many years ago, a Labour minister (Mrs Barbara Castle) declaring that 'a touch of the tiller' was all that was needed to set Britain to rights. The principle, we see, is to raise the threat and the reassurance at one and the same time, or at all events to raise the threat, with the implication that salvation is at hand for all who will think, act and vote in the right way. During the Suez crisis of 1956, the British Prime Minister, Sir Anthony Eden, made repeated, almost obsessive use of the image of 'the forest fire'; the 'forest fire' was the fighting between Egypt and Israel, and it was the mission of the honest British fireman to douse the flames and stop the fire from spreading. (In the end, I think, Eden actually believed the myth of his own metaphor.) When Mr Edward Heath was in office, he and his Chancellor told the public that their financial policies would prevent inflation from 'running rip' – using the image of the fierce, uncontrollable ocean current known as the 'rip tide'. All these are instances of what I have called metaphors of social control, intended to raise and assuage fears, or more loosely to distract perception from the realities of political and social life. Out there the winds are raging, the tide is running, the forest is blazing – but never mind, the captain is on the bridge, the masons are building a wall, a resolute brigade is standing by to save us, as long as we do the bidding of our leaders.

Metaphors of control often enter PTE in connection with vogue-words, or as they are now often called, buzz-words, those fashionable items of vocabulary that decorate the discourse of well-informed people. They come and go, like other fashions. Thirty years ago it was hardly possible to hold a serious conversation without using the word 'dichotomy'; the dichotomy of body and soul, the dichotomy of heart and head, the dichotomy of theory and practice – dichotomy meant any division of two parts, from heaven and earth to bacon and eggs. Then suddenly the word was no longer indispensable and everyone stopped dichotomizing and began to buzz other words. Among today's buzz-words are: area; dimension; situation; stance; posture; scenario; formula; model; image; concept; perception; presentation; strategy; syndrome; growth; pressure and, of course, capability. Such items are frequently, but not invariably, nouns. Currently fashionable verbs include 'implement', 'refute' (in the sense of 'deny'), 'de-fuse' (often pronounced as though a homophone of 'to diffuse') and 'denigrate' (although this word appears to be going out of fashion). Some of these fashionable words have come to the fore by a peculiar process of metaphoric heightening, in which a figurative usage is superseded by a more emphatic figure. Thus a 'position' becomes first a 'stance' and then a 'posture'; we talk about the Social Democrats adopting a multilateral stance on disarmament, or about the government's posture in labour relationships. Or again, 'line', as in 'line of research', develops into 'field' as in 'field of study', whence to 'area', as in 'area of interest', and so to 'dimension', as in 'dimension of thinking': those of us who work in the 'area of language' can testify that the invention of the word-processor has brought 'a whole new dimension to writing'. Vogue-words, like slang, are constantly being displaced by new arrivals, but such a displacement is often achieved only by a figurative expansion which is just another kind of abstractedness.

Furthermore, vogue-words often enter into collocations which are pseudo-metaphoric and at the same time highly abstract. One may talk about 'a growth area', 'a strategy of presentation', 'a peace formula', 'cultivating an image', 'de-fusing a situation', 'projecting a scenario', 'pressurizing the workforce' and so on. In many instances the effect of this is ultimately to drain the word of all figurative sense, by eroding the literal reference which is the necessary foundation of metaphor. 'Syndrome' is a good example. In its strict medical sense it refers to a combination of signs and symptoms, but in popular usage it has promptly acquired the meaning 'disease' or 'ailment', and is used by many to express the even weaker notion of 'unfortunate characteristic': thus in a BBC radio programme on the annual Boat Show at Earl's Court, a commentator, discussing the trials of dinghy sailing, was heard to refer to 'the wet socks syndrome'.[9]

It is by such declensions that some words lose metaphoric force, become inert. Others *apparently* extend their power. As an instance, take the word 'strategy'. In many contexts this looks like one of the current metaphors of control. It enters into collocations suggestive of all sorts of military notions, figuring with words like 'campaign', 'troops', 'advance', 'retreat', 'front', etc. But while 'strategy' seems in this way to be metaphorically expansive, it is also, perversely, reductive, like 'syndrome'. There are recurrent contexts in which it means no more than 'plan' or 'method'. Treasury officials talk of 'economic strategies', literary theorists of 'critical strategies', primary school teachers discuss their pupils' 'reading strategies', or their own 'teaching strategies'. At this level, of finding a noun to fill a hole, vogue-words are often freely interchangeable: a 'strategy' can be much the same as a 'formula' or 'model', while a 'perception' might just as well be a 'stance'. Viewed thus, 'strategy' is a zombie word, and the apparently lively associations into which it enters are, after all, the combinations of cliché. When some editorial commentator remarks that 'the ranks of the Labour Party are in disarray and Mr Kinnock needs a strategy to rally his forces', we can hardly think that 'strategy' is the vital, radiant centre of a shimmering tissue of imagery. It is just a handy knot in an old string bag.

The figurativeness of PTE is suspect in two ways. First, the *terms* of metaphor are often mismanaged, mistaken or blurred, so that we cannot properly identify the process of comparison or transference. Second, the *configurations* of metaphor, the deployment of successive figures in a pattern of imagery, are seldom well contrived. Our daily newspapers are hospitals and graveyards of figurative language; there we find the sick and the dead of the tropical tribe. I must resist the temptation to enter upon the fascinating topic of dead metaphor, but let me at least say something about *maimed* metaphor, that is, about the incomplete or inadequately resolved figure. Here is another piece of Daily Telegraphese, the opening sentence of an editorial: 'After a fashion, battered but very much inured to battering, the search for a Middle East peace continues apace'.[10]

I will ask you to leave aside the question of how a search which continues 'after a fashion' can also continue 'apace'; the writer possibly believes in burning his adverbials at both ends. My immediate concern is with the failure to endow 'search' with the personal or concrete character that would justify 'battered'. You can batter babies or boxers or tin mugs or motor cars, but you do not batter a search. You may as well try to thump an enquiry. If 'batter' is to take as its metaphoric object an abstract noun, then it must be a noun capable of expressing a personification or 'objectification'; hope may be battered, like a boxer, or perhaps a proposal may be battered, like a well-travelled parcel, but somehow there is no personification called 'Search', and no concrete object with search-like associations. The metaphor simply does not work out – or, to use the metaphoric description proposed earlier, it is *maimed*.

Journalists and other PTE speakers are not unaware that metaphor can become enfeebled to the point of death. Periodically there are attempts to imbue jaded old figures with new vitality. Salesmen at first 'cut' prices, and then 'slash' them; rapidly rising costs are described as 'soaring' until that becomes too commonplace, and then they are said to 'rocket'. In a report on the so-called Cyprus spy trial, a contributor to a national journal wrote of 'the haemorrhage of thousands of Secret and Top Secret Documents'.[11] The cliché metaphor for betraying an official secret is 'leaking'; documents are leaked. But if a stronger figure is sought, what could be leakier than 'haemorrhage'? That process of heightening or inflating, which I have mentioned in connection with vogue-words, is apparent here: as 'line' is to 'dimension'; as 'plan' is to 'strategy'; so 'leak' is to 'haemorrhage'. It is all very vigorous, apparently; but inflation in language is no more healthy than inflation in the currency.

The absurdity of 'tropery' is most evident in passages of extended metaphor. It is remarkable how often the figurative drive gets out of control, and indeed how often the writer or speaker seems to lose the sense of where metaphor begins and ends. Sometimes one trope or play on words can flower gaudily among a drift of shrivelled, semi-figurative clichés. Take this example, from the report of a speech by Mr Neil Kinnock:

> In particularly attacking high interest rates, Mr Kinnock said the Government's record was one of flop and failure. Great images had gone; sacred cows were turning out to be old bull. The strategy of shrinking the economy was obvious when one stripped the Queen's Speech of virile phrases about firm policies. It was a recipe for a further rundown of the economy.[12]

Here is one strenuous, self-conscious piece of word-play on 'sacred cow' and 'old bull'. But see how, in the rest of this passage, words and phrases die. What a figurative falldown! Here are the vogue-words 'image' and 'strategy', and here are vaguely vigorous notions of 'shrinking an economy' and 'stripping a speech', to say nothing of a 'recipe for a rundown'. The metaphor is well and truly – or ill and truly – maimed. In such contexts, words like 'shrink' and 'strip' lose their primary meaning without clearly acquiring a secondary, figurative meaning; and 'recipe for a rundown' is so obviously derived from the cliché–metaphor 'recipe for disaster' – which is itself based on a misuse, rather than a figurative use, of 'recipe' – that there is no life at all in the figure.

Well, a *speaker* may be excused an unlucky or impulsive choice of words; but when *writers* of PTE attempt to plan coherent figurative episodes, they are just as likely to make a botch of it. I give you two samples of writing from *The Times*. The first reflects the Conservative Party's concern with 'image' and 'presentation':

> In the last session, the Government presented its programme badly. It dug pits for itself and strewed the banana skins in strategic places for the ministers to fall in. The pits are still there, not least the pit marked 'fear of freeing the economy from state chains'.[13]

Here is a whimsical yoking of the figure of the pitfall and the figure of the banana skin. Cartoon characters drop banana skins for pompous people to slip on. Hunters dig pits for wild animals to fall into. Hunters do not generally dig pits and strew banana skins round them. Nor do they mark their pitfalls with identifying or cautionary labels. Bottles may be marked 'poison' and doors may be marked 'private', but pits are not literally marked 'sharp spikes', 'rope net' or 'gorillas only, please', and so it is unconvincing to suggest that figurative pits may be metaphorically marked 'fear of freeing the economy from state chains'. This is old bull with a vengeance – and this is *The Times*.

In this second sample, the writer has noted the disappointing results of 'productivity agreements', and goes on:

> Consequently the Chancellor's much-vaunted new growth will not be the smooth, well-balanced creature that ministers like to parade and stroke. Instead it is likely to turn out to be a lumpy unbalanced beast whose different limbs – investment, exports, and domestic consumption – grow at alarmingly different rates.[14]

This is constructed round another vogue-word, 'growth', and appears to be an exercise in galumphing allegorical humour. That at least would be a charitable explanation of the fact that this 'unbalanced beast' is indeed so unbalanced as to have only three legs (investment, exports, domestic consumption), which means no balance at all. No matter: the limbs are 'different limbs' – a right leg, a left leg and a middle leg – all displaying the important principle of 'growth'.

Writers of PTE, however, seldom attempt figurative cohesion. Their metaphor-making is generally loose, disorganized and *dead*, as in this, my final illustration. Again, the *Daily Telegraph* is the source: a columnist is discussing problems of leadership and organization facing the Trades Union Congress.

The role of the general secretary in recent years has been to steer with the help of dominant trade union bosses rather than actually leading.

The trouble, as insiders admit, is that Willis is totally bereft of such power-brokers. Todd of the transport workers has flexed his muscles but little more. Bickerstaff of NUPE is regarded as a lightweight. Clive Jenkins carries no clout whatever. Basnett has led the troops into ambush after ambush and is retiring anyway.

As if its cup of bitterness were not already running over, the TUC also has the problem of the breakaway miners to contend with. Here, if anything, it is even more powerless. When it met the NUM executive recently, Basnett murmured about a commission of conciliation, but the idea has no more chance of getting airborne than a circus elephant. 'We can't do anything on that front', admitted one union boss.[15]

If one were looking for a unifying metaphor to guide one through the exposition, this passage would be puzzling indeed. Diverse figures appear, vanish and reappear. There are metaphors – not dead, so much as dead-and-alive – of strategy and warfare, of pugilism, of navigation, of flight. There is also muddled allusion, for the cup that runneth over in the 23rd Psalm is not a cup of bitterness. I can imagine my own students accusing me of being too literary about this. 'After all, the meaning's clear', they might say. But my point, literary or otherwise, is that the meaning is not, after all, so clear; it is fuzzed, fuddled and fugitive. The purpose of figuration, in a passage of this kind, ought to be to give coherence and sharp definition to the argument – to give realities their say; instead, what we are offered is a tangle of images that abstract and distract. There is indeed 'a cool web of language winds us in' – or rather, a clammy tissue of wordage. Brininess and volubility could not be better illustrated.

I have spent rather a long time discussing a few small points – the use of a suffix, a type of phrase, some instances of metaphor. Does this adequately represent the pretensions of my title, 'Usage, users and the used'? Does it more than marginally illustrate the thesis that language, our approach to reality, embodies conditions for a retreat from the real? Clearly it cannot. But it may at least have suggested that usage is a complex topic, requiring the patient observation and interpretation of countless such small details of language, and of how they enter into organic relationship with each other. And of course it requires something more: an understanding of the social functions of language, of the psychology of discourse, of the forces that make for linguistic change.

Such complexity denies the claims of those who would like to be *prescriptive*, in the crudest, most authoritarian sense; the ills of speech and society are not cured by eliminating intrusive *r*s, or keeping prepositions away from the ends of sentences. On the other hand, I have long felt that the virtuous claim of many academics to be *descriptive* – to keep account of linguistic fact but to withhold evaluation – is a comfortable evasion, a defection from responsibility. Since we are not in Eden any longer, and cannot enjoy Adam's privilege of settling language once and for all, I would prefer that we subordinate both the *prescriptive* and the *descriptive* to the *constructive*; that is, (a) that we should describe what exists, trying to understand how it has come into its present state and how it may change, and (b) that we should assess ways of using what exists. 'Assessing ways of using' means making choices appropriate to different purposes, social contexts and styles of discourse. It implies, in fact, a *criticism of language*, of no less import and no less exacting in its pretensions than the criticism of literature. This is a subject of considerable scope; yet usage does not occupy a position of central importance in our University courses in English. But I am venturing into observations that border on complaints, and I am in any case addressing them to the wrong audience. For here I stand a-Groningenizing on this happy occasion, in the University of Kruisinga and Zandvoort, and in this most civilized of lands, whose inhabitants all, from ticket-collectors to learned professors, speak my native language with such assurance, such fluency, such grace, that I might strangely say: if Adam spoke English, then I am a Dutchman.

The text of a lecture delivered at the University of Groningen in January 1986, at a conference celebrating 100 years of English studies at Dutch universities.

3 The difficulty of explaining: a word or two about dictionaries

Anyone who spends a working life in classrooms will have a lot of explaining to do, and may want to ask a few questions about what is, after all, an extraordinary and complicated process. How do we manage to explain things? Is there a discourse of explanation, as there is a discourse of cookery recipes, small ads or scientific reports? How reliable are the explanations we give and receive? When do they convey real knowledge, and when are they no more than a usefully plausible account of things we can never really know? When, indeed, do they convey only the conveyance, so that the explanatory act lives by its palliative rhetoric, the assurance it gives as a satisfying performance? There are difficulties of explaining beyond the scope of simple explanations.

Such philosophical worries have arisen, in my case, from a very ordinary, practical, tutorial interest in explaining words and their meanings to foreign students of English: the text lies in front of the class, the words file past us, this one catches the eye or challenges comprehension, and the tutor has something to explain. It is an exacting skill, particularly because words call for explanation at more than one level. We may need to account for their linguistic behaviour, their relationship to other words, their history, their membership of families (such as synonyms), their entry into idioms or grammatical constructions. There is a community of words, in which each word has a significant place. At the same time we must furnish what is perceived as the explanation proper, an indication or description of a *reference*, which is a pointing beyond language to something in the world, whether it be the world of things or the world of notions. The naïve observer tends to assume that only one of these levels of explanation – that of reference – is of any practical importance, but the professional recognizes the frequent necessity of moving from one to the other, talking not only about what the word 'means', in a dictionary sense, but also about how it is used, and by whom, and when, and for what purpose.

Experience fosters an ability to recognize what the difficulties of explaining are going to be, and how they might be successfully surmounted. Let us, at this point, put our own intuitions to a casual test. Here is a short list of randomly chosen words:

rain check (phrasal noun)
arch (adjective)
fold in (phrasal verb; cookery term)
regale (verb)
entropy (noun)

It is likely that not all of these will be equally familiar. My suggested 'test' requires no more than a summary response, thus:

1 Mark the words you can quite readily explain.
2 Mark also those instances where you can see an obvious method of explanation.
3 Distinguish honestly between those words you really *know*, and those you *think you can explain* by hazarding a definition or guessing at contexts in which you suppose them to occur. ('X is generally defined as . . .'; 'It sounds as if it ought to mean . . .'; 'I think it has to do with . . .'.)

TECHNIQUES OF EXPLANATION: OSTENSIVENESS

My test is a rapid measure of the readiness to explain, a readiness requiring some mastery, roughly and pragmatically acquired, no doubt, of several co-functioning techniques of explanation. The first of these, indispensable auxiliary of all chalkface heroes and heroines, is the resort to 'ostensive' definition. This can mean, quite simply, pointing to an instance of what is meant by the word, or drawing it or even miming. The word 'threshold', for example, virtually obliges the explicator to point at the doorframe. 'Spindle' may call for a little blackboard artistry or a quick sketch on the back of an envelope. 'Twiddle' sets thumbs and fingers irresistibly in motion; 'leer' produces facial contortions only to be excused by the difficulty of explaining. Ostensiveness is immediate, makeshift, concrete; but there is also a kind of 'referred ostensiveness', in allusions to known instances of phenomena not immediately present or not easily drawn or mimed: 'There's one on the top of the tower outside'; 'That thing in the corridor'; 'You find them in circuses.'

There are obvious limitations to the adequacy of this form of explanation. The referents it deals with are concrete, or in some way visible; we cannot use it in the explanation of abstractions and concepts, unless, perhaps, we try to explain the concept by pointing to something that embodies it, or represents it metonymically. (As, for example, a thermometer represents 'temperature' or a globe embodies 'meridian'.) Furthermore, this ostensive technique, which appears to be highly specific, is, paradoxically, vague; or rather, it is the *least powerful* of all modes of explanation, because while it deals satisfactorily with one instance it does not generate terms of recognition to cover all other instances. I might easily explain 'desk' by pointing to one, but that single act of identification will not account for 'desk' as a superordinate term with potential reference to a variety of constructions and functions. Concomitantly, it may foster a misunderstanding, for example by seeming to indicate quite simply 'a flat surface', in which case table-tops, tea-trolleys and the lids of piano stools might all be perceived as types of 'desk'. Some trust, however, is put in the intelligence and perceptiveness of the persons receiving the information. The informer says, in effect, 'that's the sort of thing I mean', leaving the informed to make inferences, deduce categories and, in general, supply for themselves the terms of definition. This implies, oddly enough, a disclaiming of complete authority on the informant's part, and a kind of collaborativeness in the explanatory act. You ask me what a word means, and I point to a concrete instance; but I leave it to you to generalize the explanation.

THE 'TRANSLATIONAL' TECHNIQUE

Ostensive definitions directly match words with objects. In another kind of explanation, the attempt is made at a direct match between words and words. The most obvious case is translation from one language to another; if I happen to know that the French for 'ashtray' is *cendrier*, I will not waste any time in trying to explain to a potentially puzzled French student of English that an ashtray is a form of receptacle for the residuum of tobacco burnt in cigarettes and cigars. (I hope in any case that I would not be so pompous as to put it that way; but if I were, I would probably be faced with the task of explaining 'receptacle' and 'residuum', which could then involve me in a discussion of the scope of 'container' and the distinction between 'remainder' and 'remnant'.) A translation saves time and forestalls complications. Another kind of 'translational' technique requires the equation of word and word within the same language. We explain by citing synonyms, or by locating the word in a hyponymic set; thus I might relate 'amble' to 'stroll' or discuss its place in the hyponymic set governed by 'walk' and including 'stroll' 'saunter', 'plod', 'trudge'.[1]

To explain by synonyms, however, is to court the notorious danger of circular definition. In response to an enquiry for the meaning of 'arch', I suggest, perhaps, 'sly'. But 'sly' has to be explained by 'cunning', and 'cunning' by 'crafty', 'crafty' by 'shrewd', 'shrewd' by 'knowing' and 'knowing' by – can it be? – 'arch'. In this kind of explanatory exercise, the cycle of synonyms is rehearsed, and sometimes, if the explainer is unlucky or unhandy, other synonymic cycles are encountered on the way round (as 'shrewd' means 'astute' means 'clever' means 'artful' means 'cunning', etc.). This is a fascinating way of exploring the networks and intersections of our lexicon, but what is required, for the immediate purposes of explanation, is some method of breaking out of the cycle, getting off the roundabout and quitting the imprisonment of the semantic domain.

Sometimes etymology offers the possibility of a breakout, because of its indications of how words began and its occasional capacity to make transparent the referential purport of forms which time, usage and forgetfulness (or ignorance) have rendered opaque. A preferred method of explaining 'parthenogenesis', for example, might well be to take the direct etymological route which points us to the translation from Greek *parthenos*, 'virgin', 'maiden', and *genesis* 'birth'. This is probably better than trying to explain that the word refers to a type of reproduction in which the unfertilized ovum directly produces a new individual of the species; or if not better, at least an initially helpful way of prompting the understanding.[2] Certain native compounds, like 'gainsay', 'withstand', 'outwit', may also be suitable candidates for etymological analysis. But etymology is often an unreliable, frequently useless and possibly treacherous ally. It is misleading, for example, to relate 'meticulous' to Latin *metus*, 'fear', and to deduce from this fact – correct in itself – that the proper meaning of the word is 'timid'. (This is still listed in the *Oxford English Dictionary* as the primary meaning.) And it is not so much misleading as frankly useless to explain 'puce', in the manner of one current and reputable dictionary, as meaning 'flea-coloured', because it is ultimately derived from Latin *pulex*, a flea.[3]

On the other hand, explanations of the origin of a word in some cultural fact or social practice may be of great value, particularly when what is to be explained is a figurative usage. We may choose to explain 'take aback' synonymically, as roughly equivalent to 'surprise', 'astonish' (but with the additional note that it commonly occurs in the passive); or we may relate 'heavy going' to a set of synonyms with the superordinate notion of 'progress'; and still our explanations may take firmer effect from some account of sailing vessels or racecourses.[4] In many such cases there is as it were a 'social etymon', recognition of which locks knowledge of the word into a knowledge of social history and culture. Ignorance of the social etymon never prevents the use of words, but it does quite often result in a condition that has been called the illiteracy of the literate, which means the capacity to use words fluently and plausibly without wholly grasping the realities they reflect. Conversely, a knowledge of the social etymon does not guarantee accurate perception of how the word is currently used; knowing the technical origins of 'feedback', for example, or the military source of 'forlorn hope', could hinder rather than promote access to the current meanings of 'report, response' and 'lost cause, hopeless case'.[5]

'DEFINITIONAL' TECHNIQUES

Still the problem remains of improving on the explanation that simply points to the thing that merely points back to the word; or that points to a word that points to other words that point back, in due course, to the original word. It is here that we begin to resort to methods that can be called 'definitional'. ('Definitive' would be preferable, but its services are engaged elsewhere.) There are two kinds of definitional technique. One is the categorical explanation that casts its definition in a form generally equivalent to the grammatical category of the word itself. Thus nouns are defined by nominal constructions, a 'pen' being defined as 'an instrument for writing or drawing, using ink', or 'courage' as 'the power or quality of dealing with or facing danger, fear, pain, etc.'. Definitions of verbs are customarily based on the infinitive, e.g. 'impose', 'to establish as something to be obeyed or complied with'. Adjectives are more variously defined, sometimes with synonymic reference to other adjectives (thus 'courteous' = 'polite and considerate in manner'), or in some cases via participles of the type 'having', 'possessing', 'making', 'containing', 'characterized by', etc.; thus a definition of 'benevolent' is 'intending or showing good will'. 'Manner' adverbs are commonly defined (or simply located) in the context of the adjectives from which they are derived. (Look up 'slow' in your dictionary, and the chances are that a fairly long entry on the adjective will be followed by the laconic notation *slowly, adv.*) Adverbs of time and place are regularly defined by prepositional phrases ('then' = 'at that time, period', 'here' = 'at this place, point', 'henceforth' = 'from now on', 'thither' = 'towards that place', 'in that direction'). In all this we may recognize the conventional style of dictionary definitions.

The other type of 'definitional' explanation is not yet so familiar in lexicographical practice, though it has a long and fruitful history in the classroom and as the informal method of ordinary social exchanges. The contextual explanation appeals directly to common knowledge and posits some situation or experience in the context of which the use of the word may be understood. A contextual explanation of 'courage' might run: 'When you are afraid because someone is attacking you, but you do not run away, or when you make yourself overcome your fear of a painful operation, you are showing *courage.*' And 'impose': 'If you make a rule and force other people to obey it, you are *imposing* it *on* them.' These explanations suggest particular contingencies – being attacked, facing an operation, lawgiving – which illustrate the use of the word in question. Like the categorical definition, the contextual explanation has its linguistic markers, in the form of the conjunctions, etc., that introduce subordinate clauses expressing possibility, habit or condition: 'if', 'when', 'supposing', usually accompanied by the pronoun of personal address, 'you'. Another feature of this method of explaining is its use of citation. Citations are of course common in large dictionaries that employ the conventional technique of categorical definition; there is a defining sequence followed by a citation sequence. (The *Oxford English Dictionary* supplies the master pattern for this.) Contextual explanations often cite in a somewhat different way, incorporating a typical idiomatic usage within the definition itself, e.g. the explanation of 'thick' in 'When we say that someone is "thick as two short planks", we mean that he or she is very stupid'.

The two 'definitional' techniques interestingly imply different attitudes of the maker to the recipient of the definition, together with different views of the function of language and the purpose of dictionaries. Categorical definition is authoritative, not to say authoritarian; so authoritative that it apparently excludes overt appeal to shared knowledge or experience. The definer assumes all responsibility for the definition, which is purportedly comprehensive and commonly intended to document the practice of language as *writing*. Contextual explanations are collaborative, not claiming sole or complete authority, implying, if only in a vague way, some commonality of experience, suggesting, above all, the use of *speech*. The contextual explanation is democratic and functional; the categorical definition is autocratic and theoretical, in that it is concerned with abstracting an account of usage rather than with demonstrating a use. This contrast is seen in the mix or methodological farrago of our common dictionaries, which variously combine the categorical and contextual styles of explanation.

EXPLANATORY DISCOURSE

Collectively, the ostensive, translational and definitional techniques amount to a recipe for explanatory discourse. Variations on the recipe can be observed in parlour games depending on the explanation of words. There is, for example, a popular BBC TV programme entitled *Call My Bluff*, in which two teams of three players take it in turn to 'explain' to each other the meanings of words culled from the deepest thickets of the *Oxford English Dictionary*, a work which can always be relied upon for an improbable 'hoggerel' or a 'slammerkin'. The three members of the team whose turn it is to explain a word each propose a definition, and the three definitions are then assessed by their opponents, one being eventually selected as the most plausible. The explanations, nearly always amusing, tend to assume conventional forms which are easily parodied. Suppose, for example, that the task is to explain a word 'brugloo' (which, incidentally, will not be found in the *OED*). One player might distract the opposition with a definition suggesting some kind of dwelling, like an 'igloo'. Another might define 'brugloo' as a blight attacking vegetables, particularly Brussels sprouts. But a third, deliberately picking up a pen and wagging it demonstratively at the opposing side, might proceed like this:

> What I am holding in my hand is a kind of *brugloo*. Others might call it a *shlini*, or perhaps a *glatz*, but to me it's a *brugloo*. A *brugloo* is an ancient writing instrument used by the Sumerians for signing death-warrants. If you were a Sumerian High Priest in the year 3000 BC, or thereabouts, and you were going to sentence someone to be thrown to the crocodiles, you would cry 'Brugloo hakri pakri!', which means, 'Let the man be devoured by writing'. It comes from an old Indo-Aryan root, *brgl*, meaning 'to inscribe'. *Brugloo!*

This 'explanation' (a mimic performance, but attestably typical of the convention), is a compendium of all the techniques. There is ostensive definition ('what I am holding in my hand . . .'). There is an appeal to synonymy ('others might call it a *shlini*, etc.'). There is an etymology ('it comes from an old Indo-Aryan root . . .'). There is a categorical definition ('A *brugloo* is an ancient writing instrument');

and there is a contextual explanation ('if you were a Sumerian High Priest in the year 3000 BC'), which includes a citation ('Brugloo hakri pakri . . . etc.'). In the context of the TV game, the value of this account as a possible definition would be of less moment than its impact as a satisfying verbal display. All the tricks are played; the performer imposes an arbitrary authority, but at the same time woos his audience with a personal appeal. Nothing is really explained, but an explanation takes place.

SOME DICTIONARIES AND ONE OR TWO WORDS

The players in *Call My Bluff* commonly deploy the full range of explanatory techniques, piling one emphasis upon another in the hope of bluffing overwhelmingly. Teachers are more selective, picking the method that fits the moment; their aim, after all, is not to bluff but to enlighten. Dictionaries present an interesting case. They, like teachers, set out to enlighten, but, like players, often achieve a confusion that might pass for bluffing. The making and marketing of dictionaries is now a thriving industry, and the student has a fairly wide choice of reputable products. In general, the dictionaries we keep on our desks, or have conveniently to hand on our bookshelves, supply information corresponding to the explanatory techniques I have outlined. They offer etymologies, synonyms, categorical definitions, citations, and, as a rule, brief grammatical notes enabling us to understand the paradigmatic forms of the word, how it is used idiomatically, and how it commonly enters into the higher constructions of phrase and clause. They can differ a good deal in the way they present this information, or emphasize one aspect of definition at the expense of another, and that is potentially a source of confusion. Readers are safe enough if they put their trust in a single dictionary; paradoxically, it is the scrutiny of several that produces the feeling, occasionally, of being involved in a scholarly version of *Call My Bluff*.

I have been prompted to test my intuitions about this interesting matter by taking soundings among the dictionaries on my bookshelf. Several are compact, easily-handled volumes of the type commonly known as 'desk dictionaries': *Chambers Concise 20th Century Dictionary*; *The New Collins Concise Dictionary of the English Language*; *The New Penguin English Dictionary*; and the *Longman Dictionary of Contemporary English*. One or two are of slightly larger, less comfortably tractable format: *Webster's New World Dictionary, 2nd College Edition*; *Collins COBUILD English Language Dictionary*; and the *Reader's Digest Universal Dictionary*. One, the two-volume *Shorter Oxford English Dictionary*, is a bulky shelf-sitter, hardly to be handled without pressing cause. About their format and their methods of collecting and presenting lexicographical data there is no doubt a good deal to be said, but I will note only, in passing, one interesting circumstance. The *COBUILD* dictionary, with 1703 pages, contains, by the publisher's reckoning, 70,000 references – which is a comparatively small number for a work of its size. By contrast, the *Universal Dictionary*, with 1751 (slightly larger) pages is said to contain 180,000 references, rather more than twice as many as *COBUILD*. The disparity is perhaps to be accounted for by a difference of methodologies: *COBUILD* – alone among the dictionaries cited here – makes regular, sometimes exclusive use of the technique of contextual explanation, and hence implies a view of language as essentially a process of spoken communication. This makes for bulk, since, as a lexicographical colleague recently informed me, with barely suppressed irritation, 'explanations take up a lot of space'.

The words I asked my dictionaries to explain are the words I put to you a little earlier: 'rain check', 'arch', 'fold in', 'regale', 'entropy'.[6] In their treatment of the five test-words, the dictionaries differ, sometimes surprisingly, and there is no instance that does not invite remark. Here are some matters for comment:

Rain check

A very satisfactory explanation is furnished, as one might expect, by the American dictionary, *Webster*:

> 1. The stub of a ticket to a ball game or other outdoor event, entitling the holder to be admitted at a future date if the event is rained out. 2. an offer to renew or defer an unaccepted invitation.

What makes this satisfactory is the provision of the social etymon, the explanation of the practice that has given rise to the figurative expression 'take a rain check'. Equally effective is the definition – almost a verbal echo – provided by *The Reader's Digest Universal Dictionary*:

> *n. U.S.* A ticket stub for an outdoor sports event entitling the holder to admission at a future date if the original event is rained off. – *take a rain check* To postpone acceptance of an offer on the understanding that the offer may be taken up later.

There is, however, a small yet important distinction between this and the explanation given by *Webster*. The wording of the American dictionary entry implies that the rain check is offered by the baseball club, and hence, in figurative extension, by the host-figure in the social game. Against this, the *Universal Dictionary* would appear to suggest that the option is exercised by the guest-figure. The same interpretation is offered by *COBUILD*, in the form of a contextual explanation:

> If you say that you will *take a rain check* on an offer or a suggestion, you mean that you do not want to accept it straight away, but you might accept it later: an informal expression, used mainly in American English.

For want of a social etymon, we are not allowed to know *how* it comes to be used in American English. The *Longman Dictionary of Contemporary English* likewise omits explanation of socio-cultural origins, and makes a confused attempt at categorical definition:

> *n*. informal esp. *AmE* an act of not accepting something when it is offered with the condition that one may claim it later: *I don't want a cigar now, thank you, but I'll take a rain check on it.*

It is neither helpful nor to the point to define the noun 'rain check' negatively as 'an act of not accepting something' (and hence as potentially synonymous with 'refusal', 'rejection'). The example is dubious, verging as it does on the jocose; one short pace beyond taking a rain check on a cigar is taking a rain check on rice pudding, a pickled onion or a smack in the eye – though such extensions become possible when the consciousness of the social etymon is removed. As to the power to negotiate the rain check, *Longman* is with the receiver rather than the giver. *Collins* is even-handed, explaining 'to take a rain check' as 'to *accept* or *request* the postponement of an offer' (my italics), meaning that the initiative can come either from the host-figure or the guest-figure. *Chambers* ('to promise to accept an invitation at a later date') introduces a new note of obligation; I take a rain check, it seems, in the spirit of taking a vow, by 'promising' my host that I will return on some more auspicious occasion. *The New Penguin English Dictionary* is not new enough to accommodate this word, which in fact has been in circulation in British English for some decades; and the *Shorter Oxford* includes the expression in its *Addenda*, notes 'also *transf*. and *fig*.', but does not explain or even cite the transf. and fig. of 'take a rain check'. Whoever goes to a dictionary for an explanation of this word will probably go because it has been encountered in the context of this phrase, and how to

use the phrase is the object of the consultant exercise. Yet none of
the dictionaries, or rather, none of the British informants, seems to
be wholly confident as to what the phrase means, how it is used,
what kind of event or interaction it takes into scope, what roles and
responsibilities are assumed by the participants in the interaction, or
even, in the case of the *Shorter Oxford* entry, how to spell the word.
(A check is not the same thing as a cheque, and I imagine that any
American who used the spelling 'rain cheque' might invite the scorn
commonly reserved for a milque toast.)[7]

Arch

Of the five test-words, this proves to be the most difficult to
define. ('Entropy' is probably the most difficult to understand,
but 'arch', though commonly understood, eludes definition.) The
dictionaries vary somewhat in their presentation of the word's
historical credentials, some indicating its derivative contact with a
pre-nominal element, 'arch = chief, supreme', as in 'archbishop',
'arch-conspirator', 'arch-rogue', while others list the adjective sepa-
rately from the pre-nominal particle. The generally preferred technique of definition is by synonyms. Thus *Chambers* has 'cunning,
waggish, roguish, shrewd', *Collins* 'knowing or superior', *Webster*
'clever, crafty', the *Universal Dictionary* 'mischievous, roguish',
and the *Shorter Oxford* 'clever, cunning, waggish'. These attempts
to find 'translational' equivalents indicate a puzzled guessing at
two, possibly three, semantic fields. There is the sense of 'private
knowledge' represented by 'cunning', 'crafty', 'knowing', 'shrewd';
there is 'benign teasing', as in 'mischievous', 'waggish', 'roguish';
and there is the sense of 'complacent attitude', as in 'superior'.
One or two of the dictionaries attempt to separate these strains of
meaning, though it is likely that in the actual usage of the word they
are often mingled, and some tackle the evident semantic difficulty by
resorting to manner adverbs. Thus *Collins* has 'coyly playful'; *The
New Penguin* 'cleverly sly and alert', 'playfully saucy', *Webster*
'gaily mischievous', and the *Shorter Oxford* 'slyly saucy', 'pleasantly
mischievous', with the sociological note 'now usu. of women and
children'. Several dictionaries cite the common collocation of 'arch'
with nouns denoting facial expression: 'an arch look'; 'an arch
glance'; 'an arch smile'. Only two, *Longman* and *COBUILD*, offer
categorical or contextual explanations, supported by citation. The
entries read:

Longman

> adj. making fun of people in a clever or playful way; *an arch smile-ly, adv, 'I know what you're thinking!' said the old lady archly*.

COBUILD

> An **arch** look or expression is mischievous and cunning EG *She giggled and gave me an arch look*. **archly** EG *She caught his eye and smiled archly*. A tone of voice that is **arch** suggests that you think you are more important or clever than anyone else EG *His tone of voice tends to be rather arch*.

What must strike anyone reading and comparing these entries is how little the definitions and exemplifications avail, and how puzzled the enquiring foreigner must continue to be about the meaning of 'arch'. The citations may acceptably illustrate usage, but they are attempts to define by insistence – an arch look means looking at someone archly – and do nothing to assist a breakout from the synonymic circle. *COBUILD*, furthermore, makes a contextual explanation that would be challenged by many native speakers of English: 'A tone of voice that is arch suggests that you think you are more important or clever than anyone else.' The compilers support this interpretation with a marginal note stating that 'arch' is synonymically related to 'superior' and is an antonym of 'humble'. Sampling among informants in casual encounters suggests to me that the *COBUILD* reading of the word is either totally aberrant, or perhaps indicates a peripheral drift towards a new sense. It is not my own practice to use 'arch' in the sense 'I think I am more important than anyone else', but rather with the nuance 'We know, don't we, you and I?' When all is said and done, however, the amusing and perhaps disturbing fact remains: we all recognize the kind of event denoted by the adjective 'arch', but we cannot adequately define the word, and our dictionaries do not help us much. Least helpful of all, perhaps, is the dictionary (*COBUILD*) that claims as a peculiar advantage its basis in an extensive corpus of actual English usage.

Fold in

It might be thought that few things could be more easily defined than this word, and indeed all the dictionaries with the exception of the *Shorter Oxford* (which ignores it) deal confidently with a phrasal verb familiar to all cooks. We require, it seems, a synonym; a manner adverb or an adverbial phrase or clause expressing manner; and, perhaps optionally, another adverbial indicating an instrument. The synonyms are 'mix', 'incorporate', 'blend', 'put into'. The recurrent manner adverb is 'gently'; 'carefully', 'gradually', 'slowly' also occur. It is with the clauses of manner and the 'instrument' adverbials that the dictionaries suggest slightly different views of what is essential to the definition of 'fold in'. Compare:

Collins

   by gently turning one part over the other with a spoon

New Penguin

   without stirring or beating

Longman

   by turning over gently with a spoon

Webster

   using gentle, cutting strokes

Universal Dictionary

   by slowly and gently turning one part over the other

A cook may not be confused by these variants, but a cook will hardly need to consult a dictionary to discover the meaning of the term. To the practically uninformed, the variant wordings are of greater moment. The consensus, at least as represented by *Collins*, *Longman* and the *Universal Dictionary*, appears to be that 'turning (one ingredient) over (another)' is necessary to 'folding in'. *The New Penguin*, however, merely makes the negative stipulation 'without stirring or beating', and *Webster* somewhat puzzlingly indicates 'cutting strokes'. *COBUILD* is neutrally uninformative on how the 'folding in' is done: 'you put the first substance into the second substance.' The general conclusion is that if you already understand 'fold in' the dictionary will tell you more or less what it means.

Regale

Most dictionaries (*COBUILD* is the customary exception) provide etymologies along the lines of that given by the *Shorter Oxford*, making reference to Old French *gale*, 'pleasure, joy' and to cognates like 'gallant' and 'gala'. The preferred technique of explanation is by categorical definition. Thus *Chambers* has 'to feast', 'to treat to'; *Collins* 'to give delight or amusement to' and 'to provide with abundant food or drink'; *The New Penguin* 'to entertain sumptuously' and 'to give pleasure or amusement to'; *Longman* 'to entertain with'; *Webster* 'to entertain by providing a splendid feast' and 'to delight with something pleasing and amusing'; the *Universal Dictionary* 'to delight or entertain'/'give pleasure to' and 'to entertain sumptuously with food and drink'/'provide a feast for'; and the *Shorter Oxford* 'to entertain or feast (a person etc.) in a choice manner', as well as a number of historical meanings. It is generally clear that two contingent meanings are involved: first, to make sumptuous provision of food and drink, and second, to entertain lavishly, presumably with some kind of show, recital or spectacle. Current usage suggests that this second meaning, in the weakened form of 'to tell stories' or 'to sing songs', predominates over the other. *COBUILD*, however, introduces a further element of significance:

> If you **regale** someone with stories, jokes, etc., you tell them a lot of stories or jokes, even if they do not want you to EG *I used to have a dentist who regaled me with extraordinary stories*.

'Even if they do not want you to' seems to have been inferred, without much justification, from the attested example. This illustrates rather well one of the incidental failings of the technique of contextual explanation; a meaning that apparently lurks subliminally in one context (you don't like going to the dentist, so the dentist's stories are as unwelcome as his other attentions) is not generally characteristic of the word in all its occurrences.

Entropy

Very few people who are not scientists will grasp, or be capable of grasping, what this word means; though many will have vague notions of its connection with thermodynamics and the physical laws concerning the conservation of matter and energy. The method of explanation adopted by all the dictionaries is that of categorical definition. Here *Webster* is generally the most intelligible to the baffled layperson, by consistently defining 'entropy', in three given senses, as 'a measure of [something]'. The enquirer will at least learn that entropy is a kind of measurement – of diminishing energy and increasing disorganization in 'closed' systems like the universe, an engine, or, by analogy, a text. The recognizable word, 'measure', makes available at least a figurative understanding of a term which the *Universal Dictionary* elaborately defines by the *Call My Bluff* technique of *ignotum per ignotius*, the unknown by the still more unknown. What must be obvious to anyone reading the dictionaries' earnest quasi-explanations of this difficult term is that such words can never be explained *deductively* – 'here's a definition of entropy, now see if you can find an instance'; they can only be learned *inductively*, in the course of a lecture, or after the laboratory demonstration – 'and this, ladies and gentlemen, is what we call entropy'. It is of little use to know the etymology of the word, although *Webster*, once again, does some service in pointing out that R.J.E. Clausius, the scientist who first formulated the concept, named his notion in a piece of word-play, on the Greek particle *en*, as a preposition meaning 'in', 'into', and as the first syllable of the word 'energy'. Clausius' intention was thus to suggest a portmanteau of 'energy' and the Greek *trope*, a turning: 'entropy', a turn-over of energy. This again has some value in providing a figurative access to a concept which *COBUILD*'s definition happily disregards. 'Entropy', according to *COBUILD*, is 'in formal English a state of disorder, confusion, and disorganization', a definition supported by a marginal note indicating synonymy with 'chaos'. This is extraordinarily misleading. Are we to gather from it that 'formal English' usage would admit sentences like 'My room is in a state of entropy', or 'The entropies of 1789 have never been adequately described'? It looks as though the lexicographer, having in this case no corpus material to draw on, is wildly guessing.[8]

It takes only a word or two to persuade us that dictionaries often delude seekers after knowledge and wisdom, leaving them none the wiser and only a little more knowing. But this is a cynical conclusion, and indeed a disturbing one, for if it were even half true it might be thought that a dictionary is a fairly useless and certainly not indispensable piece of equipment. Dictionaries, however, are not useless, and would be difficult to dispense with. Their commonest service to us is psychological: they assure us that words exist, that they 'are English', and that we are free to use them. For the literate, it is unsettling to find that the compositionally apt word is not yet in any dictionary, either because the dictionaries are never wholly up to date or because it is sometimes very easy to invent a word. The dictionary guarantees words as a bank sponsors currency. Furthermore, most dictionaries offer some advice on the way to use words, at least to the extent of demonstrating typical constructions and typical contexts. They tell us that the appropriate preposition after 'regale' is 'with', and they indicate, as a semantic constraint upon 'arch', that it collocates with nouns denoting facial expression or tone of voice, so that 'Her hat had an arch tilt', or 'His dentures gleamed archly' would be stylistic acts committed at the innovator's own risk. What dictionaries are rather less good at telling us is the type of social interaction or communicative function in which a word may be appropriate. They will sometimes note that a word is archaic, or literary, or informal, but beyond such brief annotations we are rarely able to discover from a dictionary what sort of person might be expected to use a particular word, in what circumstances, and with what purpose in view. These are the real determiners of 'meaning', the criteria that most commonly need to be explained, and dictionaries have the perverse quality of most helping those who least need help; 'For they teach not their owne Use', as Bacon says of Studies, 'But that is a Wisdome without them and above them, won by Observation'.

This was the subject of a talk given to a research seminar at the University of Nottingham; the revised and considerably expanded version printed here formed the text of a lecture delivered in January 1989, to an audience in the Department of Applied Linguistics at the University of Thessaloniki, Greece.

4 Our true intent: or, what's the point of punctuation?

When the rustic players in *A Midsummer Night's Dream* appear before Duke Theseus, his courtiers and his formidable spouse, the Lady Hippolyta, they are understandably nervous. Indeed, the actor who is to speak their prologue, Peter Quince, is so unsettled by the grandeur of the occasion that he can hardly make sense of his lines. You may remember how he introduces their play, 'The most lamentable comedy and most cruel death of Pyramus and Thisby':

> If we offend, it is with our good will.
>   That you should think, we come not to offend,
> But with good will. To show our simple skill,
>   That is the true beginning of our end.
> Consider then, we come but in despite.
>   We do not come, as minding to content you,
> Our true intent is. All for your delight,
>   We are not here. That you should here repent you,
> The actors are at hand; and, by their show,
>   You shall know all that you are like to know . . .

At which the Duke is moved to observe, 'This fellow doth not stand upon points', meaning that the prologue-speaker has not punctuated his text correctly, and Lysander, with the toadying instinct of the true courtier, hastens to show off his own wit and flatter the Duke's:

> He hath rid his prologue like a rough colt; he knows not the stop. A good moral, my lord: it is not enough to speak, but to speak true.

Both Lysander and the Duke are of course punning, or 'quibbling', with the Shakespearean gusto that so irritated Dr Johnson. The words 'point' and 'stop' in Elizabethan usage both refer to marks of punctuation; but the idiom 'not to stand upon points' meant to proceed rudely, without regard to etiquette and 'not to know the stop' signified to be inexpert in the technique of bridling your horse. The Duke and Lysander are agreed in their judgement of the prologue: the poor chap is a mere peasant.

They are a little snobbish, perhaps, these fine gentlemen, but they are in no doubt about the point of punctuation. For them, clearly, it is an accessory to speech, an organizer of cohesion and good sense. Theseus and Lysander clearly associate punctuation with oral delivery; their allegation that the prologue's speech lacks punctuation implies a scripting of material intended to be spoken aloud. Perhaps this is how Shakespeare himself regarded punctuation: not as a device to guide the eye and the mind as we sit passively reading a text, but as a set of instructions for speakers, enabling them to phrase their discourse for the benefit of hearers. It is certainly the case that punctuation has both auditory and visual implications – the values, if you like, of the forum or the theatre on the one hand, and of the study or the library on the other. It is also the case that our literary culture has tended to merge these implications, so that quite often, when we read a piece of text, the punctuation will suggest a delivery, the sense of a voice speaking, and a semantic interpretation, a guide to relationships within the text which we perceive without necessarily feeling impelled to speak the words aloud. Texts as we know them generally carry, in the form of punctuation, recommendations for performance and indications of grammatical structure. We assume, not unreasonably, that there are conventions which writers use in planning their texts at these two levels; yet reasonable though the general assumption may be, it is far from true that the conventions are immutable. They do change in time, and they are variously handled by individual writers.

GENERAL CONVENTION AND AUTHORIAL OPTION

Here let me digress a little, to introduce two examples which may help to show how conventions change their rulings and how writers change their minds. The first example consists of a couplet from Samuel Johnson's *The Vanity of Human Wishes*. The lines I have in mind come at the end of Johnson's portrait of Charles XII of Sweden. This is the form in which they were first printed:

He left the name, at which the world grew pale,
To point a moral and adorn a tale.

And here are the same lines, as printed in a modern anthology:

He left the name at which the world grew pale
To point a moral and adorn a tale.

When I first became acquainted with these lines, as a student, the commas in the original text puzzled me a great deal. For one thing, they seemed to script a delivery marked by fractional pauses before and after the phrase 'at which the world grew pale', and by a distinctive intonation pattern. This delivery, moreover, was associated in my mind with a particular syntactic and semantic relationship, the relationship of a parenthesis or of a commentary on the general proposition of the preceding clause; that is, as though what the world grew pale at was the leaving of the name. Now, this was clearly not Johnson's intention; I think we may say with some certainty that what the world grew pale at was the name itself, not the business of leaving it. The source of my puzzlement or distraction lay in my suppositions about a modern punctuational convention that distinguishes regularly between so-called 'restrictive' or 'defining' and 'non-restrictive' or 'non-defining' relative constructions. Thus,

The bishop drew a rude picture, at which the curate laughed

may be taken to imply something slightly different from

The bishop drew a rude picture at which the curate laughed.

Similarly, this:

The postman, who is blind in one eye, misread the address

differs significantly from this:

The postman who is blind in one eye misread the address.

The second instance in each of these pairs of examples presents the relationship we call 'restrictive' or 'defining'; the curate's laughter is restricted to the picture, the one-eyed blindness defines a particular postman. In the first example of each pair, the relationship is non-restrictive, and the process of defining is not limited to an immediate antecedent. What the curate laughs at is the circumstance that the bishop draws a rude picture; what we are told about the postman is intended as auxiliary information, which will help us to understand how he came to misread an address; it is not used to define one postman among several.[1]

What I am describing now is a present-day convention in literary usage, a convention which, as we see, has led at least one editor to correct Johnson's punctuation so that the reading of 'at which the world grew pale' is shown to be unmistakably restrictive, and thus limits and virtually dictates the possibilities of intonation and delivery. In present-day English the contrast I have described is regularly observed by careful writers – so regularly indeed that we might give it the status of a central principle in punctuation. Dr Johnson's writing, and that of other eminent eighteenth-century and early nineteenth-century authors, does not observe this principle. So far as I can ascertain from random sampling, these authors customarily put relative constructions between commas, irrespective of their potential status as defining or non-defining items. 'Customarily' does not mean always; restriction through the omission of a comma is occasionally observed. It is difficult to speak with certainty about these things; the punctuation practice of our eighteenth- and nineteenth-century authors, a practice we might suppose to be built on consistent principles, will often appear idiosyncratic in particular cases. Punctuations of the past are fascinating because at times they suggest quite an unfamiliar view of discourse, a different *framing*, so to speak. Consider, for instance, the punctuation of one of the best-known sentences in English literature, the opening of *Pride and Prejudice*:

> It is a truth universally acknowledged, that a single man in possession of a good fortune, must be in want of a wife.

Why does Jane Austen put a comma after 'acknowledged', instead of letting the sentence run on, as a modern author might? One answer could be that she was 'scripting' her text, giving directions for reading aloud. Or might she have been following a convention that required the placing of a comma before a *that*-clause and after a reporting proposition? Assertions with verbs like 'say', 'remark', 'allege', 'declare', 'hear', 'learn' are not infrequently punctuated in this way in eighteenth-century prose. Some examples culled from two pages of Swift's pamphlet *The Conduct of the Allies*:

> Yet in the very same article it is said, that the *States* shall be *favoured in all the Spanish Dominions*

> It is to be observed, that this Treaty was only Signed by one of our Plenipotentiaries

> And I have been told, that the other was heard to say, He would rather lose his right hand, than set it to such a Treaty

> I have been likewise told, that some very necessary conditions were wanting in the Entrance upon this Treaty

his Secretary threatened, that if we would not further supply his Majesty, he could not answer for what might happen

his Highness very frankly promised them, that in Consideration of this Deficiency, *Britain* and the *States* should encrease their Subsidies

It is therefore to be hoped, that his *Prussian* Majesty, at the end of this War, will not have the same Cause of Complaint.

Swift's practice helps to explain Jane Austen's; when she puts her comma after 'acknowledged' and before the *that*-clause, she is observing a literary precedent, the Augustan convention still in force a hundred years after Swift's time. But what about that comma after 'fortune'? This seems to me at first sight to be a little odd; if I were going to put a comma after 'fortune', I would also want a comma after 'single man', to mark off a parenthetical qualification, thus: 'that a single man, in possession of a good fortune, must be in want of a wife.' Did Jane Austen intend that phrase to be suspended, as it were, in a parenthesis? If not, it would seem that our writer has taken the unusual liberty of separating the subject of a clause from its predicate by the insertion of a comma. Not only unusual, but, for a modern writer at least, impermissible. We would not think it correct to write, for example, 'University College London, stands in Gower Street', or 'Professor Sidney Greenbaum, is an eminent grammarian' or 'A rich man, needs a wife'. On the other hand, we are not allowed to suppose that it has always been unacceptable. Here is Swift again, in the first sentence of the fifth chapter of *Gulliver's Travels*:

The Empire of *Blefuscu*, is an Island situated to the North North-East Side of *Lilliput*.

And at the beginning of the preceding chapter:

The first Request that I made after I had obtained my Liberty, was, that I might have Licence to see *Mildendo*.

If such instances are not to be ascribed to carelessness or individual whim – hardly likely with Dean Swift, who was punctilious in matters of usage – they suggest at least some precedent for Jane Austen's practice. If we are sufficiently interested in the placing or the omission of a comma, we might, then, offer two explanations of her punctuation in this classic sentence. We might like to think that she punctuated it that way because she wanted it to be *spoken* that way – that the comma after 'fortune' indicates, for instance, an emphasis on the following 'must'; on the other hand we have reason to suppose that she was merely reflecting the punctuation standard of her time. Our modern convention admits alternative solutions, which may not have been available to Jane Austen. For instance, assuming that we do not intend to 'script' for expressive phrasing, we can take the option of presenting 'in possession of a good fortune' restrictively – that is, without encapsulating commas. The whole sentence is then comma-less:

> It is a truth universally acknowledged that a single man in possession of a good fortune must be in want of a wife.

Or we can opt for a non-restrictive reading:

> It is a truth universally acknowledged that a single man, in possession of a good fortune, must be in want of a wife.

Quite possibly (I would not wish to be dogmatic about it) these would be our primary choices, and Jane Austen's own version would have marginal status, as a punctuation representing a delivery style rather than a syntactic analysis.

There, indeed, you have two phrases that conveniently express the point of punctuation: 'delivery style' and 'syntactic analysis'. Deciding what punctuation *means* is often a matter of discerning and distinguishing between these concomitant functions. This is not always easy, even with texts written in our own time; when we look at older writings we are often faced with the oddity of having to reconcile modes of proposition and modes of emphasis or feeling. We may be certain enough of what Dr Johnson and Jane Austen *meant*, in the logical–propositional sense, but what has receded from us is any like degree of certainty about how they would have delivered the words. Hence there is a dimension into which we cannot assuredly enter, a dimension of feeling. People tell me that the first sentence of *Pride and Prejudice* is supremely ironic. I can see, without wishing to rehearse them now, the grounds for asserting this; but I would nevertheless say that our perception of the irony is fairly crude, and that the finer feelings of the sentence, contained in modulations, pauses and emphases, are much less obvious and may indeed be inaccessible to us.

The surface logic of the text is always more accessible than its attitudinal implications, which is my professorial way of saying that it is fairly easy to see how sentences hang together but not so easy to pick up the tone of voice they imply. It is also relatively easy to know when sentences do not hang together logically, and, if you are a writer, to repair the defects of your construction. If you are worried about the inadequacy of punctuation to convey emphases and intonations, you are bound to rely, ultimately, on the reader's perceptiveness and good will. But if it is a matter of eliminating ambiguities or revising a pattern of connections between word and word, you should be in full command of what you do. This brings me to the second of the two examples I had in mind when I began this now rather lengthy digression. It consists of some lines from Wordsworth's *Prelude*, cited by J.C. Maxwell as an interesting case of poetic punctuation and re-punctuation.[2] This long poem, as is well known, exists in two versions, one from the year 1805, and the other, incorporating many revisions, from 1850. Lines 457–62 in Book VIII of the 1805 text read as follows:

> Starting from this point,
> I had my face towards the truth, began
> With an advantage; furnished with that kind
> Of prepossession without which the soul
> Receives no knowledge that can bring forth good,
> No genuine insight ever comes to her.

Note here the semi-colon in the third line of the extract. Its purport, I think you will agree, is to suggest to the reader that the antecedent of 'furnished', the word to which it is logically connected, is 'I'; it is the poet who is 'furnished with that kind of prepossession'. Now consider the corresponding passage, lines 322–7, in Book VIII of the 1850 version:

> Starting from this point
> I had my face turned toward the truth, began
> With an advantage furnished by that kind
> Of prepossession, without which the soul
> Receives no knowledge that can bring forth good,
> No genuine insight ever comes to her.

Wordsworth, it seems, has changed his mind about his meaning, and in doing so has changed his punctuation. Ignore the lesser revisions and concentrate on one point, the gap between the words 'advantage' and 'furnished'. Here is neither semi-colon nor any other point of punctuation. Consequently, 'furnished' is no longer to be referred to the antecedent 'I'; it now has a restrictive, or defining relationship with 'advantage'. The sense is no longer that the poet is 'furnished *with* an advantage', but rather that the advantage in question is 'furnished *by* a kind of prepossession'. It makes a considerable difference. The propositional content of the verse is affected and reflected by this change in punctuation; indeed, I know of few passages which more strikingly answer the question, 'What's the point of punctuation?' Its point here is quite obvious. It is an agent serving the author as he seeks to explore and re-articulate his own meaning.

THE PROCESS OF ARTICULATION

Now, with that word 'articulate' we may return to the true beginning of our end, our Shakespearean prologue with its uncertain command of points and stops. Peter Quince is 'inarticulate' in a very special sense. He can find words and phrases, but he cannot connect them properly. Latin *artus*, the dictionary tells us, means 'a limb', and *articulus*, 'a joint'; it can also mean 'a division of discourse'. To articulate, then, involves a control of the means by which a subject-matter is portioned and linked; a control of textual components, accompanied by a command of devices that express linkage or disjunction. The terminology of punctuation is generally related to these complementary activities of dividing and connecting. The word 'colon', for example, is yet another word meaning a limb, or member, and in classical rhetoric denotes a stretch of text corresponding to what we would call a clause; in time, however, the reference of the term has shifted from the piece of text to the sign indicating the demarcation of the piece of text; from the compositional unit to its concomitant mark of separation and subdivision. A comparable ambiguity can be discerned in the word 'point'. A 'full point', or as we should now say, 'a full stop' related originally to the completion of a unit of meaning. The point of the point was that the mark on the page conventionally indicated the conclusion of a semantic process; but the word 'point' also indicates the process itself, as we acknowledge when we talk of 'making a point' or 'coming to the point' in argument or exposition.[3]

In the classical rhetoric to which I have just referred, terms like 'period' and 'colon' express the notion of discursive unit, rather than of any mark by which the unit is delimited. *Periodos* in Greek means 'a circuit', 'a cycle'; for the Greeks, a stylistic 'period' was a circuit of meaning, a 'cycling' of the immediate matter of discourse. Periods might be phased, as it were, in constituent processes or sub-periods called 'cola'. The relationship between *period* and *colon*, as discerned by Aristotle and his contemporaries, closely resembles the relationship we in our time perceive between *sentence* and *clause* – our grammarians tell us that a sentence consists of one or more clauses.

The difference, if any, is that in the Greek view the relationship is rhetorical as well as grammatical, so that the 'cola' are often seen to enter into the 'period' as elements in a design involving verbal parallels, inversions, repetitions and so on. The notion is well illustrated by the following passage from the *Rhetorica ad Herennium*, a textbook from the first century BC, formerly but no longer attributed to Cicero. Its author explains:

> Colon or Clause is the name given to a sentence member, brief and complete, which does not express the entire thought, but is in turn supplemented by another colon, as follows: 'On the one hand you were helping your enemy.' That is one so-called colon; it ought to be supplemented by a second: 'And on the other you were hurting your friend.' This figure can consist of two cola, but it is neatest and most complete when composed of three, as follows: 'You were helping your enemy, you were hurting your friend, and you were not consulting your own best interests.'
>
> *Rhetorica ad Herennium*, IV.xix.1[4]

This is a manufactured example of what we have come to know as 'the periodic style', a manner of writing in which periods, or completed cycles of expression, are parcelled out in cola which are quite often in rhythmic and grammatical balance. There is indeed a figure of rhetoric called 'isocolon', involving the exact balancing of clauses, word for word. We see it in the example from the *ad Herennium*: 'You were helping your enemy, you were hurting your friend.'

In the English translation of that example, the period is punctuated by commas which mark off the 'cola'. For us this is obligatory; not so for the Roman writer, in whose text the three clauses follow in sequence without intervening marks of punctuation. For the ancients, the primary significance of 'comma' was a short piece of text – corresponding to our 'phrase' – and only in the second place a mark of punctuation used to portion out the text. Again, let the author of the *ad Herennium* supply the commentary:

> It is called a Comma or Phrase when single words are set apart by pauses in staccato speech, as follows: 'By your vigour, voice, looks you have terrified your adversaries.' Again: 'You have destroyed your enemies by jealousy, injuries, influence, perfidy.'

This is the style the Elizabethan rhetorician George Puttenham has in mind when he translates the name of the figure called *Brachylogia* as 'the cutted comma'. The first-century Graeco-Roman rhetorician, Demetrius, speaks of a 'forcible style' which is characterized by 'commata', comma-linked phrases, rather than by periodically-patterned 'cola'.[5] The term 'comma', used in this way, labelled a rhetorical function. It could also be used as we now employ it, to denote the mark rather than the textual unit. Aristotle mentions the importance of such marks in resolving ambiguities. The particular example he cites is a sentence from Heraclitus which may be paraphrased in English as follows:

Although this reason is apparent at all times men are devoid of understanding.

Aristotle observes that 'it is hard, since it is uncertain to which word another belongs, whether to that which follows or that which precedes'; implying that the sentence needs to be disambiguated, either by putting a mark of punctuation after 'apparent' ('Although this reason is apparent, at all times men are devoid of understanding') or after 'times' ('Although this reason is apparent at all times, men are devoid of understanding').[6] In such cases, the comma is not a stylistic element; it is a way of showing which word belongs to which construction.

The Graeco-Roman writers thus appear to have conceived the articulation of texts in terms of a threefold hierarchy: the *period*, the *colon* and the *comma*, these concepts referring in the first instance to units of construction, and subsequently to the marks of punctuation by which the units were distinguished. Period and colon outline the larger shapes of discourse; the comma, as a punctuation mark, has more to do with the local, short-term management of meaning. My full stops and colons, or, more probably semi-colons, show how I view the build-up of my text; my commas are more likely to show how I choose between grammatical options or between alternatives of expressive phrasing, as I work my way through the text. There is, one might say, a punctuation for exterior form and a punctuation for interior detail. Our perception of this is specifically expressed in our use of those marks of punctuation called *stops*, the central devices in any punctuational system. In the late sixteenth century, writers appear to have used systems of three or four stops. George Puttenham, for instance, describes a three-stop system:

Much . . . might be sayd for the use of your three pauses, *comma*, *colon*, & *periode*, for perchance it be not all a matter to use many *commas*, and few, nor *colons* likewise, or long or short *periodes*, for it is diversly used, by divers good writers.[7]

Puttenham does not mention here the semi-colon, though it was certainly in use by his time. Towards the end of the sixteenth century writers began to use the semi-colon regularly, as partner to the colon in a discursive system of four stops.[8]

THE FOUR-STOP SYSTEM: HISTORICAL EXAMPLES

Let us look at some examples of texts ranging from Tudor times down to the Regency. Here is a neat instance from Robert Burton's *Anatomy of Melancholy* (1621):

> I am not poor, I am not rich; *nihil est, nihil deest*, I have little, I want nothing: all my treasure is in Minerva's tower.

A complete period is divided, at the colon after 'nothing', into two segments, the first of which is subdivided, by the semi-colon after 'rich', into parallel 'cola',which are further subdivided, by the commas, into 'commata'. Rehearse the structure: we begin with a component consisting of two exactly balanced clauses, the clauses separated by a comma, the piece of text ending in a semi-colon. Next, after the semi-colon we have a longer component – twice as long, in fact, consisting of *four* clauses in two balanced pairs, separated by commas, the whole component ending in a colon. In content, this component is a repetition or paraphrase of the first, and the second pair in the component is a translation of the first pair. This completes, we may say, half of the argument of the total proposition. The completion is marked by the colon, after which follows the second part of the argument, a single clause which functions like an explanation or a reply in dialogue, answering the question raised by the clauses before the colon: 'I am neither rich nor poor. How so?' Answer – 'I am a scholar' ('All my treasure is in Minerva's tower'). Historical examples frequently suggest that the colon has this dialogic force of introducing a reply, a reason, a summation. In a well known sentence from Milton's *Areopagitica* the initial proposition precedes the colon, which is followed by the argument expanding and explaining the proposition, laid out in two parts separated by a semi-colon:

> And yet, on the other hand, unless wariness be used, as good almost kill a man as kill a good book: who kills a man kills a reasonable creature, God's image; but he who destroys a good book kills reason itself, kills the image of God, as it were in the eye.

Sir Thomas Browne reverses this process, first setting out the argument round a semi-colon division, and then bringing in the summary after the colon. (The example is from his *Religio Medici*, 1642):

> Thus there are two books from whence I collect my divinity; besides that written one of God, another of his servant nature, that universal and public manuscript lies expanded unto the eyes of all: those that never saw him in the one, have discovered him in the other.

Such relationships between the structure of the argument and its punctuational framing are commonly discernible in Renaissance prose. A magnificent example is this extract from Richard Hooker's *Of the Laws of Ecclesiastical Polity* (1593):

> Now if nature should intermit her course, and leave altogether though it were but for a while the observation of her own laws; if those principal and mother elements of the world, whereof all things in this lower world are made, should lose the qualities which they now have; if the frame of that heavenly arch erected over our heads should loosen and dissolve itself; if celestial spheres should forget their wonted motions, and by irregular volubility turn themselves any way as it might happen; if the prince of the lights of heaven, which now as a giant doth run his unwearied course, should as it were through a languishing faintness begin to stand and to rest himself; if the moon should wander from her beaten way, the times and seasons of the year blend themselves by disordered and confused mixture, the winds breathe out their last gasp, the clouds yield no rain, the earth be defeated of heavenly influence, the fruits of the earth pine away as children at the withered breasts of their mother no longer able to to yield them relief: what would become of man himself, whom these things now do all serve?

Here indeed is a macro-period, a huge sentence built on the basically simple pattern 'If X, then what of Y?' Hooker builds up a long introductory sequence of if-clauses, separating each from its neighbour by means of a semi-colon, and separating by commas the subordinate or coordinate clauses within the 'if' units. These units grow gradually longer. The last of them, the one beginning 'if the moon should wander' has no less than six clause-components divided by commas, and here once more there is a general process of building up clause length, so that the last in the series ('the fruits of the earth') is twenty-three words long. Then, after all these 'ifs', bridled by semi-colons and by commas controlling the text between the semi-colons, then comes the colon: followed by a brief propounding of the question. This is a classic example of the periodic style, using the major stops.

Eighteenth-century examples are in many cases less clearly indicative of the marshalling of argument and more suggestive of what I have called the 'delivery style'. In the following sentence from the preface to Fielding's *Tom Thumb the Great* (1730), semi-colon and colon do not appear to have any propositional significance; rather it would seem that they measure pauses:

> As to this history's not bearing the stamp of the second, third, or fourth edition, I see but little in that objection; editions being very uncertain lights to judge of books by: and perhaps Mr. M---r may now have joined twenty editions in one, as Mr. C----l hath ere now divided one in twenty.

A modern writer would put a comma where Fielding has a semi-colon ('I see but little in that objection, editions being very uncertain lights to judge of books by'), and a semi-colon for Fielding's colon ('being very uncertain lights to judge of books by; and perhaps Mr. M---r etc'). Similarly, in this passage from Johnson's *The Vision of Theodore the Hermit of Teneriffe* (1748), the eighteenth-century punctuation looks odd to modern eyes, unless we regard it as an index to the delivery style:

> As I sat thus, forming alternatively excuses for delay, and resolutions to go forward, an irresistible heaviness suddenly surprised me; I laid my head upon the bank, and resigned myself to sleep: when methought I heard the sound as of the flight of eagles, and a being of more than human dignity stood before me.

Modern practice would perhaps suggest the insertion of a full stop, in place of the semi-colon after 'me', and the replacement of the colon after 'sleep' with a semi-colon or a comma. The eighteenth-century punctuations exemplified by Fielding and Johnson no doubt seem to us too deliberately measured, too 'heavy' for the argument or narrative they present. The weight of the four-stop system is still apparent in the following sentence from Jane Austen's *Northanger Abbey*, but here enters another, lighter motif:

> There were still some subjects, indeed, under which she believed they must always tremble; – the mention of a chest or cabinet, for instance – and she did not love the sight of japan in any shape: but even *she* could allow, that an occasional memento of past folly, however painful, might not be without use.

Note, incidentally, the comma between the reporting verb, 'allow', and the following *that*-clause. Jane Austen obediently follows the Augustan convention, except that into this sentence she introduces an oddly discrepant element, the dash. It invites a repunctuation in a more modern style, replacing the semi-colon with a comma and the colon with a semi-colon:

> There were still some subjects, indeed, under which she believed they must always tremble – the mention of a chest or cabinet, for instance – and she did not love the sight of japan in any shape; but even *she* could allow that an occasional memento of past folly, however painful, might not be without use.

It is more than possible, of course (Jane Austen being Jane Austen), that the 'Augustan' punctuation is a kind of solemn mimicry upon which the dash irreverently breaks, in the headlong spirit of Catherine Norland herself. That is an entertaining thought, but it hardly affects the undoubted fact that with this sample of usage at the turn of the eighteenth and nineteenth centuries we are beginning to witness a weakening of the old four-stop method of marshalling a text.

WHATEVER HAPPENED TO THE COLON?

I do not mean to imply the rhetorical rule of colon, semi-colon and comma came to an end in Jane Austen's day; there are examples enough in nineteenth- and twentieth-century prose to prove me wrong, were I to assert any such thing. What I would venture to assert is that since the nineteenth century, at least, the four-stop system has been weakened by a general reduction in the scope and power of the colon, which has become less prominent in the organization of discourse and more closely tied to particular functions. At the present time, I would say, it is most commonly used to cite, to specify, to introduce a consequence or a conclusion, as in these examples:

> The following persons have access to the files: the chairman, the managing director, the company secretary, and heads of department.

> Only one person could have written the poem: Shakespeare.

> He became addicted to cocaine: it killed him.

> Somebody had to admit it in the end: the earth was round.

It is generally not used to link the cola of an extended period, nor, as a rule, does it mark antitheses, comparisons or expansions. Thus, it is improbable that anyone would choose to write:

The climate is benign: the food is excellent: the people are friendly.

More probable is this:

The climate is benign; the food is excellent; the people are friendly.

And still more likely, this:

The climate is benign, the food is excellent, the people are friendly.

The general abandonment of the colon, for anything other than the purposes of citation or specification, has left us with a three-stop system in discursive prose. The semi-colon, as a result, has become a rather complex mark of punctuation. It has some of the disjunctive force of the colon; it also has some of the linking significance of the comma. Consequently there is a rivalry between the semi-colon and the comma, a rivalry that may well cause the semi-colon in its turn to be relegated to the stylistic margin. If that happens, discourse of the 'periodic' kind will have recourse to two stops only, the full point and the comma; which means that the cola of long periods would be managed by the comma alone. This I would regard as an impoverishment of our punctuational system, or perhaps I should say of our punctuational rhetoric. A three-stop system (period, semi-colon, comma) serves formal and oratorical prose rather well. Here is a familiar modern instance:

We shall fight in France, we shall fight on the seas and oceans, we shall fight with growing confidence and growing strength in the air, we shall defend our island, whatever the cost may be, we shall fight on the beaches, we shall fight in the landing grounds, we shall fight in the fields and in the streets, we shall fight in the hills; we shall never surrender.

In this extract from one of Winston Churchill's wartime speeches, the cola are scripted by commas, not semi-colons, and correspondingly a semi-colon enters at the point where a colon might have occurred, before the concluding, summating clause. This is certainly formal oratory, but the style is not entirely the *megaloprepes*, the elevated style described by the Greek rhetoricians. In its headlong progress from 'We shall fight' down to 'in the hills' it has something of the *deinos*, the *forcible*, which Demetrius recommends. If we were to re-punctuate this passage, substituting semi-colons for commas and a colon for the one semi-colon, it would be more grandly measured, loftier, perhaps, but less urgent. Given the occasion and the challenge he has to meet, Churchill is justified in his punctuation. He rides his oration like a charger; he knows the stop.

THE PETER QUINCE PROBLEM

But that phrase must remind us of where we started, with Peter Quince and his want of articulation. After all our discussion of stops, can we help him out? Can we find the right punctuation for this notorious passage, one of Shakespeare's teases? We may remind ourselves of the text:

> If we offend, it is with our good will.
>   That you should think, we come not to offend,
> But with good will. To show our simple skill,
>   That is the true beginning of our end.
> Consider then, we come but in despite.
>   We do not come, as minding to content you,
> Our true intent is. All for your delight,
>   We are not here. That you should here repent you,
> The actors are at hand; and, by their show,

The task of reforming this gabble is harder than perhaps it looks; in fact it resembles what textual scholars do in fierce earnest when they struggle to restore meaning to passages that seem irretrievably corrupted. The eighteenth-century scholar Edward Capell said of this passage from *A Midsummer Night's Dream* that 'its punctuation, which is that of his First Quarto, can be mended by nobody'. That conviction was not shared by Charles Knight, a mid-nineteenth-century editor of Shakespeare. He offered this version:

> If we offend, it is with our good will that you should think we come not to offend; but with good will to show our simple skill. That is the true beginning of our end. Consider, then. We come: but in despite we do not come. As, minding to content you, our true intent is all for your delight. We are not here that you should here repent you. The actors are at hand . . .[9]

To this attempt he added the comment, 'we fear we have taken longer to puzzle out this enigma than the poet did to produce it'. And, indeed, you may be disposed to say, as I am, that Knight's solution, ingenious though it may be in some respects, is not the last possible word on the matter. Apart from anything else, I suspect any punctuation that leaves unmodified the paradoxical pronouncement

'That is the true beginning of our end' – even if 'end' is read, no doubt correctly, as meaning 'purpose'. (So that the line might be paraphrased, 'That, at the outset, is what we intend to do'.) We have to correct Quince's text so that all absurdities, real or apparent, are banished. If we make a skip forward, well over a century, we find the following version proposed as 'Quince's prologue rightly punctuated' by the editor of the Arden edition:

> If we offend, it is with our good will
> That you should think we come, not to offend,
> But with good will to show our simple skill:
> That is the true beginning of our end.
> Consider then, we come – but in despite
> We do not come – as minding to content you;
> Our true intent is all for your delight:
> We are not here that you should here repent you.
> The actors are at hand . . .[10]

A convincing feature of this is the use of the four-stop system; colon and semi-colon control the text in plausible style. Less convincing, perhaps, is the dash (but this objection is no stronger than the merest hunch about the probabilities of Shakespearean punctuation). Least convincing is the retention of the problematic line, 'That is the true beginning of our end'. Although I am in broad agreement with the Arden editor's revision, I am unwilling to accept any punctuation that keeps this proposition intact. I can only feel that Shakespeare intended it as a joke – a sample, in fact, of the joke that generally governs the text, the joke that arises fortuitously when, thanks to the speaker's mismanagement of his script, self-contradictory propositions appear to be made: 'If we offend, it is with our good will', 'We do not come as minding to content you', 'Consider, then, we come but in despite' ('but', in this bungled instance, acquires the sense of 'only'). If we perceive these as instances of comic ambiguity to be corrected by punctuation, we must surely perceive 'That is the true beginning of our end' in the same way, as a 'howler' committed by an unpractised rhetorician.

Before proposing a modified version of the Arden solution of the Peter Quince problem, I should like to suggest two explanatory procedures. One of these is to attempt a reconstitution of the sense of the passage by means of paraphrase. To articulate the passage convincingly, we must have in our minds a clear idea of a scheme of emphases, repetitions and disjunctions. It is likely that there are several possible schemes, or 'immanent' texts, each expressed by different surface punctuations. My paraphrase, therefore, must be taken as representing a personal – if, as I hope, plausible – reading of the rustic prologue and its anxious, stammering attempt at a *captatio benevolentiae*:[11]

> If we offend, please believe that we come with the best of intentions – not to offend at all, but in the sincere hope of entertaining you to the best of our simple abilities. That, truly, is what we are now about to attempt. Please, then, bear in mind our aim. We have not come here with the idea of displeasing you; we wish to give you pleasure, and our whole intention is that you should be delighted. We do not want you to be sorry we came here. The actors are standing by. . .

This is an interpretation that has now to be mapped onto Quince's text, with the help of the kind of punctuation that Quince's creator might have regarded as standard – in effect, the four-stop system. But there is another 'explanatory procedure' that must first be taken into account, and that is the elucidation of two related points of rhetoric and grammar. The rhetorical point is that Tudor English, no less than Modern English, allowed the device of 'fronting' – that is, of indicating a particular emphasis or focus by placing at the beginning of a clause an element not occurring there in the 'normal' word order; for example, we might write 'For your delight we come', instead of 'We come for your delight'. Now in Quince's prologue there is one place at which the possibility of fronting makes acceptable sense out of an unacceptable line. Suppose that, instead of 'That is the true beginning of our end, etc.', we read: 'That is the true beginning. Of our end consider, then, etc.' If this looks odd, it is no doubt because such a reading postulates the existence, in Tudor English, of a phrasal verb 'to consider of (something)'. If we can make that assumption, then there is no difficulty about the 'fronting' from 'Consider of our end' to 'Of our end consider'. Now, 'consider of' did indeed exist in Early Modern English, and the *Oxford English Dictionary* attests occurrences which include a striking instance from the translators' preface to the King James Bible (1611): 'They set them forth openly to be considered of and approved by all.' Thus, granted a dual licence from rhetoric and grammar, we may at last propose a version that separates beginnings from ends:

> If we offend, it is with our good will
> That you should think we come; not to offend,
> But with good will, to show our simple skill.

> That is the true beginning. Of our end
> Consider, then: we come, but in despite
> We do not come, as, minding to content you,
> Our true intent is all for your delight.
> We are not here that you should here repent you.
> The actors are at hand . . .

This is an attempt, not only to punctuate in a way that denotes a plausible articulation of the text, but also to do so in a style which I believe to be typical of the late sixteenth century. Does my suggestion do better service to Peter Quince than the others? I do not know. What must certainly be apparent, however, is the point of punctuation, which is to give discourse its meaning by putting it into a frame. To shift the frame is perhaps to shift the meaning, but a frame there has to be, or there is no intelligible picture of sense. In the end, of course, the sense may not have been worth framing; but that is another matter.

The text of a lecture delivered at University College London, February 1989.

5   The possibilities of paraphrase

AN IDLE PROCEDURE?

The 'heresy of paraphrase', it used to be called, by sage and serious critics; 'heresy', because the language and content of a literary work, being conceived as one, are indivisible, and there is no separable quantum of 'meaning' that can be made more readily accessible by altering the words in which meaning is couched. Richard Wilbur, speaking up for poets, puts the case thus:

> It does not upset me to hear poetry paraphrased and its 'subject matter' stated. But I don't usually care for the sort of poem which too readily submits to paraphrase. A poem ought not to be fissionable. It ought to be impossible satisfactorily to separate 'ideas' from their poetic 'embodiment'. When this can be done to a poem, it is a sign that the poem began with a prose 'idea' – i.e. began wrongly – and that the writer was not a poet but a phrase-maker.[1]

With this reasonable statement, made from the insider's point of view, no teacher of English could quarrel. To accept it, however, is to invite the awkward inference that qualities in language characterized as 'poetic' or 'literary' are not isolable or definable, hence perhaps not even teachable; that indeed there is no 'poetic language', but only the language of particular poems, indissociable from their unique status as acts and artefacts. The awkwardness is felt especially by the language teacher, to whom paraphrase – a discredited procedure for literary critics – is a customary tool. In the widest sense – of reformulating, defining, expanding, expatiating, mimicking, making parodies, transposing and translating, seeking parallels – we use paraphrase as a method of teaching the idiom and usage of English. And as we affect to teach the whole language, it is hard for us to accept that there is a privileged domain from which our methods are debarred; that literary utterance cannot be fairly characterized as 'usage' or 'idiom'. Our position is that there is an element of 'literariness' in language, a deposit of practice, as it were, that invites analysis by any means at our disposal. So we may ask of paraphrase – is it inevitably heretical, or may it not sometimes serve a heuristic purpose?

ABSURDITY IS THE MOTHER OF INSIGHT

By way of general discussion, and to make an apparent case *against* paraphrase, let us take a few lines of verse, one of the most familiar passages in the Romantic canon, the opening of Keats's 'Ode to a Nightingale':

> My heart aches, and a drowsy numbness pains
> My sense, as though of hemlock I had drunk,
> Or emptied some dull opiate to the drains
> One minute past, and Lethe-wards had sunk . . .

An attempt to paraphrase these lines will reveal difficulties possibly unsuspected by the reader who knows them well and who may consequently take them for granted as comfortable old exponents of the Romantic death-wish. There is a perverse intricacy in the passage, and any effort of reformulation is simply inadequate to the text, e.g.:

> I feel great grief and weariness, as though I had just drunk poison or a drug, and were drifting into the sleep of death

or:

> Poignant sadness fills me, and an aching sleepiness, as though I had just taken a toxic substance or a narcotic drug, and were sinking into oblivion.

The most careful attempt to express accurately and adequately the 'meaning' of the poetic text founders in absurdity. Paraphrases of the kind suggested here do not bring a poem more firmly into our possession, and may even mislead us if we rely on them as a form of explanation and commentary. Their necessary tendency, indeed, is to omit, or 'filter out', things essential to the communicative art of the text. Taking Keats's lines, consider – the consideration is inevitably somewhat ponderous – what features are lost in the proposed attempts at paraphrase:

1 In the poetic text there is a lexical pattern (and concomitantly a syntactic design) involving the nouns 'heart', 'sense', and the verbs 'ache', 'pain'. These items somewhat resemble the casual collocates of 'ordinary' language (e.g. 'heart and soul', 'body and soul', 'sense and feeling', 'aches and pains'), and we may therefore be lulled into a careless reading; but they invite scrutiny, as terms elevated into precise significance. The reader must assume that for Keats 'heart' and 'sense' have particular values – e.g. 'heart' = 'psychological state or event' and 'sense' = 'physiological correlate', or 'heart' = 'emanation of feeling' and 'sense' = 'recipience of sensation'. At all events, there is here a duality and complementing of meaning that evades the blurring paraphrase of 'I feel grief' or 'Sadness fills me'.

2 The pairing of 'heart' and 'sense' involves the companion pairing of 'aches' and 'pains'. As noted above, there is in ordinary language a banal collocation of nouns ('We all have our aches and pains to put up with'); but in this poetic text the collocates happen to be verbs, each coloured by distinctive properties of semantics and syntax. One ('aches') is intransitive, the other ('pains') is transitive; one is 'stative', the other 'dynamic'; in one case the verb in relationship to its subject suggests energy proceeding from an endogenous source (cf. 'my head reels', 'my foot hurts', 'my hand itches'); in the other the relationship is that of an agent and a recipient ('the whisky turned my head', 'a stone bruised my foot', 'the nettles stung my hand'). The poetic relevance of all this is that it confirms a design in the lexicon, a design that presents 'heart' as the active principle, 'sense' as the receptive principle; feeling comes *from* the heart, sensations come *to* or operate *on* the sense. But the agent of experience operating on the sense in Keats's lines is extraordinary – no object or instrument, but a *-ness*, abstract and vague. We cannot paraphrase 'a drowsy numbness pains my sense', or arrive at its meaning by diligently seeking out word-by-word equivalences. To grasp it we must respond sensitively to the paradoxical teasing of the text.

3 The fact is that paraphrase can do no more than fumble at what is a profound and significant ambiguity in these lines, an ambiguity well expressed in the oxymoron of 'numbness' (subject/agent) and 'pains' (verb). How can a 'numbness' (absence of sensation) cause 'pain' (presence of sensation)? Is the experience through which the poet is passing pleasant or unpleasant? Certain words ('dull', 'drowsy' = the agreeable onset of sleep) suggest pleasant experiences, while others in the immediate context ('aches', 'pains') unmistakably denote

suffering. Does hemlock starkly kill, or does the opiate agreeably coddle? What is the poet saying by means of those extraordinarily well-matched mismatchings? 'This hurts, and is desirable?' 'This is pleasant, and yet hurtful'? The opening of 'Ode to a Nightingale' displays a curious shiftiness, an elaboration of defining that postpones definition until the poem's fruitful contradiction is overtly formulated in its fifth and sixth lines:

'Tis not through envy of thy happy lot,
But being too happy in thine happiness . . .

4 Some literary language is designedly vague – in no bad sense of fudging accuracy, but in its prudent avoidance of specific terms, its reliance on the competence of the reader to recognize time-honoured generalities. Thus 'hemlock' has respectable status as a literary word for 'poison' – reminding us, quite possibly, of Socrates's resigned and stately death – and 'opiate', or rather 'some opiate', is a dignified abstraction that avoids the necessity of going into grim chemical details. Undoubtedly there are moments in the life of literary language when specification would be disastrous:

My heart aches, and a drowsy numbness pains
My sense, as though of Brasso I had drunk,
Or emptied all my Valium to the drains
One minute past, and Lethe-wards had sunk.

This is absurd, and grievously unKeatsian. We may struggle in paraphrase with words like 'poison', 'drug', 'toxic', 'narcotic', etc., but the struggle is vain, because Keats's lines do not really imply these things; the poetic vocabulary makes symbolic *resonances*, not precise references to the pharmacopoeia. Of course any person of literary competence understands this, and only a fool would want to ask Keats (a medical student, after all!) what particular opiate he had in mind. Reference may be paraphrased; 'resonance' cannot.

5 Nor can paraphrase capture the localized symbolism of literary allusion. Keats alludes to *Lethe* – the river of forgetfulness which all travellers must pass on their way to the underworld; supposedly, then, a symbol for death. But there are two components here: oblivion and extinction. Is it so certain that Keats implies the latter with the former? Does he wish for a truly *lethal* administration of hemlock? Does he really mean the blank discontinuity of death, or is his *Lethe* a way of *forgetting* and *transcending*, rather than dying into non-existence? Forgetting appears to be the keynote of the poem ('Fade far away,

dissolve, and quite forget . . .'). It develops the theme of escaping from the cheerless present; an escape which the poet effects not by opiates, or even by alcohol ('not charioted', he tells us, 'by Bacchus and his pards'), but by the power of the poetic imagination, a power that will not lead him into the blackness beyond Lethe but, for one brilliant moment, into the moon-world of the nightingale. It is worth noting that Keats refers to Lethe in a coined word *Lethe-wards*, a formation obviously based on or analogous to 'towards', 'downwards', 'homewards'. The suggested movement or transition is *towards* Lethe, not into or across the fatal river; it is *downwards* – as the verb 'sink' confirms; and we may suppose that it is a gradual or drifting movement rather than a sudden descent.

So, after all this, what are we to say of paraphrase? Having pointed out its manifold imperfections, can we improve it in a version expanded to accommodate all the noted points?

> I feel poignant emotions, while a desensitizing lethargy disagreeably attacks my nervous system, as though I had just taken poison of that noble kind so movingly associated with the death of Socrates, or had ingested a powerfully hypnagogic drug and had begun to drift slowly, vaguely, downward towards oblivion, if not actually into death.

???

Well, says the questing spirit, forget the paraphrase, let us take the easy option and read the poem. And not surprisingly, for all we have done here is provide detailed attestation to the truth of Richard Wilbur's words: 'It ought to be impossible satisfactorily to separate "ideas" from their "embodiment".'

Yet there is something interesting and quite important to add. If there is any merit in these observations on Keats's lines, if these deliberations express any insight into the language of the poetic text, the value derives ultimately from those limping, inadequate, foolish attempts at paraphrase. The consciousness – sometimes embarrassed, sometimes humorous – of what is defective and awry in paraphrase creates a sharp focus on the text. The paraphrase is a vain attempt to reflect what is in the poem; the vanity becomes apparent to us, and we set about trying to identify and explain what we have missed. So a process of discovery begins. We discover patterns, couplings, networks in the 'literary' vocabulary; we note how the 'ordinary' word is thereby endowed with complex poetic significance; we observe the presence in the text of accredited 'literary' words and traditional symbols; we note the nonce-item and the special coinage; the figurative and generalizing power of the literary text declares itself in specific and intermeshing details. Paraphrase may have no critical status, may be utterly ludicrous as an account of what the poem is and does, but it can still be the step that initiates a sophisticated response to language. In this, as in so many fields of study, absurdity is often the mother of insight.

PARAPHRASING 'ORDINARY' LANGUAGE

For foreign students especially, the paraphrase of quite a small part of a poetic text may prove a daunting task, since the crudest essay in reformulation requires a refined linguistic competence that the learner does not always possess. It is obviously a self-defeating exercise if, before students can attempt a paraphrase or use one, they must have continual recourse to a dictionary. (One of the more depressing experiences of taking a poetry class with foreign learners is to observe the frantic paginal whirring of *Duden*, *Larousse* and *The Oxford Advanced Learner's Dictionary of Current English*.) Some teachers, in any case, seem to regard the comprehension of literary language as God-given, and therefore none of their instructive business: 'Either you have the sensitivity or you don't'; 'If people don't respond to poetry in their own language, they obviously won't respond to it in English'. From which assurances we may turn, relieved, to teaching language of the everyday transactional sort.

But such a retreat from the problem is both vain and unnecessary, for 'ordinary' language (however one may define that concept) is full of the seeds and weeds of literariness. Everyday speech includes turns of phrase, idioms (for which foreign students have a bottomless appetite), folk-sayings, proverbs, encapsulations of the common experience, the accredited thought, the conventional wisdom, miniature acts of literary creativeness. These 'encapsulations' invite paraphrase, and the invitation does not overawe foreign learners. Ask them to paraphrase a sonnet, a passage from a story, a speech from a play, and they may look askance, but require of them something straightforward and banal like the rewriting of a proverb – for instance, 'It's the early bird that catches the worm' – and they will cheerfully oblige, with many comments, applications and striking international instances. It may not occur to them that in the simple, routine paraphrasing of 'ordinary' language, they are beginning to learn something about 'literary' language and English manifestations of 'literariness'.

Take the proverb suggested above: 'It's the early bird that catches the worm.' Asked to explain this, each student will produce a rendering, as competence and temperament dictate, and the versions will range from something like this:

If you get up early in the morning you will achieve your task

to something like this:

When we are promptly attentive to our business, we are rewarded with success

(two actual instances recorded in my class notes). Of such exercises two things may be observed. The first is that nobody, not even the most inept and linguistically incompetent student, ever supposes that he or she is dealing with a purely factual statement, i.e. that when we say 'It's the early bird that catches the worm' we are talking about birds as such and worms *per se*. This is perhaps an obvious point, inasmuch as when a teacher says to a class 'Here is a proverb' they understand that they are being invited to consider a non-literal category of utterance. However, it is observable that if one presents the example without the predisposing stimulus of a label such as 'proverb', 'popular saying', 'motto', etc. – if, for example, one should quote 'Blood is thicker than water' – students will still respond with a non-literal (transferred, generalized, metaphorical) interpretation. Possibly all folk-sayings and gnomic utterances have tell-tale characteristics of form and structure that key the appropriate response. A profounder possibility, however, is that when we encounter a piece of language that seems far too obvious to make much sense, we try to render it sensible by putting it into a non-literal frame. Blood is undeniably thicker than water, as a matter of physical fact, but there seems little point in saying so unless we mean blood figuratively and water metaphorically. Taken that way – not *literally* but *literarily* – the saying becomes more meaningful. The willingness to construct a viable meaning in this way is surely an index to the literary competence that we all possess in some measure.[2]

A second interesting aspect of the attempt to paraphrase proverbs is that the versions offered can usually be arranged in a progression running from the most specific, or narrow paraphrase, to the most general, or broad; from a particular or local interpretation (perhaps making birds into students and worms into examination results) to the account that transcends particularities of person, time and place (birds as general agent, worm as a gratifying general consequence of action). Presented with a narrow and a broad paraphrase, and asked to assess their acceptability, students will generally reply that both are acceptable, and indeed that both might apply simultaneously to the test-proverb; perhaps some will add, on reflection, that the interpretation of the latter will of course depend on contexts and circumstances of usage. In saying this, they acknowledge the essentially *literary* nature of proverbial utterances. The proverb lives as a poem lives, both by specifying and generalizing. And its language, therefore, is the language of literary discourse – patterned and multivalent. 'It's the early bird that catches the worm' and 'My heart aches, and a drowsy numbness pains my sense' are types of literary statement, differing in scope and complexity, but affined in their deliberate arrangement of words and their implication of meanings that transcend brute literality.

Students are amused if one makes the simple point that many proverbs are not, so to speak, reversible. We say 'It's the early bird that catches the worm', but no one is inclined to consider the vermicular viewpoint of 'It's the tardy worm that cops the bird'. This rewriting would not be accepted, other than as a Woosterish sort of joke. The reason for this is surely that the proverb 'It's the early bird that catches the worm' is a particular realization of the paradigm, or archetype, of hunter and quarry, pursuer and pursued. The paradigm implies a psychological sequence: the hunter or pursuer or agent comes first in the natural order of things. Now many folk-sayings, perhaps the greater number, can be referred to such archetypes of the perceived 'natural' order: working, playing, hunting (or trading), preparing and consuming food, providing shelter, forming relationships and alliances, maintaining social hierarchies, making war and keeping the peace – all the primary provinces of human activity and organization create the 'paradigms' from which proverbs are derived, and also the complexes of fact and feeling which enter into poems and stories. Proverbial encapsulation and free poetic elaboration have the same cultural sources. Sometimes the two coincide, as in a poem by Robert Frost called 'Mending Wall', which is constructed round the saying 'Good fences make good neighbours'. The poem makes a commentary on the proverb, criticizes its application, and might be described as a protest against the literal interpretation or the excessively narrow paraphrase.

Though paraphrase is a general term, covering a variety of techniques and practices, two styles are commonly apparent. One is the explanatory/interpretative type, that tries to express something 'in other words', possibly with complementary illustrations. The other is a mimetic/parodic type, depending on a technique of word-for-word substitution that often has comic results: 'It's the auroral avian that mugs the maggot'. These also are 'other words', but they explain nothing; rather, they laugh at literariness, or possibly, through their manifest absurdity, pay subtle tribute. One curious effect of the comic substitution technique is to destroy all figurative scope. 'Early' may imply 'early in the morning', 'punctually', 'promptly', 'opportunely', 'before others can act', 'with a proper sense of urgency', etc., adjusting its meaning to changeable contexts of application; 'auroral' is a funny way of saying 'at dawn'. The scope of the paraphrase narrows to zero; the true literariness of the proverb is reduced to the falsity of a pseudo-literary gesture. But this kind of game is not without its uses.

THE SCOPE OF THE LITERARY UTTERANCE

The scope, i.e. the breadth of application, of literary utterances is worth a moment's consideration. One well known feature (indeed a diagnostic symptom) of literary texts is that while they may intensively state a case, they also have the inherent power to illuminate a universe of parallels, analogues and variants. They become emblems of general and continuing experience. If, quoting Samuel Johnson, I declare 'Slow rises worth by poverty depress'd' (and we may remind ourselves that Johnson himself was paraphrasing Juvenal) I may mean, specifically, that poor Bloggs has had a raw deal in life, or my remark may be a contribution to a general discussion on the difficulty of making one's way in the learned professions. The classic line provides us with a saying of fairly wide scope.

In common usage we exploit the scope of literary language as it occurs in tags and adages, well known quotations and the general patchwork of the anonymous folk-tradition. A personal example: when my daughter was very small, I would sometimes play with her a game requiring the accompaniment of a familiar nursery rhyme:

> Rock-a-bye-baby on the tree top,
> When the wind blows the cradle will rock,
> When the bough bends the cradle will fall,
> Down comes the baby, cradle and all.

To play our game, the child would lie in my lap, along the cleft between my legs. I would begin by moving my legs gently from side to side ('Rock-a-bye-baby'). Then I would begin a slow alternate tramping of my knees ('When the wind blows . . .'). This would be followed by a slow parting of the legs ('When the bough bends . . .'), and a hysterically gleeful pantomime of dropping and catching on the word 'down', the focus of the game.

This fairly typical piece of parent-and-child play represents a practical application – one might say an 'action paraphrase' – of a piece of verse with much wider scope. 'Rock-a-bye-baby' invites interpretation as a paradigm of false security in any form: complacency in politics, false optimism in business, self-satisfaction in the performance of work, failure to read the obvious signs of rift in personal relationships – to all such situations the old rhyme might provide a fitting commentary. To use it as a sort of timing-device for a child-distracting game is to narrow its scope considerably.

Taking this one step further, suppose that in the course of these amusements I had devised a verbal paraphrase to match the action. I was never rash enough to propose any such heretical procedure, but had I done so, I might possibly have produced something like this:

Rock-a-bye-daughter, here in my lap,
When I waggle my knees you may take a wee nap,
When I open my legs you will take a big drop,
And your lapping and napping will come to a stop.

Having narrowed the scope of the original text with an action-paraphrase, I now suggest a verbal paraphrase that is concomitantly narrow. This could be applied *only* in direct connection with the rocking game, the successive phases of which it specifies. The relationship of this verbal paraphrase to the original text is tenuous; the expression 'Rock-a-bye' and the familiar metre serve to invite comparison with an underlying model. The removal of these props would destroy all suggestion of mimetic paraphrase, and with it all allusive power. What we then make is just another action rhyme:

Swingaroo, kiddo, so deep,
While I wiggle my knees, you can sleep;
When I open them – PHEW!
You're going to drop THROUGH!
And land in a horrible HEAP!

This, like 'Rock-a-bye-daughter' (and unlike 'Rock-a-bye-baby'), may be bad verse, but such spoofings are not *unliterary*. We may still find in them a literariness of structure that allots significance to certain items of vocabulary or conveys, at particular points, a sense of gesture. What is lost is the power to generate many meanings – or, as we have put it earlier, to create the *resonance* of literary language.

THE MESSAGE OF MIMICRY

The point of the mimetic paraphrase may be to have fun at the expense of the original, i.e. it may be frankly parodic, an exercise in literary vandalism. This is not the whole point, however. The explanatory paraphrase, through its inadequacy, directs us to the fullness of the text; comparably, a mimetic paraphrase, act of hooligan mockery though it be, pays tribute to the refinement of the original: if, that is, the original has real merits. Here is a poem that is often used as a text for foreign students of English, because of its ostensible (but in fact quite deceptive) simplicity.

Richard Cory

Whenever Richard Cory went down town,
   We people on the pavement looked at him:
He was a gentleman from sole to crown,
   Clean favoured, and imperially slim.

And he was always quietly arrayed,
   And he was always human when he talked;
But still he fluttered pulses when he said
   'Good morning,' and he glittered when he walked.

And he was rich – yes, richer than a king,
   And admirably schooled in every grace:
In fine, we thought that he was everything
   To make us wish that we were in his place.

So on we worked, and waited for the light,
   And went without the meat, and cursed the bread;
And Richard Cory, one calm summer night,
   Went home, and put a bullet through his head.

                          Edwin Arlington Robinson

This poem seems readily susceptible to explanatory paraphrase, encapsulating as it does some kind of moral or 'wisdom'. When students are asked to state the meaning of the text, their answers range from the laconic 'Wealth doesn't make you happy' to somewhat fuller explanations, e.g. 'Rich persons may seem to enjoy every advantage in life, yet still have some despair not seen by those who envy them'. Occasionally these summaries have an ideological ring, suggesting that the material sufferings of the proletariat do not impair their moral soundness, whereas the well-to-do are corrupted by their possessions and become spiritually dead. Those who are thus disposed to interpret the poem antithetically – 'we, the strong ones, survived, but he, the moral weakling, perished' – are not as a rule deterred when a teacher asks them to consider that the conjunction introducing the final couplet is not the adversative *but*, but the continuative *and*, suggesting something slightly subtler than a crude adversarial reading. There is certainly a predisposition to read the text as some form of moral injunction; yet it could be argued that the dramatic – indeed, melodramatic – final stanza is an existentialist statement, or a comment to which we may attribute a morality or not, as we please. ('We unaccountably went on living and he inexplicably chose to die.')

Discussion of the paraphrasable meaning or 'moral' of this poem nearly always reveals that it is not, after all, so simple. It is when one begins to discuss its vocabulary and its lexical patterning, however, that one is reminded how the plainest texts often seem to be the most impenetrable. For some foreign students the vocabulary of 'Richard Cory' may have cultural and social overtones that are not easy to interpret. I once read this poem with a group that included a pupil from one of the poorer Third-World countries. He found 'imperially slim' unconvincing as an image of class ascendancy, since most of the wealthy and powerful people in his society were distinguished by the portliness of the well fed; and his interpretation of 'he glittered when he walked' was that the sweat shone on Cory's forehead (Richard being intrinsically a fat cat, whatever the poem might say to the contrary). We may smile at these misconstructions, but they should make us ask how often, from our own cultural presuppositions, we might go astray in attempting to read an exotic literature.

The central difficulty of the language used in this poem, however, is not primarily cultural; even native students can go astray, merely by taking the poem for granted as an exercise in the mimicry of the naïve. If it is indeed naïve in its diction and idiom, the naïvety is oddly complicated, not to say troubled. There is a speaker-in-the-poem, a 'person on the pavement', behind whom lurks (like some ventriloquist or puppeteer) the poet, Edwin Arlington Robinson. Robinson makes his speaker-on-the-inside construct the kind of text one might well imagine to be the production of a literary man-in-the-street – clichés, posh phrases, proper words and all. (Thus it is in the character of the 'narrator' to describe Cory as 'quietly arrayed', 'richer than a king' and 'admirably schooled'.) At the same time, the poet Robinson exploits this mimetic vocabulary as an idiom for the creation of ambiguities, ironies and fine implications of lexical patterning. The last two lines of the first stanza exemplify this. The phrase 'from sole to crown' clearly imitates 'from top to toe', and might be regarded as the narrator's conscious 'literary' striving to improve on a common phrase. Validly so – but there is something more; by reversing the perspective of the phrase (i.e. 'top to toe' = 'downwards', but 'from sole to crown' = 'upwards'), Robinson adds to the figurative intimations of the text. The people on the pavement 'look' at Cory, and the 'looking' is that of subjects contemplating a ruler who is in some way placed above them. ('To look up to someone', we may recall at this point, implies respect and admiration.) 'Crown', furthermore, connotes regal attributes, and this suggestion of royal eminence is further reflected in 'imperially'. Through his speaker's blunderingly earnest attempts at literary description, i.e. through one act of mimesis, Robinson constructs a parallel act, contriving semantic links and overlaps that build the image of Cory as an inaccessible, aristocratic, indeed regal personage. That one word 'crown' quite effectively illustrates how the poem speaks with two voices. The simple insider means only 'top of his head'; the artful outsider, the poet, means us also to think of the conventional symbol of monarchy.

To get at these manipulations of meaning by discussing each in turn takes a long time, and in the end may leave a class bemused and unconvinced. There is another way of drawing attention to the lexical peculiarities of a poem like 'Richard Cory', and that is to make a mimetic paraphrase. Here is an instance of a rival text, a bad poem created in order to suggest how the real poem works.

Roger Crotty

If Roger Crotty went down town some day,
    We ordinary folk would stand and gape;
He was a gentleman in every way –
    Clean-shaven, smart, and such a lovely shape.

His suits were always tasteful, never loud,
    And when he talked, he sounded just like you,
But he'd this way of moving through a crowd
    And dazzling one and all with his 'How do?'

He'd all the earmarks of a millionaire,
    The style, the education – oh, the lot;
Put it like this, if he'd have said 'Hi there!
    Change places?' we'd have done it like a shot.

Still, there it was. We struggled to get by,
And ate some awful meals, which made us grouse,
But Roger Crotty, one night in July,
Committed suicide – in his own house.

This has the merit of being so awful that it makes students laugh. They feel superior to the silly act, and can be made to realize that this feeling stems from some competence to recognize qualitative differences between the deft original and the banal imitation, the language of which certainly resembles the style of the street but is far removed from the studied idiom of poetry. Then every line of the paraphrase evokes comparison with the original. We may, for example, contrast 'gape' with the oddly inert 'look at', asking what is present in one and notably absent from the other. 'Look at' is difficult to paraphrase (as, indeed, it is in the proverb 'A cat may look at a king'). Or, a slightly more complex task, we may try to explain how and why 'clean favoured' means a great deal more than 'clean-shaven' – more, perhaps, than a portmanteau packing of 'clean-shaven' and 'well-favoured' ('handsome'). These are random instances indicating the general thesis that systematic comparison of the two texts would define the literary peculiarities and procedures of the true poem.

Perhaps in token of an analysis we may take up two points. First, as to titles: names are not paraphrasable (proper nouns, the philosophers tell us, have unique reference), but in the world of myth, names are regarded as having peculiar efficacy in consubstantiating the person they denote (whence the common taboo prohibiting the naming of the godhead or the devil). This mythic view of language is reflected in poetry, which often posits a quasi-magic relationship between words and things. Thus if we change the name 'Richard Cory', we seemingly change or dislocate the relationship between the title and its poetic expansion. Could the poem – the original poem – be called 'Ricco Corti'?; no, too Italianate and even gangsterish. 'Rory Coonan' then? 'Reuben Cohen'? 'Rudi Kafka'? No, clearly, such inventions could never be considered in connection with the original poem. We feel a decorum in the association of the name 'Richard Cory' and the 'quietly arrayed', 'admirably schooled' personality it denotes. Then change the name to 'Roger Crotty' and in effect a new poem must be designed, bespeaking Crotty-like attributes.[3] The whole subject of titles, particulaarly name-titles, is interesting and fruitful, because it has much to reveal about literary resonances, those associative waves that ripple through a text.

For a second point of general interest, consider the final stanza of the poem. The original text, like so many in this moralizing, punch-lining genre, is *focused*, all its rays of meaning converging to a point. We may compare it with nursery rhymes like 'Rock-a-bye-baby' in which there are one or two words ('fall', 'down') that attract emphasis and are spoken with peculiar energy in performance. In 'Richard Cory' there is a brutally exact emphasis on the word 'bullet', which we read against the background of 'light', 'meat' and especially 'bread'. ('We got bread, he got a bullet'; the emphasis is even supported by alliteration.) The precise act of self-destruction figures suddenly and surprisingly (largely because of those designedly drifting constructions, 'so . . . and . . . and . . . and') against the dull doggedness of working, waiting, going without, cursing. In 'Roger Crotty' there is (a) no surprise, and (b) a ludicrous change of focus; no shock effect but 'how shocking – *in his own house*!'. 'Roger Crotty' is trivially blurred; 'Richard Cory' is most precisely focused. Here is a notion worth wider exploration, and the mimetic paraphrase is one way of exploring it.

THE POSSIBILITIES OF PARAPHRASE

In summary, the following points emerge:

1 'Paraphrase' may be understood in a broad sense, to include techniques of explaining, summarizing, imitating, rewriting. (The latter I have scarcely touched upon.) A distinction is made between 'explanatory' and 'mimetic' paraphrase.

2 In the teaching and study of 'ordinary' language we have constant recourse to paraphrase; any attempt to answer such questions as 'What do we mean when we say . . .?' involves paraphrasing. Thus language teaches language, one usage amplifies another, one style comments on another. This is in effect the case for paraphrase, and for extending its use to the exploration of 'literary' language.

3 Paraphrase, however, will not reveal all the secrets of literariness. Some literary works are more obviously amenable to paraphrase than others. It seems notably applicable to work that presents an argument, defines a condition, or points a moral.

4 Explanatory paraphrase should fall within the competence of the student, representing his or her attempt to 'engage' with the text and account for its language. Such paraphrases provide the basis for discussion and elaboration of the concept of literary language. They are at least a useful language drill; at their best they are a step towards the comprehension of literary values.

5 Mimetic paraphrase should be the teacher's province (unless the students volunteer to attempt it). Strictly speaking, it requires native competence, some gift for parody and burlesque, and a sensitivity to the humorous nuances in language: specifically, an awareness of the difference between the ordinary and the banal, the original and the bizarre. Any competent teacher should have the sense of fun and the skill required to contrive the entertainment that is also a form of instruction. The teacher who cannot use language to inform, inspire and amuse is a dead duck – i.e. a dolorous bird that neither flies nor quacks.

Originally a lecture delivered to foreign teachers of English attending a course at the University of Nottingham, this was subsequently published in a very slightly revised version, as one of the chapters of C.J. Brumfit and R.A. Carter, eds, *Literature and Language Teaching* (London: Oxford University Press, 1986).

6 On parody: a discourse with interludes

The lecturer:

The heroine of *La Bohème* sings 'They call me Mimi, but my name is Lucia'. I sympathize with the young lady, for I am in a comparable predicament: they call me Billy – indeed, you have billed me as Bill – but my name is Walter. Like the poet Goethe, albeit with considerably less distinction, I house in my single person two souls. Billy is a frivolous fellow who loves gossip, television and bedtime, and would rather eat his victuals than write a lecture; Walter, whom you see before you, is urbane and scholarly, a signer of cheques and contracts, an ornament to the Faculty Board, a worthy contender for academic honours. Today you are to hear from both of them, for each in his fashion is interested in parody: Bill, the scribbler, for the fun and the mischief and the challenge of it; and Walter, the scholar, from a long interest in the nature of literary language and the creative variations of mimesis. Walter is thus qualified to discourse on parody, and Bill, as the mood takes him, to supply interludes of illustration.

Walter:

Let my discourse begin, then, with the statement of a drastically, perhaps provocatively simple thesis: that all imaginative writing springs from one question and one executive recommendation. The question is 'what if?', and concerns the substance of the fable; the recommendation is 'as if', and concerns its language and mode of expression. What if two dozen people of diverse temperaments and social ranks were to find themselves making a tedious and possibly dangerous journey together? What if a seaman were shipwrecked and stranded among people no more than six inches tall? What if a labourer in a fit of drunkenness were to sell his wife? These questions our literature has engagingly answered. But then again, what if Geoffrey Chaucer were to be fogbound at Luton Airport? What if Jonathan Swift were to find himself in charge of a TV panel show? What if Thomas Hardy were to write a muck-raking column for the *Daily Sleaze*? These are perhaps not questions for serious literature, but they are indeed the kind of question raised and answered by the literary *genus* we call parody. It is in the nature of the parodic 'what if' to take the wonderful one step further, into the wild and weird.

'What if?' is the necessary directive to the imagination. 'As if' is the challenge to competence, to what we know about linguistic usage and literary convention. 'As if' means finding a voice, a manner of speaking, a *performing* style. I stress 'performing', because all literature, from anecdote to epic, is performance. We sometimes speak of 'telling a story in one's own way', but this is largely an illusion. In telling a story – as opposed, perhaps, to giving an account of something that happened in the street – 'one's own way' is often debarred by precedent, by convention, by the aesthetic demand for a convincing presentation. In any case, though I may wish to speak in my own voice, how can I know what my own voice is? Is it not the penalty and perplexity of being myself that I cannot know myself?; that I must sometimes suspect that I have no real existence except as a conditioned response to the demands of changing contexts?; that I try to account for the elusiveness of what I am by resorting to the myth of the divided personality? No one who tells a story can confidently assert that it is told entirely 'in his or her own voice'. The telling, the 'as if', is a recollection and mimicry of other voices, perhaps of many voices. 'As if' is the stimulus to experience and memory, to the stored knowledge of phrasing, inflection and gesture, gleaned through countless social interactions and through an accumulating sense of literary convention. From this we generate the forms of what we take to be self-expression. But we have been serious for long enough: let us take a frivolous interlude.

Bill:

All right – but if you talk of 'what if' and 'as if', how's this? What if World War III were to break out in the middle of a lecture? Eh? Right in the middle of your Friday grammar lecture, sir, someone pokes his head round the door and tells you the balloon has gone up? I mean, how do you deal with that? What do you say to the boys and girls? Can you hear yourself? –

Incident on Friday Morning

I don't know if you heard –
Class! People!
Could we have some quiet?
We'll get on a lot better.

There's too much talking on the back row!

Thank you.

I don't know if you heard what Mr Featherstone said.
Did you?

For the benefit of those who did not hear –
And I think that includes *you*, Miss Mobbs –
You were too busy talking –
I will repeat it.

World War Three began five minutes ago,
And a nuclear bomb is coming this way.

Quite a large one, I believe.
Isn't that so, Mr Featherstone?
As far as we can tell.

Now *don't* bother to write it in your notebooks.
This is not an invented example.
Rest assured, when I say
A nuclear bomb is coming towards us,
I am not violating Grice's Maxim of Quality.
This is *true*,
In addition to being a well-formed sentence.

Well, the implications are obvious.
Aren't they?
Do I need to spell them out?

Some of us will not be able to finish our Term Projects.
Which is a little unfair.
I mean, to those who gave them in on time.
Still, there it is, you can't do a great deal in four minutes.

Three minutes, Mr Featherstone?
Three minutes, class!

Failure to submit a Project

Normally invites a zero mark.
As you know,
Don't you,
Miss Mobbs?
Under the circumstances, however, I am prepared to modify
  the rules.
Those failing to submit a Project
Will be awarded the average of their existing course-work
Minus ten per cent.

This is the best I can do for you,
So do not grimace, Miss Mobbs.

Two minutes, forty-five seconds, class!

While you are helping Mr Featherstone to stack the tables,
Might I suggest that you do some work on *prepositions*?
Collect suitable illustrations –
For example, 'We lie *under* the table,'
'The ceiling falls *on* the table,'
'A beam comes *through* the table' –
Preferably from naturally occurring speech.
We can discuss them later,
When we will also be able to practise our phonetic transcription.

Mr Featherstone has brought an adequate supply of candles,
And you will be able to work in pairs.
Miss Mobbs, you will have to work with me.

Two minutes, class!

In the event of the campus being directly affected
I suggest you spend tonight reading –
Shall we say pages 207–50 of *A University Grammar of English*
By Quirk, R,
and Greenbaum, S?

One minute, class!

Thank you, Mr Featherstone.
You wish to leave us?
You doubtless have your own arrangements at the Porter's Lodge?
Of course.
And I do not suppose you want to work on prepositions.
Not at this juncture.
Quite.

Come then, Miss Mobbs,
Or may I call you Jacqueline?
We have a lot of ground to make up.
Let us go to work on the concessive conjuncts.

Fifteen seconds, class!

Shut the door, someone.
It's getting horribly noisy out there.[1]

This is the sound of someone's voice, I suppose. But whose? Who speaks like that? Does Walter ever speak like that? Or is this something else, very recognizable and quite abstract, the *idea* of a teacher speaking to a class? The 'as if' that carries the voucher of a 'could be'?; why yes, says John Doe, who has never been in a seminar room, I can just imagine them going on like that, it's typical. So is this parody? Of a sort, yes. Quite a subtle sort, as a matter of fact. It's a parody of some people's notions of how other people speak. It's an imitation of a mimicry. But we are getting complicated; let's go back to our discourse.

Walter:

Imitation, obviously, is the essence of parody. The name itself means 'song alongside', and this singalong – singalonga Shakespeare, singalonga Keats – demands that words echo words, or that sense shadows sense, or both. The parodist imitates language, but it is clear that the imitation must be of a quite specific kind. If I imitate a *notion* of speech, a mental image of expression accessible only to myself, I am not quite engaging in parody. Bill may be certain that 'Incident on Friday Morning' is parody, but I am not so sure. Properly speaking, parody deals with what is readily attestable. It may of course address itself rather loosely to the sort of thing people say or write – that is, to verbal experiences accessible to anyone who reads newspapers, watches TV chat shows, listens to conversations in shops and is generally receptive to the enormous provision of cliché and banality which is indispensable to the conduct of everyday affairs. More specifically, the linguistic object of parody may be the usage of a class of persons in certain occupations (e.g. civil servants); or of some particular speaker or writer (the Prime Minister, Ernest Hemingway); or more narrowly, and more attestably, it may be the language of one text (the Book of Genesis, 'Ode to Autumn', *The Waste Land*). The more specific the object, the clearer the intention to parody; the clearer the intention to parody, the greater the risk of failure on the parodist's part, and the greater the burden of recognition laid on the parodist's audience. Obviously you cannot relish an imitation or assess its effectiveness unless you are fully aware of what is being imitated. The audience must recognize the object of the mimicry. Their recognition is promoted by the parodist's acknowledgement of the mimic act. It is characteristic of the language of parody, and something that distinguishes it from pastiche or outright forgery, that the imitation is never quite exact, but always accommodates the false accent, incongruity, deliberate infelicity – much as the skating clown, by often stumbling and almost falling, more intensely evokes the grace and gesture of the accomplished skater. It is time for another interlude.

Bill:

When I was a boy we used to talk about 'taking people off'. Did you ever hear that expression? We would say 'He does a good take-off of Charles Laughton', or 'She takes off Greta Garbo to a T'. Everybody did George Formby take-offs. Usually they were nothing like George Formby (and the mimics of Laughton and Garbo weren't so very clever), but you could see the principle. You picked up a few things – a grin, a pout, an intonation, a notorious phrase ('Mr Christian!', 'I want to be alone', 'Can you hear me, mother?') and you added a few things of your own, and you stirred it all about.[2] Most people gave up doing take-offs when they were fifteen (taking off your head teacher was a risky way of winning popularity), but some went on to do take-offs of more distant objects, like poets and famous authors.

I was on a train one day, going for an interview, and I had on my best blue suit. Thinking that lunch might calm my nerves, I made my way, rocking and lurching against old ladies and sharp edges, to the restaurant car, where they were just dishing the soup. It is very difficult to get British Rail soup up from the plate and safely into your mouth while the train driver is maniacally building up speed between Kettering and Luton. On this occasion, falling at my third attempt, I spilled a large spoonful of soup over my neat blue worsted, and in a particularly uncomfortable place. For the rest of the journey I had to sit embarrassedly watching embarrassed people trying to spare me embarrassment by not looking at my embarrassing stain. This was the beginning of a take-off. How would the poets have coped with this?, I thought. Would Byron have mastered it? Would Lord Tennyson have survived it, mellifluously? Or what about – yes, what about Hopkins?

It took surprisingly little working:

G. M. Hopkins Takes Lunch in the Restaurant Car

Ah, waiter, are there any, where are, tell me, come,
   Napkins, lovely all-of-a-starch-staring
Linen, preferably, or pauper-seeming paper, waiter? Wearing
   My gaygear goodsuit, ah, my dear, dim was it? dumb?
Well, this train's tripping and track-truckling as I sipped
   Soup did, ah God, the hot of it! – yes, slipped, flipped
Into my lap, slapping, of this clear consommé, some
   Spoonflung flashes, splashes for bosom's bearing.

Bring me a – coo – lummy – here dab, here dry with a kerch-
   ief, tea-towel, toilet roll, oh dear-then-a-doyly, but merely
A move (with a mercy, man) make! Oh what a slanting that sheerly
   What with the canting curve of the, what with the lilt of the lurch,
Hurled leaping lapward, all in a skirl, the dear drenching.
   There was a splash to abash one quaintly, ah, there was a
      quenching!
Since when on seat's edge sodden I pensive perch,
   Picking at lunch unlovely, unappetizing nearly.

Now if you never heard George Formby, or never saw Charles
Laughton in *Mutiny on the Bounty*, the most charitable thing you
might assume about any imitation of them would be that the imitator
was in his dotage. So with this Hopkins take-off. A reader who has
never looked into Hopkins will make nothing of it. It can't be funny
– it can't even be serious – it can only be 'drivel', a word much beloved
by John and Joanna Citizen when they are confronted by things that
pass them by. On the other hand, the reader who is acquainted with
Hopkins may perceive here not only the general features of Hopkins's
extraordinary poetic style, but also echoes and traces of his actual
vocabulary in diverse poems. In this way, the take-off becomes a kind
of tribute – or at least a sort of password among friends of the author:
'You know how old Hopkins goes on? Well . . .'. You like the chap's
stuff so much, you imitate his language, you try to speak as he might
speak, you catch at the smallest turn of phrase.[3]

Walter:

But language is not the only thing that parody imitates. There is
another level to its mimetic act: that of content. Frequently it appears
that the content is the least important element in parody, a frivolous

excuse for a jovial exercise in language. Indeed, I can easily propose to you parodic subjects that are merely fanciful. Write a parody of Milton buying a copy of *Playboy*; of Dr Johnson at a football match; of Ernest Hemingway trying to clear a blocked sink-trap. In such cases the fancied topic is so remote – psychologically, materially, historically – from the known concerns of the proposed speaker, that we may describe the content of the parody as *displacing*. Shakespeare never wrote a sonnet on rice pudding; if you attempt to write one for him, you will be attempting something in Shakespearean style on an absurdly unShakespearean content, a displacing content.

There are, however, possible instances of parody in which the content would be typical and plausible – or as the late lamented Philip Larkin might have said, not untypical and not implausible. Frances Bacon wrote short essays on gardens, on studies, on revenge, on death, on other such matters civil and moral. A parodist might conceivably write in Baconian style on unemployment, on the stock market, on vegetarian diet, on toothache. D.H. Lawrence wrote many poems disparaging humanity by comparison with animals – snakes, lizards, tortoises, mosquitoes and other livestock. His considerable output in this vein invites parodic essays on June bugs, hamsters, shubunkins, newts, or the creepies that crawl up the bathroom plumbing.[4] In such cases, we may say, the content is *apposed*. You will not find anything quite like it in your source; but it has a discernible if distorted resemblance to what you do find, a burlesque likeness.

Parody of an apposed content is frequently destructive in intention. This was Mark Twain's method in attacking Fenimore Cooper, whose Leather Stocking novels he detested. Twain's parodies, crackling with contempt for his victim, take wicked effect simply by exaggerating the marvellous attributes of that all-purpose Fenimore Cooper character, the romantic Man of the Woods.[5] It only needs the skill of expression, the 'as if', to make the absurd content absurdly plausible; and here I am reminded of something Aristotle says, that a convincing impossibility is better than an unconvincing possibility. The example he quotes is of Odysseus being put ashore from a ship while he is asleep.[6] Impossible really, says Aristotle: in such a case the sleeping man would surely wake up; but in the context, it seems, the impossibility is convincingly rendered. Aristotle rightly challenges crude notions of what we would now call 'realism'. Again and again, literary discourse turns on the convincing impossibility; a man wrestles with a monster in a submarine cave where a fire is burning; a knight-errant disguises himself by the silly-simple expedient of reversing the syllables of his name (i.e. by converting 'Tristram' into

'Tramtrist'); a castaway finds 'a single footprint' in an unbroken tract of sand; a seafarer, thought to be lost, comes home at last, and finding his wife married to his best friend, settles down as their neighbour and to the day of his death conceals his identity. These are more or less convincing impossibilities in Beowulf, in Malory, in Defoe, in Tennyson. Each of these instances, by the way, is vulnerable to parody; for in parody the frankly impossible is made to mock the fairly improbable. This was quite a long stretch of discourse – let us take another break.

Bill:

And while we are at it, let me tell you of a time before word-processors and photocopiers, when teachers were obliged to duplicate their class handouts with the help of a crude machine called a Roneo (or perhaps a Gestetner), which in itself was a miracle of technology by comparison with an earlier method involving jelly and methylated spirits. They were primitive and uncertain times, when you used primitive and uncertain typewriters to hack messages into a waxed sheet called a stencil, which you then secured to the revolving drum of the Roneo, having first larded the apparatus with a noisome black ink. The Roneo was not a forgiving machine. Stencils got creased or torn, the ink blubbered all over your shirt cuffs, the paper would jam in the feed, and the text, when it arrived, would be illegibly pale or indecipherably black. Because of these inconveniences, the Roneo machine purchased for the English Department at the University of Nottingham was never a popular facility. I was, I think, the only person to use it, and to do so I had to visit the ill-lit, ill-ventilated store cupboard which it shared with the superannuated remnants of other academic endeavours. It was during these claustrophobic sessions that I invented Umffrei.

Umffrei was – I should say *is*, for he still works from time to time – a medieval bard whose poetic language is a parodic dialect called Muddle English. In this he discourses, with innocent emphasis, on current phenomena – on cars, pianos, TV shows, the space age, tennis stars, pop singers and other urgently trivial matters. Many of his utterances are about modern machinery. Here he apostrophizes the Electrolux:

> Vakum Clenere
>
> Ha, vakum clenere, synge thi songe,
> A luvsum laye hyt ys, I wene.

Wyth brethynges amorous and stronge
Thow makest mone a mornynge longe
Til al mi hows ys clene.
    Then welcum, welcum, vakum-wight
    That suckest uppe the mucke aright.

A serpente ys thi luvelie necke,
Thi bodie ys a litel bulle;
On duste thow dynest, manye a pecke,
Thow gobblest everie spotte and specke,
Thi belye waxeth fulle.
    Then welcum, welcum, vakum-wight
    That suckest uppe the mucke aright.

Foteless thow farest thurgh mi halle,
Thow grazest on the grittie grownde,
And, grettest wondyrment of alle,
Thi tayle thow pluggest yn a walle,
Yf anye poynte be fownde.
    Then welcum, welcum, vakum-wight
    That suckest uppe the mucke aright.

A derksum closet ys thi den,
Wherin thow liggest stocke-stille
Til hit be Saterday, and then
Thow farest foorth, and alle men
Cryen, wyth gode wille,
    Ha, welcum, welcum, vakum-wight
    That suckest uppe the mucke aright.

I have discovered that the most appreciative readers of Muddle English are those who do not know too much about Middle English. Scholars tend to be a little restive, and feel obliged to point out that the grammar, dialect features, and so forth, are not strictly consistent or accurate. Indeed they are not, and this is just the parodic point. In parody there has to be a *designed imperfection* – Walter's clown on the ice – that proclaims to the world at large: 'This is a SPOOF. Read in accordance with the rules of SPOOFING. If you don't know the rules, KINDLY LEAVE.' This 'vakum clenere' piece, incidentally, illustrates Walter's remarks about 'displaced' and 'apposed' content. Inasmuch as no medieval lyricist could ever have written about vacuum cleaners, the content is well and truly displaced. But then again, medieval authors did write about strange beasts – your gryffoun, *par exemple*, or your wyvern, or your cockatrice – and rightly seen, an Ouvere or an Alecktrollockes is just another strange beast. So this could be a case of an 'apposed' content. I suppose it depends on how you want to play the game.

Walter:

Yes – but beyond playfulness, what is the purpose of parody? Many would insist that it is inevitably aggressive, an adjunct to satire. Certainly there are parodies which suggest, if not hatred, at least some asperity of feeling towards a person, a style, a work. Twain was piqued by Cooper's popularity, and showed it; Fielding took his comic stick to Richardson; the Canadian humorist Stephen Leacock, a classically educated man, so resented the cultural pretensions of classicists that in untypically sardonic mood he wrote parodies of the Homeric-epic style; and certain poems – among which Edgar Allan Poe's *The Raven* comes most readily to mind – have always attracted hostile parody, much as factory windows attract stones.[7] But is parody always aggressive? Quite as often, it seems to me, it pays the teasing tribute of recognition – acknowledging whatever is difficult or distinctive in a style. The parodic stimulus is commonly a curiosity to see how things work linguistically, and the imitation, the learning of the steps, is consequently a mode of insight and assessment. I would stress this, particularly to an academic audience. The literary critic expresses his judgements in evaluative adjectives, telling us, it may be, that such and such a style is expansive, occasionally florid, but always controlled. Along comes the linguist with his dry look and his pursy mouth, to state that 47.6 per cent of the sentences are complex hypotactic structures, 21.3 per cent of which are introduced by non-finite adverbial clauses. The parodist sidesteps all this pomp and circumstance and makes his judgement mimetically. For him, knowing is doing. But the doing is also fun – and fun, let us say, in a spirit of informed and informing pleasure, is too often and all too lamentably absent from many of our current studies in literature. I have only to open certain works of literary theory (I refuse to be specific) to feel that Count Dracula has found a new *métier* and that poor pleasure has been received into the drained and ghastly company of the undead.

I must not invite misunderstanding. I do not mean that it is the primary business of literature – still less of literary criticism – to feed us with fun. But simple restorative fun *is* one of the better motives of parody, and it is twinned with another, equally laudable impulse:

to be reconciled, to come to terms with the small setback, the minor grievance, the occasional nuisance, the bunions and blisters of life, the small inconsequential sufferings that are inflicted on us and cannot be helped. Parody is a way of getting the little bad feelings out of your system. For the big bad feelings there is prayer. Let us take another break.

Bill:

I used to read and admire Browning a great deal. I still admire, though perhaps I no longer read so much. Reading Browning takes time – time to tease out the windings of syntax from the intricate prosodic patterns he creates. Take, for example, 'Love among the Ruins', with its alternate long and short lines, its abruptly juxtaposed rhymes, and its sentences that run discursively over the line-ends and the rhyme-pairs.[8] I thought of this poem once when I was in a large library and found myself wandering around rather bemusedly, benumbed and disorientated in this maze of books. The parody I subsequently wrote has nothing at all to do with the content of 'Love among the Ruins'. I merely borrowed the prosodic form of that poem because it seemed to fit very well a rather different content – the tale of a man 'Lost among the Bookstacks':

> Where the bookstacks packed with racked and hardbacked
>   prose –
>   Rows on rows –
> Stand like regiments of sheen and shade arrayed
>   On parade,
> And the closets and the cosy carrels stand
>   Of a band
> Of explorers bent on laying down their youth
>   For the truth,
> Foraging through fact and fancy, with their notes
>   Full of quotes
> And those little packs of cards that plainly show
>   All they know,
> I am brooding o'er a learned journal, which
>   Makes me itch,
> Makes me fidget, fret, and wish to go elsewhere –
>   To my chair
> And a winsome whisky and a cheery fire,

    Or yet higher,
Up the sleepy stairs with unresisting tread,
    Into bed,
Where the stupid mindless blankets round my chin
    Snug me in –
Feeble-fleshed and sleepy-souled, I quit my seat,
    And my feet
Plod along the padded alleys where no sound
    Falls to ground,
Though a whisper bores a hole precise and clear
    In the ear,
Lanes of learning so intense, so dense, so still
    I feel ill
Thinking of the weary effort, all the pains
    Of the brains
Of the centuries of students here interred
    Word by word
In each monograph and thesis, in each schol-
    arly vol.,
Plump with paragraphs like porridge oats or stew
    Mixed in glue,
And among them, even, here and there, a line
    That is mine –
Goodness me! The mulling over, midnight oil
    On the boil,
Inspiration, desperation, bubbling hot,
    Soon to clot,
Panning into waxy wisdom, coolly poured,
    Duly stored –
Was it worth the effort, children? Did the grind
    Of the mind
Lead to fame and frequent laurels? Did you romp
    Into pomp?
Was there praise from ravished readers, near and far?
    There you are,
Dreaming in your decent leather, with a bold
    Touch of gold,
While before you with my weary eye and sigh
    Here am I,
Promenading round and round your boundless maze
    In a daze,
Lost, befuddled. Where's the exit? Should I shout?
    Get me out!

I keep this piece by me almost as a piece of verse in its own right; the connection with Browning seems remote, almost unnecessary to the reading of the text. What does strike me, however, is that Browning's metre, both in its sound when spoken and in its shape as laid out on the page, has become a metaphor for the arrangement of the bookstacks and the halting–hastening progress of someone rambling among them. It's odd that parody can work in this way, saving a versifier the trouble of finding an effective form.

Walter:

For such a complicated activity, parody has diverse and sometimes quite complicated forms. It is possible, in all solemnity, to demon-strate, by letter and diagram, parodic models. I will spare you the diagrams if you will tolerate a little commentary.[9] What is common to all parodic models is the assumption of two mimetic planes, one of expression and one of content. These, identified in a source-text, are echoed or reflected in a *derived expression*, and in a content either of the kind I have called 'apposed', or of the sort I have called 'displacing'. By the derived expression I mean the deliberately flawed mimicry which mingles accurate observation of a source-language with the happy interpolation of an extraneous idiom. This mimicry of expression is the main point of numerous parodies where the content is of the displacing kind, as in the Hopkins-on-the-train poem. In another model, unfortunately not properly illustrated by any of Bill's interludes, the expression and content of the source material are shadowed by a derived expression and an apposed content. These are two basic models, one appropriate to a simple joke about language and style, the other adapted to the more involved mockery of language and content together. On these bases more or less complex variants can be constructed. In some cases, what is imitated on the plane of expression is not an idiom, a variety of language, but simply the form of a poem, to which a displacing content is attributed. 'Lost among the Bookstacks' is a parody of this kind; its source connection is not so much with Browning's poetic *language* as with Browning's prosody, or a particular example of it.

There are more complex forms, in which the parodied expression and content are derived from different sources. If such intricacies are of interest to you, you might do worse than seek out the parodies of the now almost wholly neglected J.C. Squire. Squire wrote spoofs with titles like 'If the author of the Spoon River Anthology had written

Elegy in a Country Churchyard', and 'If Lord Byron had written the
Passing of Arthur'.[10] These mimicries involve expressing the content
of one author in the style or in the well known form associated with
another; so that an episode from Tennyson's 'Idylls of the King' is
rewritten in the stanza form of Byron's 'Don Juan', and in imitation of
Byron's breezy, macaronic verse-idiom. It is extremely skilful, but the
sadness of it is that time overtakes these things. Tennyson and Byron,
dare I say it, are not very widely read now, and so Squire's dexterity
is no longer appreciated, indeed no longer wanted. His book gathers
dust on the library shelf, along with the jocosities of C.S. Calverley
and Thomas Hood and Bret Harte, unborrowed except by passing
eccentrics with a taste for the byways of literature. But new parodic
energies are awakened, the impulse never dies; even as I speak, some
sprightly scribe in study or bed-sit is taking a poke at Pinter, laying into
Larkin, or even – for hope springs eternal – shooting an amiable shaft
through Jeffrey Archer. Parody rides on, and what is more important,
parodic activity, pseudoparody, the ringing of echoic bells from text to
text, also goes on.

Indeed, there is something about this lecture that strikes me a little
disturbingly. Has it, too, been a parodic act? May we not say that
from the moment I proposed to you the twin *personae* of Walter and
Bill, speaking now as one, now as the other, now as a composite, I
have been making mimetic sport with the discursive structure, the
antiphonal projection, that we call a lecture? A parodic discourse
on parody, illustrated by parodies – it sounds like mimesis run mad
– yet it is in this way, of imitation folded in speculation cloaked in
convention, that literature at large makes its arguments. As to our
little interludes of parody, it cannot be said that they are anything
more than bagatelles – doodles on thought and experience, trivia: yet
even from them shapes of the imagination arise – situations, objects,
personages speaking in many voices. And if we can say this of such
rhymes and rigmaroles, how rich and how complex in its creative
method must be the great text itself, on which these marginalia are
fitfully scribbled – the page of literature. Literature has absorbed
parody as part of the history of the art. There is parody in Chaucer,
in Shakespeare, in Ben Jonson, in Fielding, in Pope. Modern writers
like Tom Stoppard make extensive use of parody; his play *The Real
Inspector Hound*, for example, is from beginning to end parodic of
theatrical convention. Sometimes parody, standing up in its own
virtue, outlasts its object. An example is Stella Gibbons's novel *Cold
Comfort Farm*, now perhaps a little neglected but surely due for a
re-emergence. If it does come into favour again, I am sure that few

will know or greatly care that much of it is parodic of the writings of Mary Webb. Parody, beginning in a spirit of fun, amiable mockery, or literary scavenging, may end in creative art.

Lecturer:

And now I, too, must make an end. How shall I do it? Shall I say, Walter thanks you for your patient hearing? Or should it be, Bill is obliged and hopes he has managed to entertain you a little? I suppose we should be smart enough to compose a parody of a man struggling to find a full stop, but our wits are dry. I think we should merely pause here, leaning, with suspended voice, on a languid semi-colon;

This was one of a series of public lectures arranged by the Department of English at the University of Liverpool. I had been asked to contribute a talk about parody. In the advertisements for the series, my name was listed as *Bill Nash*, 'Bill' being a familiar address used by close friends. This touch of pleasant informality amused me and prompted the duologic form of the lecture.

7 The meanings of metadiscourse

Every student who has silently suffered a course of lectures, surreptitiously watching the clock – which seems to exact half an hour's patience for five minutes' progress – or perhaps trying to read favourable portents in the lecturer's gestures, phrasings, inflections – every such student, I say, knows what metadiscourse is, although the word may be quite unfamiliar. Metadiscourse is 'Last week' and 'Now I propose to turn to' and 'What are we to understand by this?' and 'If I may put it metaphorically', all the way through to 'And so to conclude . . .' followed by 'Finally . . .' and 'Next week we shall go on to examine . . . etc.'. I am sure you must have heard all this before; if you have not, then either the technique of lecturing has been wholly transformed since I was a student, or you have not been paying attention to the endearing ways of your instructors. Lecturers are necessarily addicted to metadiscourse. It is hardly possible to make one's way without it, and I shall not be at all surprised if, before the end of the present hour, you begin to pick up some of my own metadiscursive mannerisms. But do not immediately assume that I am only talking about some common, easily parodied tricks of the professorial trade. Metadiscourse is generally involved in many of the things we say and most of the things we write; and it conveys, as I hope to show you, various meanings.

You will have gathered that what we mean by metadiscourse is a kind of commentary, made in the course of speaking or writing. The essential feature of this commentary is that it is not appended to the text, like a footnote or a postscript, but is incorporated with it, in the form of words and phrases fitted in to the unfolding message. These words and phrases carry out functions somewhat different from the straightforward expression of a content. When I deliver a lecture or write an academic article, one of the things I may want to do is to provide my audience with verbal signposts, like 'in the first place',

'in due course', 'as we have seen', 'two considerations remain' –
phrases which help the reader or listener to form a mental map of
the discursive country I propose to travel through. Such phrases are
items of metadiscourse. I also make use of metadiscourse when I see
fit to elucidate or elaborate expressions which strike me as potentially
obscure; I say 'as it were', and 'so to speak', and 'to put it another
way'. Something of the same sort happens when I stand back from
my text for a moment in order to make a brief evaluation of what is
being stated; I say 'fortunately', or 'we may be assured', or 'despite
all evidence to the contrary'. And if I am just a little unsure of myself,
just a little afraid of smart-alecs and hostile critics, I have recourse to
still more words and phrases: 'admittedly', 'in most circumstances',
'to the best of my knowledge'. All these devices imply a working
relationship with an audience, the negotiation of an 'I' and a 'you' with
the intention of establishing a 'we'. Such negotiation is yet another of
the tasks of metadiscourse; I exemplify it when I say 'imagine', or 'if
you will allow me', or 'let us consider'.

VARIETIES, TACTICAL AND LEXICAL

After that recital you may well want to know if there is anything in a
text, certainly an academic text, that is not definable as metadiscourse
– and this, indeed, is a question that must haunt the handling of our
theme. The word 'metadiscourse' may have a reassuringly objective,
'scientific' ring, but its usage suggests boundaries of definition no
more firmly drawn than those of, say, 'rhetoric' or 'style'. One reader
may perceive a clear stylistic intention in something which another
reader dismisses as a commonplace, 'automatized' use of language.
Similarly, I, as a lecturer, may be at pains to make what seem to me
to be important contextual signals which, however, you, as audience,
casually ignore. It is by no means certain that we will all perceive
metadiscursive intention in the same way and in every instance.
To define my own perceptions of metadiscourse and metadiscursive
functions, I need a little terminology, and for this purpose I shall
draw mainly on my own invention and occasionally on some existing
usages. I am going to suggest that 'metadiscourse' principally implies
two processes, and that we can relate these processes to those divisions
of oratory known in classical rhetoric as *taxis* and *lexis*. By *taxis* the
Greek rhetoricians meant the structure of a speech, its programme or
running order of 'here beginneth' and 'firstly' and 'consequently' and
'on the other hand' and 'in conclusion'; the Romans called this the
dispositio. *Lexis* signified the diction and style of the piece, as adapted

to the orator's perception of the formality of his topic and the status of his audience; the Latin word was *elocutio*. Now many of the words and phrases we characterize, in their context, as 'metadiscourse' quite obviously function as marks of text structure, or *taxis*, while as many again seem to occur as explanatory or corrective comments on diction and style, that is, *lexis*. Accordingly I propose from this point onwards to speak of 'tactical metadiscourse' and 'lexical metadiscourse'.[1]

Tactical metadiscourse tells audiences what point they have reached in the narrative or exposition, how they got there, and – perhaps most important of all – what they are to expect. A very common tactic, taking different stylistic forms in various types of speech and writing, is to buttonhole the audience with an announcement or a reminder of a theme. Think of your own everyday experience and the number of times you may have said, by way of introduction to a joke, 'Here's one I bet you haven't heard', or, in establishing a topic of discussion, 'You know that book you lent me last week?'. Such phrases are specimens of tactical metadiscourse, serving both to nominate a topic and solicit the attention of an audience. Moves of this kind are conventionalized in some kinds of writing, particularly academic writing. Looking through offprints and typescripts of articles sent to me by colleagues I find these examples, among others:

In this article I should like to study the following points and questions . . .

In this article I want to argue for a multi-levelled approach to the linguistic study of irony. Previous studies have tended to discern the presence of irony in a text chiefly by reference to the levels of syntax and the semantics of speech act analysis.

This analysis will focus on the narrative structure of Ernest Hemingway's *The Old Man and the Sea*. More specifically, it will examine a passage taken from the central section of the novel.

The assumption which the present paper takes as its starting point, is the fact that the present-day teaching of writing does pose considerable problems. These problems involve teachers and pupils alike, they affect adult literates and semi-literates.

The main aim of this article is to provide an analysis of one aspect of linguistic organization in a literary–critical text. The particular aspect of language that will be examined is *modality*, and the analysis will be conducted with a view to explicating the techniques and strategies which characterize this type of academic writing.

The primary aim of this chapter is to provide a quantitative account of the ways in which modal verbs are used by writers of academic articles and textbooks in biological and physical science. A secondary aim is to sketch some possible consequences of this analysis, and of studies of the modals in general, for teachers and learners of English for Science and Technology.

In this section we discuss the principles that guide the construction of sentences as the basic building blocks of text. We start off, in 2.1, by presenting a tripartite structure for all three levels of analysis of the essay (the essay as a whole, the paragraph, and the sentence). This tripartite structure will allow students to gain the fundamental insight that the marshalling of information within the sentence can make a direct contribution to the writing of effective texts. In 2.2 we then demonstrate how this view of the sentence can modify and expand the student's basic notion of what constitutes a grammatically correct English sentence. In 2.3 the role of the sentence as a grammatical and rhetorical unit in text construction is clarified in a broader perspective by means of four requirements which every sentence should satisfy. Finally, attention is paid in 2.4 to subordination as a backgrounding strategy and the prominence and coherence function of the initial and final constituents in the sentence.[2]

Between these passages there are some remarkable similarities, if not of actual wording then at least of what might be called verbal strategy. The author takes a stance ('I should like to', 'I want to'), defines what the topic in 'this' case will be (the word 'this' occurs in nearly every passage), points to his main and secondary themes or indicates the general and more specific interest, glances at previous work in the field or refers to current problems, states (in the case of the last example) how the investigation will be carried out, and by what steps. This is tactical metadiscourse as commonly displayed in one part of a text, the opening. In reading the final example in my list, we may readily imagine ways in which, as the exposition develops, further marks of *taxis* might be incorporated. The authors here make use of the scientific convention of numbering the successive sections and sub-sections of a text; but they also make use of verbal comments on their intention and performance, for example 'we start off', 'we then demonstrate' and 'finally'. In this way they adduce the topics to which they will successively turn. It is not difficult to specify the kind of phrases that could be used to introduce the changing topics;

prominent textual signals would be such expressions as 'turning to another matter', 'a quite different aspect of the subject', 'now on a related point', 'in consequence of what has just been said', and, of course, enumerative words and phrases such as 'in the first place', 'next', 'thirdly', and 'in conclusion'. Another kind of tactic is the reviewing phrase: 'so far we have considered X', 'at an earlier point I suggested Y', 'bearing in mind our preliminary explanations I want to define Z'. Tactical metadiscourse thus involves some general preview of a theme, some statement of objectives, some indication of an expository plan, some enumeration of topics, some review of progress as the material is unfolded. (See summary table, p. 114).

Lexical metadiscourse also takes diverse forms, as illustrated by a few extracts culled from an essay by Bertrand Russell, called 'In praise of idleness'. I have emphasized the words and phrases that seem to me to have a metadiscursive function:

As long as a man spends his income, he puts just as much bread into people's mouths in spending as he takes out of other people's mouths in earning. The real villain, *from this point of view*, is the man who saves.

Usually two opposite kinds of advice are given simultaneously by two organised bodies of men; *this is called politics*. The skill required for this kind of work is not knowledge of the subjects as to which advice is given, but knowledge of the art of persuasive speaking and writing, *i.e. of advertising*.

From the beginning of civilisation until the Industrial Revolution, a man could, *as a rule*, produce by hard work little more than was required for the subsistence of himself and his family . . .

It is obvious that, in primitive communities, peasants, left to themselves, would not have parted with the slender surplus upon which the warriors and priests subsisted, but would either have produced less or consumed more.

The conception of duty, *speaking historically*, has been a means used by the holders of power to induce others to live for the interests of their masters rather than for their own. *Of course* the holders of power conceal this fact from themselves by managing to to believe that their interests are identical with the larger interests of humanity.

Assuming, as we may, that labour is on the whole disagreeable, it is unjust that a man should consume more than he produces.

Of course he may provide services rather than commodities, like a medical man, *for example*; but he should provide something in return for his board and lodging. *To this extent*, the duty of work must be admitted, *but to this extent only*.

In America men often work long hours even when they are already well off; such men, *naturally*, are indignant at the idea of leisure for wage-earners, except as the grim punishment for unemployment; *in fact*, they dislike leisure, even for their sons. *Oddly enough*, while they wish their sons to work so hard as to have no time to be civilised, they do not mind their wives and daughters having no work at all.

The wise use of leisure, *it must be conceded*, is a product of civilisation and education.

What are, in essence, revivalist appeals are made . . .

For the present, possibly, this is all to the good. A large country, full of natural resources, awaits development, and has to be developed with very little use of credit. *In these circumstances*, hard work is necessary, and is likely to bring great reward. *But what will happen when the point has been reached where everybody could be comfortable without long working hours*?

Broadly speaking, it is held that getting money is good and spending money is bad.

Academic institutions, therefore, *useful as they are*, are not adequate guardians of the interests of civilisation in a world where everyone outside their walls is too busy for unutilitarian pursuits.[3]

What the emphasized expressions have in common is the writer's consciousness of what he is writing and his perception of the need for further elucidation, for qualification, for emphasis, for evaluation, for the involvement of the reader in the assertions of the text. There is, in short, a variety of functions suggesting a variety of technical terms, and I would like to keep my terminology as simple as possible.[4] Let us confine ourselves to a few serviceable definitions. Some of these phrases indicate the particular conditions, the limits of time, place and so on, under which a proposition can be thought to hold good. Let us then call them 'limiters': 'from this point of view', 'speaking historically', 'to this extent' (and with a more emphatic limitation 'to this extent only'), 'for the present, possibly', 'in these circumstances', 'broadly speaking'. Not unlike these limiters are the 'hedges' which protect an author's position, saving him from the accusation of making unsafe categorical statements. If you say 'never', you are speaking categorically; if you say 'well, hardly ever', you are hedging. 'As a rule', 'it must be conceded', 'useful as they are', are typical hedges. 'Concede' is a characteristic hedging verb; it goes along with 'admit' and 'allow' and 'grant' and 'accept' and 'confess'. The opposite of the hedge is the 'emphatic' which focuses attention on or implies the particular saliency of some proposition or formulation: 'it is obvious that', 'of course', 'in fact'. Emphatics in their turn are semantically related to the 'evaluatives' which imply the writer's assessment of the plausibility, permissibility, peculiarity, etc., of what he asserts: 'naturally' and 'oddly enough' fall under this type. Other types are important because of what they imply about the relationship (dominant or deferential) between author and audience. One such class of expressions I will call 'formulators', because the author in various ways defines the meaning of a word or phrase as he wishes the reader to understand it. In Russell's text we have, after the assertion that 'two opposite kinds of advice are given simultaneously', the mocking definition 'this is called politics'. In the same extract the trick is repeated when he alludes to 'knowledge of the art of persuasive speaking and writing', and adds, 'i.e. advertising'. Note, 'this is', and i.e. – 'that is'. In another passage Russell uses 'what are': 'What are, in essence, revivalist appeals.' There is a hint of apology, in this last instance, as though Russell were saying 'there is no other name that I can think of'. That kind of semi-apologetic reliance on the reader's good will is apparent in phrases not occurring in our extracts but common enough as formulators: 'so to speak', 'as it were' and 'to coin a phrase' are symptoms of an author's consciousness of an unusual formulation, while 'in other words' and 'in short' suggest reformulation or revised definition. In all these instances, the author implies some degree of diffidence, even deference, but at the same time establishes a claim on words.

In fact, the formulators reflect the author's sense of being in charge of his discourse and imposing his will – with a gesture of apology maybe, but imposing it, none the less – on the reader. In this sense, just as emphatics are the opposite of hedges, so formulators are the opposite of 'appeals'. An 'appeal' is my term for the kind of rhetorical question that draws the reader into the text with an apparent request for opinion or arbitration: thus 'what is the significance of this?'; 'how are we to understand these words?'; 'what might the consequence of such a supposition be?'. Russell obligingly supplies a quite lengthy example: 'But what will happen when the point has been reached

when everybody could be comfortable without working long hours?'
We know, of course, that he is going to answer this question for us,
but our presence as readers is nevertheless acknowledged. The author
is not proposing something axiomatic, thereby closing the possibility
of further discussion; he is asking a question, ostensibly appealing for
an opinion, and thus indicating that on this point the discourse is still
open.

In such a case the author's stance is seemingly deferential. By
contrast, the address to the audience, particularly in spoken discourse,
may take the form of a 'directive' – 'Write this down', 'Remember
this' – in which case deference gives place to authority; or it may
take shape as an 'aside', when its stance is more or less neutral,
neither deferential nor particularly authoritarian. There are at least
three distinct types of aside. There is the 'explication', characterized
by such phrases as 'by which I mean': 'Elizabeth I was emotionally
unstable, by which I mean that she was given to violent bouts of
bad temper.' This kind of aside is akin to formulators like 'so to
speak' and 'as it were'. Then there is the 'parenthetical comment',
of which a typical marker is the phrase 'by the way': 'The father of
American liberty was George Washington – who, by the way, was a
slave-owner.' Then again there is the 'anticipatory' or 'promissory'
aside, which incidentally marks a topic for subsequent discussion,
booking, as it were, an as yet unspecified place in the expository
scheme. Key phrases here are 'in due course' and 'at some later
point': 'The economic miracle – an expression to which I shall return
in due course – has yet to occur in Britain.' Asides, directives and
appeals are forms of comment on the substance or wording of a
text, all of them, however, implying the presence of an audience.
One might add that while all of them can occur freely in spoken
address, written discourse is more self-conscious in its selection of
these types, seldom using directives, for instance, in the course of an
essay or an article.

THE TACTICS OF FICTION

These examples may appear to be demonstrations of the obvious. The
role of metadiscourse in lectures, in scholarly writings, in expository
prose, is something we take pretty much for granted; you may even
have been a little surprised that I should have gone to such lengths
to point out some very ordinary stylistic symptoms. We assume from
the outset that the expository text will be *mediated* to us; that the
author will assume the role of guide, regularly coming between us

and the text, taking his distance from his writing, on the one hand, and his audience, on the other. This expectation does not colour our encounters with other kinds of text. Here, for example, is the opening of a short story:

> The woman went almost running along the road from the Necropolis to the city, unaware of her speed, which was that of desperation seeking outlet. A funeral procession, walking ahead, slowed her down; women in white linen beat their bared breasts with rhythmic ululations; the bier with the gilded and painted mummy-case was drawn by softly-pacing mules. It would be unseemly to overtake, still more to join them; she had to keep behind their crawl till they turned off towards a tomb. Then she hurried again, as relieved as if she had some appointment to keep, till she reached the suburbs. Here she collected herself; it was the Egyptian quarter, where she might be known, though she was a Greek and lived in the Bruchion.
>
> Mary Renault, *According to Celsus*[5]

That is clearly not 'mediated', in the sense in which I have just used the word; it is *immediate*. No author here intrudes between the text and the reader. The author is concealed somewhere in the text itself. We may think of a lecture as a triangular relationship – in one angle the topic, in another the demonstrator, in the third the audience. But in this story-opening, no such relationship is discernible. The author has drawn a circle, you might say, and then stepped into it and disappeared. No guidance is given. We are not told what the story is to be about. The woman mentioned in the very first phrase is not identified. We may assume that this will be her story, but it may turn out to be someone else's. We do not know, at this point, the name of the city in which the funeral of an unspecified person is taking place, nor can we tell whether that city, that funeral and that person will have any relevance to the narrative. We are required to guess, or to be patient or both. Because this is fiction, we are ready to accept the role of the hoodwinked or temporarily blind spectator.

On the other hand, narrators will sometimes assume a posture not at all unlike that of the expositor going through the motions of mediation. There are stories that open in a style that presents at least a semblance of metadiscourse. Observe, for instance, Conan Doyle – or, if you like, observe the narrator, Dr Watson – beginning his story called *The Adventure of the Speckled Band*:

In glancing over my notes of the seventy-odd cases in which I
have during the last eight years studied the methods of my friend
Sherlock Holmes, I find many tragic, some comic, a large number
merely strange, but none commonplace; for, working as he did
rather for the love of his art than for the acquirement of wealth,
he refused to associate himself with any investigation which did not
tend towards the unusual, and even the fantastic. Of all these varied
cases, however, I cannot recall any which presented more singular
features than that which was associated with the well-known Surrey
family of the Roylotts of Stoke Moran. The events in question
occurred in the early days of my association with Holmes, when
we were sharing rooms as bachelors, in Baker Street. It is possible
that I might have placed them on record before, but a promise of
secrecy was made at the time, from which I have only been freed
during the last month by the untimely death of the lady to whom
the pledge was given. It is perhaps as well that the facts should now
come to light, for I have reasons to know that there are widespread
rumours as to the death of Dr Grimesby Roylott which tend to make
the matter even more terrible than the truth.

By contrast with the opening of Mary Renault's story, this is heavily
and obviously mediated. Conan Doyle uses his narrator to prime
the reader, very much as lecturers prime their audiences. The story
begins with a kind of preview, reminding us of the usual content
of these narratives and giving some indication of what we are to
expect in this one. The narrator says, in effect, 'I have been looking
through my notes . . . I propose to give you an account of something
unprecedented . . . it relates to certain well-known people . . . the
time was . . . the place was . . . my reasons for giving it now are . . .'.
This is straightforward tactical metadiscourse. Or perhaps it is not
so straightforward; for the narrator, in ostensibly tipping his hand, in
fact gives nothing away. There is, it would seem, a predictive map,
and yet the reader cannot really anticipate the development of the
narrative or preview its topics. This 'well-known Surrey family' is not
in the least known; the 'widespread rumours' have reached no one's
ears; and the 'singular feattures' Watson refeers to miight refer to any
kind of mysterious happening. On reflection, this seems to be a kind
of parody of the conventional metadiscursive opening, and its object,
we might think, is to win the reader's confidence. We place a certain
reliance in the stodgy and meticulous Dr Watson. If Holmes were
allowed to tell the tale on his own account, we might not be so trusting,
because Holmes, apart from being a drug addict, is an egocentric given

to manic fits of mental activity and depressive bouts of boredom. He might say anything. Again, if the story were presented without a mediating narrator, we might find it all too fanciful; in this tale, let me remind you, snakes come spiralling down the bell-rope in the middle of the night. Incredible. But Watson, ah, yes, Watson is an honest straightforward sort of chap, short on imagination, perhaps, but long on truthfulness, a trained physician and a military man who might well be expected to make an objective, 'mediated' report of the matters to which he turns his attention. Yet the apparent mediation is deceptive; the style of this opening may suggest methodical introduction of the matter in hand, but serves only to tantalize the reader with the hint of pleasurably strange events in the offing.

Fictional metadiscourse is often complex, both in its designed effect on the reader, and in the forms it takes. Some narrative devices are not easy to label and tabulate, but are undoubtedly metadiscursive. Let us look at just one more story-opening:

> Imagine, if you can, a small room, hexagonal in shape, like the cell of a bee. It is lighted neither by window nor by lamp, yet it is filled with a soft radiance. There are no apertures for ventilation, yet the air is fresh. There are no musical instruments, and yet, at the moment that my meditation opens, this room is throbbing with melodious sounds. An armchair is in the centre, by its side a reading-desk – that is all the furniture. And in the armchair there sits a swaddled lump of flesh – a woman, about five feet high, with a face as white as a fungus. It is to her that the little room belongs.
>
> An electric bell rang.
>
> The woman touched a switch and the music was silent.
>
> E.M. Forster, The Machine Stops

In this instance the mediation of a narrator is instantly apparent. 'Imagine, if you can', he says, addressing an audience, and 'at the moment that my meditation opens', establishing his status as the teller of the tale creating a framework for subsequent reference. He is a kind of demonstrator, though what he has to demonstrate is not the preliminary material of a lecture, but something more analogous to the stage directions that precede a play: in short, a setting. There is here a moment of transition from one kind of narrative to another, from setting to sequence. That moment comes with the marked change of tense in the short second paragraph – 'An electric bell rang' – and again in the third – 'The woman touched a switch and the music was silent'. Here we demonstrably shift our ground from the author's domain – of being conscious of preparing to tell a story, and of telling the reader something about it – to the domain in which the story appears to be telling itself; or let me use images I have suggested earlier, and say that at this point the narrator abandons his position in one of the corners of the 'mediating' triangle, and abruptly steps into the magic circle of the 'immediate' narrative. By such devices, Forster in this story establishes for the narrator a role which vacillates between the omnicompetence of the maker controlling and directing his own creatures, and the surrendered power of the artist or thinker whose conceptions become mysteriously capable of managing their own affairs. Towards the end of the story, when his central character is quite literally at death's door, he intervenes with this comment:

> It was thus that she opened her prison and escaped – escaped in the spirit, at least so it seems to me, ere my meditation closes. That she escapes in the body – I cannot perceive that.

As a symptom of the intervening commentary – the metanarrative – note the momentary switch to the present tense. (It occurs in those two sentences: in the next, we return to the past.) We must notice also the reiterated assertion that this is a 'meditation', on an action conceived in the imagination of the narrator. His comment is at one level comparable with a routine move in a lecturer's metadiscourse, the move that says 'To sum up . . .', or 'From all this we may conclude'. At another level it is less assured, less a matter of routine. The narrator, unlike the expositor, apparently regards the text as something capable of eluding his control, even while he declares his control of it; the narrative potentially generates its own solutions, and the narrator, from whose imagination the story springs to life, must at length deny himself the right to sum up, to assert, to conclude. 'So it seems to me', he says, and 'I cannot perceive that' – using expressions that mark, metadiscursively, his surrender of total rights over the text.

THE VOICE OF POETRY

It appears that in the kinds of writing we honour with the epithet 'creative' there may be a role for metadiscourse, the functions of which transcend those of simple commentary. Particularly when the text or utterance is poetic, it begins to seem that the metadiscourse is no longer something separable from the meaningful substance of the text, but tends to become an integral element in the poetic procedure. It comments, but at the same time is part of what is commented on. This is perhaps a confusing proposition. How can something be at one and the same time metadiscourse and – forgive the coinage

– infradiscourse?; how can it mediate and yet be fused with the immediate? Well, let us take an example. Here is one that ought to be familiar to you, a modern anthology piece – Henry Reed's 'Naming of Parts':

Today we have naming of parts. Yesterday
We had daily cleaning. And tomorrow morning,
We shall have what to do after firing. But today,
Today we have naming of parts. Japonica
Glistens like coral in all of the neighbouring gardens,
       And today we have naming of parts.

This is the lower sling swivel. And this
Is the upper sling swivel, whose use you will see,
When you are given your slings. And this is the piling swivel,
Which in your case you have not got. The branches
Hold in the gardens their silent, eloquent gestures,
       Which in our case we have not got.

This is the safety-catch, which is always released
With an easy flick of the thumb. And please do not let me
See anyone using his finger. You can do it quite easy
If you have any strength in your thumb. The blossoms
Are fragile and motionless, never letting anyone see
       Any of them using their finger.

And this you can see is the bolt. The purpose of this
Is to open the breech, as you can see. We can slide it
Rapidly backwards and forwards: we call this
Easing the spring. And rapidly backwards and forwards
The early bees are assaulting and fumbling the flowers:
       They call it easing the Spring.

They call it easing the Spring: it is perfectly easy
If you have any strength in your thumb: like the bolt,
And the breech, and the cocking-piece, and the point of balance,
Which in our case we have not got; and the almond-blossom
Silent in all of the gardens and the bees going backwards and
       forwards,
       For today we have naming of parts.[6]

There was a time, forty years or more ago, when it would have been quite unnecessary for any lecturer to venture explanatory comment on the situation which frames this poem, since the very title, 'Naming of Parts', would strike a responsive, if somewhat doleful, chord in the minds of the ex-servicemen who then made up the bulk of most academic audiences. 'Naming of parts' was something recruits had to learn in the course of so-called 'weapon training', and the parts were – as the poem tells us – the parts of a rifle. Recollections of this standard episode in service life constitute, we may say, the scenario and the script upon which Reed draws with amusing accuracy. No one who had ever been through these experiences could easily forget the boredom, the sense of futility, the feeling of being incarcerated in the absurd, the pathetic longing to be somewhere else, all of which the poet is able to retrieve, vividly, touchingly and funnily. Yet even today the poem makes its appeal and the poet makes his point with generations who, happily, have never been drilled by sergeants, never been bullied by corporals, never been obliged to contemplate a rifle, let alone suffer the embarrassment of publicly naming its parts.

How does he do this? The essential matter, surely, is that there are two quite distinct spheres of reference in the poem, one of authority, speaking aloud, and one of submission, speaking to itself. Two voices are represented, in alternations regularly scripted in the pattern of each of the first four stanzas, where the second voice, the inner voice of the hapless young soldier, enters in the middle of the fourth line; the final stanza, of course, represents in its entirety this second voice. The question may arise of how – apart from clues of layout and punctuation – we can recognize the intermittent lapses of the authoritarian voice and the incursions of the voice of submission, which is also the voice of defiance and subversion. There are of course clues of language and apparent speech-style. One of the speakers appears to have an uneasy acquaintance with educated English usage. He says 'which in your case you have not got', and 'you can do it quite easy'. He issues commands – 'do not let me see anyone using his finger'. The frequent 'you' and 'your' suggest that he is addressing an audience; the 'we' of the opening lines apparently includes the commander and the commanded. The other speaker, by contrast, expresses himself with literary elegance. He (for we assume masculinity) commands no one, and indeed addresses no one in particular. He never says 'you', and his 'we' does not suggest the inclusion of the sergeant-instructor; it would appear rather to imply something not unlike the Rastafarian 'I and I', a reference to the speaker himself and to members of his spiritual family. This may, of course, sympathetically include the reader, even the reader who knows nothing of weapon training and military service.

A prominent feature of this second, 'inner' voice is that it periodically echoes the discourse of the first, 'outer' voice. Now that discourse, we can hardly avoid noticing, is full of metadiscursive tags and turns of phrase. Lecturers say 'Last week we considered some aspects of Romantic poetry. . . . This week I shall consider in detail the Odes of Keats. . . . Next week I propose to examine some lyrics by Shelley'. Military instructors follow the same metadiscursive convention when they declare 'Today we have naming of parts. . . . Yesterday we had daily cleaning. . . . And tomorrow morning, we shall have what to do after firing.' It is a different scenario, if you like, but the same process of tactical metadiscourse. There is also something familiar about the instructor's discourse-controlling lexis. There are formulators – 'we call this easing the spring'; there are asides – 'which in your case you have not got'; there are directives – 'and please do not let me see anyone using his finger'; there are explications – 'the purpose of this is to open the breech, as you can see'; there is the monotonous recurrence of 'this' and 'this is', characterizing the mediated commentary as opposed to the immediate expression of observation and feeling.

The other voice, however, the voice of immediate submission, is not represented as wholly independent of the first, authoritarian voice. We have noticed already how one speaker echoes the other, in sad, lyrical mockery as blundering instructorese and the bald phraseology of the training manual are transformed into subversive emblems of yearning and *ennui*. The aside, 'which in your case you have not got', becomes 'which in our case we have not got', and what we have not got, seemingly, are the silent, eloquent gestures of the branches, suggesting such silent, eloquent gestures as a bored recruit might like to make to an all-too-vocal non-commissioned officer. The directive 'do not let me see anyone using his finger', which has a hint of coarseness almost verging on *double entendre*, is transmuted into an evocation of the still beauty of the flowers, which, like the lilies of the field toil not, neither do they spin, and certainly never have to work a safety-catch. And of course there is the outrageous yet almost plaintive pun on the formulation, 'they call it easing the spring'; here the poet is obliged to call on the services of a capital letter to ensure that the reader has fully established the contrast between springs as mere mechanisms and Springs as seasons of growth and fullness and hope.

'Naming of Parts' and its companion poem 'Judging Distances' make up a kind of poetic diptych entitled *Lessons of the War*. What Reed successfully achieves in this little work is first of all a comically accurate imitation of the metadiscourse of lessons, which then provides a frame of reference for the oblique intimation of serious feelings, the text of a different kind of lesson. The typical language and moves of common metadiscourse, its processes of mediating, are mocked, but the mockery is transmuted into the immediate ironic sadness of what I have ventured to call the 'infradiscourse'. The reader consequently experiences humour and pathos almost simultaneously, a blend of feelings which, I dare say, would not have been so effectively conveyed had the poet chosen to express himself in one voice alone, that of the unhappy conscript. The language of poetry and literature makes continual raids on 'ordinary' usage, endowing simple scripts with complex significance. This poem is an instance of the raiding habit of the literary artist; here metadiscourse is revalued in an unfamiliar, poetic frame.

But it depends, you will tell me, on what we mean by metadiscourse, and if you tell me that, you bring me almost full circle to the point at which I confessed that the boundaries of metadiscourse seem at times to be so uncertainly drawn that there are texts in which nearly everything might be considered metadiscursive in function. There may indeed be a case for saying that metadiscourse takes shape in the mind of the reader or listener as much as in the intentions of the writer or speaker. Let me finish, therefore, by trying to say what, in general, metadiscourse 'means'. It means what I have called 'mediating'. It means any form of language which can be interpreted either as a commentary on the process of making a text – for 'text', where necessary, read 'speech' – or as a negotiation of relationships with an audience. 'Let me tell you a little story' is metadiscourse. 'Arms and the man I sing' is metadiscourse. 'Today we have naming of parts' is metadiscourse. 'And next week . . .' – but this is where I came in, and I leave you to finish the message in your spare time, which in your case, I imagine, you have not got.

METADISCOURSE: SUMMARY TABLE

The following are typical moves. (NB: The terminology is purely descriptive, and does not purport to represent a standard model of metadiscourse.)

'Tactical metadiscourse'

preview	e.g.	'In this lecture I propose to discuss . . .'
topic enumeration	e.g.	'First we shall . . . Then we proceed to . . .'
topic shift	e.g.	'Now as to . . . Turning to another matter . . .'

review	e.g.	'We have seen how . . . Up to this point I have . . .'
conclusion	e.g.	'To sum up . . . Let me end by saying . . .'
forecast	e.g.	'In my next chapter . . . When we resume . . .'

'Lexical metadiscourse'

limiters	e.g.	'To this extent only . . . Up to a point . . . Historically speaking. . . In this particular instance'
hedges	e.g.	'Admittedly . . . As far as I know . . . By all accounts . . . Most people would agree'
emphatics	e.g.	'Of course . . . Quite obviously . . . It must be stressed that . . . Without the least doubt'
evaluatives	e.g.	'Strangely enough . . . By a stroke of good fortune . . . I am happy to say . . . Naturally'
formulators	e.g.	'so to speak . . . what might be called . . . for which I propose the name . . .'
appeals	e.g.	'How are we to read this? . . . One might ask what sort of response is expected . . .'
directives	e.g.	'Consider this . . . Let the reader be advised . . . We ought not to accept . . .'
asides	e.g.	explications: 'by which I mean', 'in other words': 'Caligula was psychotically disturbed; in other words he was raving mad.'
		parenthetical comments: 'by the way', 'I might add', 'incidentally': 'Gregor Mendel, incidentally an Augustinian monk, was the father of modern genetics.'
		promissory asides: 'as we shall presently see', 'in due course', 'for the time being', 'until later': 'Let us for the time being defer consideration of X.'

The text of a lecture contributed to a series on 'Language', delivered to first-year students at University College London, February 1990.

8   On writing well

Then know that I one Snug the joiner am . . .

For a while I was not sure how I would open this lecture. I had even begun to be anxious about it, but one should never fret over such matters; the words you need will always turn up in the nick of time, perhaps as you are being introduced to your audience, or preferably just a little earlier, while you still have leisure to write them down. Have faith, and you will find a way to start. On this occasion, as it happens, I have been lucky enough to discover my opening with days to spare. The necessary nudge came from one of last week's newspapers – *The Independent*, dated 20 November 1986 – where I found the following:

> 'Poetry is, for me, the highest kind of writing. The novel is next, the stage play third, and the television script after that', said Nigel Williams on this page last week.

Now here is a starting point. You have asked me to talk about writing well; then what *kind* of writing must I concern myself with? For it appears, on the authority of Mr Williams, that there are kinds, ranked in order of excellence. There is poetry, there are novels, there are plays, there are television scripts; there is a corpus, it seems, of the Proper Stuff, and I would not for a moment wish to challenge Mr Williams's taxonomy of taste. Nevertheless, I have to wonder about other kinds of writing, in which excellence is also possible. What about the critical essay, the study, the report? What about histories and biographies; scholarly commentaries; instructional texts? For that matter, what about that most consoling and vexatious product of verbal craft, the letter? Where do these come in the scale of merit? Are they also Writing with a capital W, or are they merely the Other Stuff – necessary activities of a literary kind, in which, however, the use of language has no intrinsically creative value?

I cannot really accept the distinction I have projected, between the Proper Stuff and the Other Stuff, but since it does exist in common prejudice and presupposition, let me say that I am here to speak up for the Other Stuff. If it were indeed true that all forms of writing other than poetry, fiction and drama are at best mechanical routines, at worst artless prattlings, then there would be little point in my trying to talk to you about Writing Well. I am a scholar of sorts, an essayist of sorts, a deviser of monographs – of sorts; I am Snug the joiner. But I believe that there is a measure of art, and of disciplined skill, in every kind of writing, not least in the writing that scholars do. I believe that it is possible for an essay, a thesis, an academic article, to be well written. More than that, I believe that in all cases the good writing is not merely a decoration, an appropriate costume, but an integral property of the text, the expression of an inner principle. I believe that we can see *how* texts are well written, and that we can translate our perceptions into practice. I believe that in the ordinary way, in the customary traffic of our lives, we can learn to write well; and I believe that there is a moral obligation upon us to do so, for we are students of English, and this is the one talent we can return with interest.

Need I put it to you with such emphasis? It is almost a matter of definition that students of English are people who want to write, who value this activity, who constitute, indeed, a Writing Class. Their enthusiasm is wholly admirable. But anyone who has attempted to teach composition will tell you that the enthusiast often draws inspiration from a potentially dangerous and deceitful source: the fabulous well of *self-expression*. More than once I have had students tell me that the point of writing is to express your feelings and your personality. Now I would be the last to deny that in writing, as in other arts, there can be self-help and self-healing; but I am sometimes obliged to remind my students of T.S. Eliot's rueful comment, that far from writing to express a personality he wrote to escape from one. To this I have to add, that a naïve insistence on self-expression not only obstructs the learning of a craft, but actually cripples the power of writing as a means by which we explore and share our experience.

You may well protest that writing is, after all, done by persons – not, as yet, by machines – and that all writings which are uninformed by a personality are dead, or at least deadly dull. I will agree with you. I think so too. But perhaps we can usefully distinguish between the *self* of the author, and the *persona* that dwells in his text; between the *auctor*, John Doe or Richard Roe, who scratches his nose, mislays his spectacles, has indigestion, loses his temper, and the transcending *auctoritas* that takes shape in the cumulative choice and combination of words, so that the text itself has personality, and speaks. To establish that authority, you must often leave your 'self' far behind, in the course of endless negotiations with language; in order to achieve something truly original, you may be forced entirely to disregard your notions of yourself as originator.

I am not saying anything new or remarkable; nor will I in the whole of this address. If I have a doctrine, I suppose it is this: use quite ordinary language – the 'standard' language, if you please – in patterns that make it seem out of the ordinary. For upwards of two thousand years, every Tom, Dick and Aristotle has been saying something of the sort, and I can only repeat the lesson in my own terms. An illustration is called for, and so I invite you to consider a piece of writing perhaps not quite as familiar as last week's newspaper. It is a passage from A.E. Housman's introduction to his edition of Manilius; a neglected prose classic, I think, or at least an unsurpassable model of the grand old academic art of giving your fellow scholars a ferociously elegant going-over. Here is Housman in comparatively benevolent mood, reflecting on the strengths and weaknesses of one of his heroes, the great classical scholar and critic Richard Bentley. (Bentley, the autocratic Master of Trinity College Cambridge, was a contemporary of Alexander Pope, who accused him of having 'humbled Milton's strains', because he had somewhat rashly practised his critical arts on the text of *Paradise Lost*.) Thus Housman:

> The faults of this edition, which are abundant, are the faults of Bentley's other critical works. He was impatient, he was tyrannical, and he was sure of himself. Hence he corrupts sound verses which he will not wait to understand, alters what offends his taste without staying to ask about the tastes of Manilius, plies his desperate hook upon corruptions which do not yield at once to gentler measures, and treats the MSS much as if they were fellows of Trinity. Nay more: though Bentley's faculty for discovering truth has no equal in the history of learning, his wish to discover it was not so strong. His buoyant mind, elated by the exercise of its powers, too often forgot the nature of its business, and turned from work to play; and many a time when he feigned and half fancied that he was correcting the scribe, he knew in his heart (and of his Paradise Lost they tell us he confessed it) that he was revising the author.[1]

Never mind if the style is a little old-fashioned, and frankly rhetorical; about such writing there is an air of almost frivolous ease. The football crowds applaud the skill of their teams with cries of 'Easy! Easy!'; and

I must confess to a comparably exultant impulse when I observe the assurance, the control of his linguistic resources, with which a skilled writer moves towards his goal. Easy, yes; but so shrewd.

Of the many things in this passage that invite comment, I will pick out only one, in pursuit of my theme that distinctiveness – or originality, or 'flair', call it what you will – is best achieved by putting ordinary words into productive patterns. Take, then, the sentence that lies at the heart of the passage (lines 8–9: 'though Bentley's faculty for discovering truth has no equal in the history of learning, his wish to discover it was not so strong.' Here is a judgement, incisively and authoritatively expressed; yet it is not urged upon us by an 'I', and there is no expression in it that is not familiar to us as everyday standard English. No author intrudes here, but there is authority, none the less; there is no extraordinary word, and yet the style is memorably pointed.

How is this achieved? Let me suggest, by one simple basic device. In patterning this particular sentence the writer has elected to put the subordinate clause before the main clause – and that is almost all of the secret of it. To be convinced of this elementary point, you need only try the experiment of reversing the order of the clauses: 'Bentley's wish to discover truth was not so strong, though his faculty for discovering it has no equal in the history of learning.' The words are the same, but they do not make an impact comparable with that of Housman's sentence, which smiles, and smiles – and shows its teeth. There is surely no harder blow than the knock that follows a caress. The sentence-pattern makes this effect; and within the broader pattern there are other configurations. There is, for example, a discernible if relaxed parisonic relationship between the two halves of Housman's sentence. By that I mean, that the two clauses are approximately in balance, element by element, with each other: 'faculty for discovering truth' is closely matched by 'wish to discover it'; 'has' corresponds to 'was'; 'no equal, etc.' finds a somewhat looser parallel in 'not so strong'. Indeed, it is possible to abstract a formula for the repeated syntactic procedure: we have Noun ('faculty', 'wish') + Non-finite Qualifying Clause ('for discovering truth', 'to discover it') + HAVE or BE ('has,' 'was') + negatively-marked Object or Complement ('no equal', 'not so strong'). The nuclear constructions are 'faculty for discovering' and 'wish to discover', and in those constructions we find the essential semantic counterpoise of 'faculty' and 'wish'. It is the main business of the whole passage, one might say, to bring those two words into opposing play; in retrospect it appears that the text is conceived and designed round that opposition.

But now consider one of those gifts of idiomatic chance that sometimes fall our way, whether we deserve them or not. The noun 'faculty' must collocate with a participial (or, if you prefer, gerundial) construction – 'a faculty for doing'; the noun 'wish' is similarly tied to a construction with an infinitive – 'a wish to do'; we simply cannot say 'a faculty to discover', 'a wish for discovering'.[2] Thus, the primary contrast of 'faculty' and 'wish' entails another contrast, of participial and infinitive constructions, and what these imply semantically: the opposition of the contingent, ongoing *process*, the 'doing', and the permanent, definitive *state*, the 'do' – the *posse* and *esse* of Bentley's nature. The phrases appear to uncover these meanings inevitably, though we may regard them as a species of happy accident, because it is simply not possible to construct 'faculty' and 'wish' in any other way. But think what would have happened if Housman had first lighted upon 'ability', rather than 'faculty', and had rested content with that word?; the phrasing would have read 'ability to discover' versus 'wish to discover' – *state* versus *state* – and an important nuance of meaning would have been lost. Possibly Housman's phrasing was an ordinary matter of luck; more probably it was a case of what Petronius calls *curiosa felicitas* – painstaking felicity. You can be lucky in your writing, but you have to work to make your luck.

Housman's text was published in 1903, yet it is hardly possible not to sense, in those Augustan cadences, a debt to much earlier styles in prose. It carries echoes of other writers (Samuel Johnson comes to mind); it displays the property some literary theorists call 'intertextuality'; it is, in short, representative of a tradition. It reminds us that in writing there is practically no task, no enterprise you can name, that has not already been undertaken. We are always in the grip of inherited principles which in part sustain us, if we understand them sympathetically, and in part lay constraints upon us. Sometimes, chafing at the constraint, we try to break free of it, to create new modes of writing; generally we accept it, and try to work skilfully within it. This is the classic way, of attempting original discourse within traditional precepts.

When you go to your room to write, therefore, you may sneck the window and bar the door, but you are not alone; there are ghosts – kindly, fussy ghosts – looking over your shoulder, whispering, counselling, correcting, telling you that this is how it has always been done and insisting that you pay your dues. But all your debt is not to the past; obviously, you have a duty to the here and now. You are an author, addressing a supposed audience, on a certain topic. Here is the writer's eternal triangle: I, you and the other one, the shape taking shape on the page. It is a relationship implying more variables than one might easily list – of attitude, of context, of shared culture, of purpose. Do I write to inform, to persuade, to entertain, or with a combination of these purposes? Do I know my audience, or are they only imagined faces in the void? Can I assume that we have a great deal in common, by way of interests, experience, reading, assumptions about life? Do I intend to treat my subject seriously, lightly, humorously, ironically? It is not only the ghosts looking over my shoulder that I have to appease; it is the wraiths of expectancy waiting *out there*, beyond the walls of my study. I am doubly governed; by the traditional directives of a genre, whatever it may be, and by the pragmatic demands of this particular composition.

Even as I speak to you, I am illustrating the demands of a certain compositional type. Against my everyday practice, I am speaking from a script – against my everyday practice because this is a special occasion and I do not want to fall over any of the stumbling blocks impromptu lecturers place for themselves. At the same time, I do not want this lecture to be like an essay which I dutifully read aloud before going off to lunch. What I have in mind is a venture for the voice, a performance necessarily involving the responses of you, my listeners. Now, if I were to re-deliver a passage presented to you barely a minute ago, you would quite certainly notice something that might have escaped your conscious attention at the first hearing: a fluctuation in my use of personal pronouns, beginning with 'you', as in 'When you go to your room, etc', and shifting at a certain point in my script-paragraph to 'I', as in 'Do I write to inform? etc.'. With the text before you, you would be able to trace this movement from 'you' to 'I', noting the intervention of a sentence that innocently contains the neutral and inclusive pronoun 'one'. ('It is a relationship implying more variables than one might easily list'.) The point of appeal shifts from 'you' to 'one' to 'I' – from the audience, to the duality of audience and speaker, to the speaker alone. I can assure you that this alternation of pronouns happened without reflection on my part, and yet it clearly happened in response to a design. I stand here monologuing, but my intention is to convey through my text a sense of dialogue, of interaction. My script must in some way encode a sense of speaking, and of being heard.

I have raised a long familiar problem. The Greeks and Romans knew all about it; here is Pliny the Younger, for example, discussing the matter from the point of view of the audience:

as everyone remarks, we are much more affected by the living
voice; for although what you read may be more precisely expressed,
there is something in the delivery, the look, the gesture of a
speaker, that makes a deeper impression on the mind.[3]

In translating loosely, I have somewhat blurred the distinction Pliny
makes between *acrior* – 'sharper', 'keener', used of writing – and
altius – 'more deeply', used of speech. It is an interesting reflection
that writing makes a keener cut but speech leaves a deeper mark
– almost the opposite of what we commonly suppose; yet totally
consistent with the teachings of ancient rhetoric, in which *hypocrisis*
('action', 'gesture') was an essential element in the art of exposition
and persuasion. The very terms we use to describe patterns of literary
expression – words like 'scheme' and 'figure' – go back to Greek and
Latin words signifying 'attitude', 'physical posture'. And although
the dominant arts of language are no longer those of pleading a
case, debating an issue, or even giving a lecture, no writer seeking
to engage the sympathetic attention of an audience can avoid the
problem of using language in such a way as to create the illusion of
gesture and personal address. It *is*, of course, an illusion, an artifice.
Writing that merely transcribed 'natural' speech would be dull and
ineffectual; it would sacrifice the *acrior* without achieving the *altius*.
But the long centuries of tradition have taught us the devices that
stimulate the emphasis, the urgency, the apparent disjunctions, of the
spoken language.

The possibilities are many; let Housman once again provide
us with an example from his cool and counterbalanced prose.
I draw your attention to this sentence, at the close of the
text:

> and many a time when he feigned and half fancied that he
> was correcting the scribe, he knew in his heart (and of his
> Paradise Lost they tell us he confessed it) that he was revising
> the author.

Note, first of all, the artifice of those deliberate parallels: 'feigned
and half fancied', 'correcting the scribe' – 'revising the author'. Into
that carefully inscribed design Housman introduces, of all things, a
bracketed parenthesis. The impulse of an afterthought is allowed
to break in on the well-regulated pattern. Now, the information
Housman wants to adduce could have been managed in a different
way. He could have dispensed with the brackets and interpolated a
subordinate construction, like this:

> he knew in his heart, as indeed he is said to have confessed of his
> Paradise Lost, that he was revising the author

or like this:

> he knew in his heart what he is reported as having confessed of his
> Paradise Lost, that he was revising the author.

Instead, he prefers to break the thread of successive dependences with a parenthesis containing a co-ordinated independent sentence. This is no smoothly delivered aside; it sticks out – there is no other word for it. A striking feature of this 'extruded' sentence is that it has what is sometimes called a *marked theme*. Thematic marking, or 'fronting', occurs in emphatic spoken English, in sentences such as 'Stupid, I call it', 'About that I wouldn't know', 'Three months he got', 'White as a sheet, she was', in which an Object, a Complement or an Adverbial is moved from its expected position and emphatically placed at the beginning of the clause. Housman, using this device, reminds us of the colloquial habit; the positioning of the phrase 'of his Paradise Lost' at the front of the sentence is a clear gesture of emphasis. And in being so positioned it becomes ambivalent, for it is not wholly clear whether the phrase is an adjunct to 'they tell us', or to 'he confessed it'; that is, whether we should assume a reading 'they tell us of his Paradise Lost that he confessed X', or 'they tell us that he confessed X of his Paradise Lost'. Does it amount to the same thing? Or are there two subtly different shades of meaning? The phrase as it stands is unclear, yet forceful; a rhetorical gesture, mimetic of speech, has somewhat blunted the edge, the *acrior*, but has added to the impact, the *altius*, of the text. And note, incidentally, that instead of the impersonal passives which I suggested in my rewritings ('he is said to have confessed', 'he is reported as confessing') we have the active voice – 'they say he confessed it' – which will always tend to suggest the habit of speech rather than the language of books. In short, by this one stylistic act, of contriving a seemingly casual, speech-resembling parenthesis in the course of a literary text, Housman produces the illusion of appealing with a gesture to a live audience. From the words on the page one can almost reconstruct the pause and the admonitory signal of the raised finger or the turning hand.

Well, to repeat an earlier remark – easy; but so shrewd. You have to be smart to be a writer; and the smartest thing of all is that you must not be seen to be doing anything out of the ordinary. The smartest writers (unlike lecturers) seldom show off; they merely control. And what is it they control? More than you might think it possible for a human being to keep in mind. First, there are the resources of grammar; I mean of phrasing, of sentence-structure, of the linking and integration of the units of grammatical form, of the provisions for expressing notions that dress the stage of daily experience – ·time, place, perspective, agency, possibility and so forth. My own students sometimes look askance when I speak of the 'resources' of grammar; because they think of grammar as a set of rules rather than as a box of tools. But for the writer it is a cabinet of resources; it is the great corpus of possible ways of putting things; and writers know in their bones, if not with their brains, that there is always an alternative.

I will suggest an example, not from the experience of writing, but from the rather more mundane business of shopping. Some time ago, when I was wheeling my wire basket through the check-out at our local supermarket, I thought I had been overcharged. 'There's a mistake here', I said, using what is called an *existential sentence* – as though the mistake had been hovering like a bluebottle and had just alighted. 'You what?' said the cashier, in blunt East Midland. I said 'A mistake has been made', resorting this time to the passive, but still naming no one and blaming no one. I was reluctant to get down to pronouns. Only when she still feigned incomprehension did I actually say 'You have made a mistake', using a simple declarative sentence, in the active voice, with a pronominal subject. The three successive constructions, three different ways of putting a point, tell the story of the situation and my attempts to manage it. It was an episode in daily life, and to handle it I used the grammatical resources of my mother-tongue.

Now the writer's 'situation' is his *text*, and the management of it requires the awareness of manifold resources and choices. I say 'awareness' – but how 'aware' must the practitioner be? Do I really mean that every would-be writer, each able Jack or clever Jill, must devote days and nights to the study of *A Comprehensive Grammar of the English Language*? Well, Jack and Jill could do a lot worse; but I do not quite mean that. If I did, the achievements of many a one would speak against me. You can certainly be a writer without being a grammarian, though all competent writers know their grammar, if only through blind experience. There is this to be said, however, for making some study of grammar, that it helps you to appraise other people's work and enables you to monitor your own, by sharpening the perception of linguistic structures. We control our knowledge more comfortably, and doubtless more efficiently, when we can refer it to the labelled boxes of concept, class and category. When you know the resources of grammar – however that verb *know* is to be understood – you are at ease with possibilities. There is no stretch of text that you cannot negotiate, no demand for expression that will find you wholly powerless. You are in control, anticipatory control, of the sentences you make.

You should also be in control of the words you use; but the lexicon is a wayward thing, all the more wayward for being involved with grammar in the evolution of that odd phenomenon we call 'idiom'. Here we need another example, a bad one; and since I cannot look to any respectable author for a sample of sustained malpractice, I had better produce my own. This passage was devised for the instructional benefit of foreign students of English. The vices it ludicrously illustrates, however, are far from imaginary:

> Virginia Woolf, one of the two talented daughters of Sir Leslie Stephen, was a big wheel in the Bloomsbury Group, a set of artists and writers who in their own day and age were pretty far out. Her special thing was the so-called 'stream of consciousness' technique, a way of writing that records in minute detail the impressions unfolding to the senses and minds of her characters. Some readers find this absolutely mind-blowing, while others incline to the belief that she goes a bit over the top. Beautifully crafted novels like *To the Lighthouse* and *Mrs Dalloway* still go down a treat, and the critical essays collected and published under the title of *The Common Reader* reflect the workings of a fastidious and well-informed mind. Her posthumously published *Writer's Diary* affords enthralling glimpses into the private thoughts of a top-notch authoress feeling the pressure and always at the perilous edge of breakdown. In the end the strain got to be too much for her, and in 1942, at the height of the battle for European civilization, she did away with herself.

We would all agree, I hope, that this is a farrago of ill-chosen words. The most practical way of defining its many defects would be to rewrite it; and this, indeed, was the original intention of the exercise. I have no intention, however, of involving you in the debate that would inevitably follow if we were now to undertake a joint act of revision. I have put the text in front of you only so that you will understand what I mean when I say that a writer's vocabulary should be precise, unhackneyed and appropriate to its discursive function. At least two of these criteria raise questions hardly to be answered in the next five minutes. We all know that precision, like beauty, may be in the eye of the beholder; and as far as 'hackneyed' language is concerned, we must all be aware that our habitual usage not only includes many clichés and vogue-words, but can even depend on the existence of such things.

Nevertheless, I think my cautionary text will readily afford examples of the imprecise ('pretty far out', 'her special thing'), and you will no doubt agree that we would all do well to avoid 'enthralling glimpses', to try not to 'feel the pressure', to resist the temptation to call novels 'beautifully crafted', and to look carefully at all phrases that are much licked and thumbed in this 'day and age'.

What I expect will strike you most of all about this example of how not to write is its absurd want of decorum. Decorum, as you will know, is the ancient term for what we now call, less elegantly, 'appropriateness' – the conformity of a style to its social and intellectual object. Ben Jonson speaks of 'keeping a decorum' – that is, of sustaining a certain level of address, involving the use of one strain of vocabulary. This is what our sample passage almost triumphantly fails to do. To write on the one hand of 'the workings of a fastidious and well-informed mind', or of 'recording in minute detail the impressions unfolding to the minds and senses of her characters', and on the other of 'a big wheel', 'going down a treat', 'a top-notch authoress', is to produce a stylistic medley only describable in Dogberry's phrase, 'most tolerable and not to be endured'. It is true, certainly, that for various reasons (humour, irony, emphasis, the relaxing of formal pretensions) we occasionally break decorum. I have done so several times in this lecture. I did it, for example, when I spoke of A.E. Housman giving his fellow scholars 'a ferociously elegant going-over'. 'Going-over' is strictly speaking indecorous – not the sort of word to be used in Gower Street on formal occasions when one is wearing one's literary waistcoat; but in this case the indecorum is under control, a kind of deliberate dialect. Its intention of joking emphasis is, I hope, unmistakable, and it is an isolated outbreak in a well-mannered and indeed rather demure context. I can perhaps claim to have been precisely indecorous. But if you allow your vocabulary to romp at random, unruled by considerations of appropriateness to a context and a purpose, then you will preclude all possibility of obeying a sovereign principle, one so vastly important that all I can do here is mention it and leave it unexamined. It is this. Let the determinant of your vocabulary be not the word, not the phrase, not the sentence, even, but a stretch of text, conceivably page-long; so that what you create as you write is not a series of discrete points of diction, but a network of meanings that run echoing through the whole compositional process.

That requirement is in fact contained in the notion I keep putting to you in the form of the word 'control'. I have urged you to control the resources of grammar, to control the options and the waywardness of the lexicon; to these recommendations I would now add, that you must above all control the shaping of the text. A good piece of text has a discernible pattern of connections, junctures, points of emphasis; a rhythm that reflects sentence organization, which in its turn reflects the organization of meaning; a grouping of material, like the groupings of a picture or the episodes in music, expressed through punctuation. This is not a matter of hit-and-miss assembly, not a question of luck, unless it be – to quote that phrase again – *curiosa felicitas*, the luck you make for yourself. There are devices of language, text-controlling devices, on which the skilful writer learns to call.

I have one more illustration for you. Before I begin to discuss it, let me make a declaration of personal interest – or rather, disinterest; you will see presently why I do so. I am not a Roman Catholic. I have no interest in Jesuits and little enough in hagiography; and though I greatly admire his accomplishments as a literary artist, I am not a particular devotee of the writings of the late Evelyn Waugh. Yet when I first picked up a copy of his *Edmund Campion* in a bookshop, I read the first page, propped myself against a shelf to read the next twenty and knew that I would have to buy the book. Never mind the personalities of authors, never mind self-expression; it is the text itself that speaks, with powerful authority. In this typical extract, Waugh is speaking of the fate of English Catholics in the reign of Elizabeth I:

> These were the conditions of life, always vexatious, often utterly 1
> disastrous, of the people to whom the Jesuits were being sent,
> people drawn from the most responsible and honourable class,
> guilty of no crime except adherence to the traditional faith
> of their country. They were conditions which, in the natural 5
> course, could only produce despair, and it depended upon their
> individual temperaments whether, in desperation, they had
> recourse to apostasy or conspiracy. It was the work of the
> missionaries, and most particularly of Campion, to present by
> their own example a third, supernatural solution. They came 10
> with gaiety among people where hope was dead. The past
> held only regret, and the future apprehension; they brought
> with them, besides their priestly dignity and the ancient and
> indestructible creed, an entirely new spirit of which Campion is
> the type; the chivalry of Lepanto and the poetry of La Mancha, 15
> light, tender, generous and ardent. After him there still were
> apostates and there were conspirators; there were still bitter
> old reactionaries, brooding alone in their impoverished manors
> over the injustice they had suffered, grumbling at the Queen's
> plebeian advisers, observing the forms of the old Church in 20

protest against the crazy, fashionable Calvinism; these survived,
sterile and lonely, for theirs was not the temper of Campion's
generation who – not the fine flower only, but the roots and
stem of English Catholicism – surrendered themselves to their
destiny without calculation or reserve; for whom the honourable 25
pleasures and occupations of an earlier age were forbidden;
whose choice lay between the ordered, respectable life of their
ancestors and the faith which had sanctified it; who followed
holiness, though it led them through bitter ways to poverty,
disgrace, exile, imprisonment and death; who followed it gaily.[4] 30

I hope you will feel that this is powerful, indeed noble writing; and I
hope you will keep that feeling as I try to dismantle a few mechanisms.
To 'alienate' the text a little, I will ask you to begin at the end and
work backwards. This is a useful procedure, by the way; it can reveal
points of significance, much as looking at a picture in the mirror or
scrutinizing a transparency from the wrong side can fix attention on
things you have taken for granted. The right way round is the way of
amiable deception; to get at the facts, go widdershins.

Look at line 23. You will see there the noun 'generation', followed
by the relative pronoun 'who'. You will note that the pronoun is
emphasized – if you like, focused – by a parenthesis in 23–4,
separating it almost awkwardly from the verb 'surrendered', of which
it is the grammatical Subject. The effect of this, if one reads the
passage aloud, is to enforce accent on a word that would normally go
unaccented. Now follow the text to 25, where we find a semi-colon,
and after it another relative link, 'for whom'; follow to the next
semi-colon in 26, and we find 'whose'; go to 28, another semi-colon,
another 'who'; and so to the last semi-colon in 30, where 'who' once
more appears. This part of the text is governed by a sequence of
who-constructions: 'who', 'for whom', 'whose', 'who', 'who'. At its
first occurrence the device is marked – with the parenthesis of 23–4
Waugh throws a *sforzando* accent, for the reader's benefit, on the
preceding relative. Further, he contains his array of pronominally
governed constructions in a guiding harness of semi-colons. As a
reader, you go from semi-colon to semi-colon, picking up at each
stage your clue to the next construction. The writer, controlling the
structure of the text, thereby controls the reading of the text.

If you now trace backwards from the last semi-colon in line 30, you
will find that what I have called the 'harness' controls more than half
the passage; in particular, it steers the reader through the last long
sentence from line 16 onwards. But here we run into a descriptive

difficulty. It is not really the case that the text from 'After him' to 'followed it gaily' consists of a single sentence. There are many sentences in that part of the passage; but they are sentences that the writer chooses to bring into a close grouping that implies unbroken continuity of theme. It may help if we make an *ad hoc* distinction between 'sentence', in our common understanding of the written or typographical form, and 'period', a set of sentences, or 'cola', comprising an integrated 'sentential process'. In the sentential process of lines 16–30, we can trace the cohesive links from colon to colon, and the constructions that work cohesively within the cola. Thus in the first colon, line 16–17, we read 'there still were'; in the second, a linking variant, 'there were still', and within that same colon a triple span of participle clauses, 'brooding . . .', 'grumbling . . .', 'observing . . .'. This leads to an important transition in 21, with the anaphoric pronoun 'these', marking the contrast between 'the bitter old reactionaries' – 'these' – and 'Campion's generation' – 'who' – with a relative pronoun that brings us step by confident step, as we have seen, to the end of the passage. All paths from line 23 onward radiate from a single word, 'generation'. Simple devices of grammar and punctuation control the text – but not these alone; for there are also subtle counterpoises in the vocabulary. Compare, for example, 'bitter' in 29 ('bitter ways') with 'bitter' in 17 ('bitter old reactionaries'); 'poverty' in 29 with 'impoverished' in 18. Consider how 'exile' in 30 obliquely reflects the 'alone' of 18 and the 'lonely' of 22; how 'imprisonment' in 30 shares at least an associative border of meaning with 'sterile' in 22; how 'death' in 30 stands in antonymic contrast to 'survived' in 21. Is it not apparent that the writer has conceived a pattern of lexical items illustrating and giving coherence to his contrast between the 'old reactionaries' and 'Campion's generation'?

Now let me direct your attention to the beginning of the passage. There the unit of organization is not the period, in the sense I have suggested, but the independent sentence. Look how the first three sentences begin: 'These were . . .', 'They were . . .', 'It was . . .'. I need hardly comment on structural resemblances. I will point out, however, that while 'these' and 'they' in the first two sentences are 'anaphoric', backward-pointing, 'it' in the third sentence is 'cataphoric', forward-pointing. 'These' refers to a foregoing paragraph, 'they' to the word 'conditions' in the foregoing sentence; whereas 'it' refers to something that follows, the clause reading 'to present . . . a supernatural solution'. This third sentence thus marks a turn towards a new topic, which is stated in the fourth sentence: 'They came with gaiety among people where hope was dead.' In the fifth sentence the compositional principle changes markedly, as we shift into the periodic mode; which brings us to the sixth sentence, or rather to the pattern of interlinked periods which we have already examined.

But now look again at those first three sentences, at a stylistic feature they have in common. In each case, the construction of a sentence is interrupted quite near the beginning by an interpolated expression. Thus in sentence 1, the construction 'the conditions of life of the people to whom the Jesuits were being sent' is interrupted by 'always vexatious, often utterly disastrous'; in sentence 2, the reading 'They were conditions which could only produce despair' is interrupted by 'in the natural course'; in sentence 3, 'It was the work of the missionaries to present' is broken by 'and most particularly of Campion'. This begins to look like a mannerism. It appears again in 13–14, with a somewhat longer intrusion ('besides their priestly dignity . . . indestructible creed'); but then, as I have tried to show, in lines 23–4, with an even longer interpolation ('not the fine flower only . . . Catholicism') this mannerism emerges decisively as a key element in a controlling design. All writers develop habits; they let their thoughts run in customary verbal channels. The weakness of this is mannerism; the potential strength is the ability to draw meaningfully on the habitual resource, as surely Waugh does here. I need hardly say that I admire this passage as a magisterial example of what I have jocosely called the Other Stuff. Nor need you remind me that Waugh is not an Other Stuff writer, but a novelist, a distinguished exponent of Mr Nigel Williams's second variety of excellence in the Proper Stuff. If time had allowed, we might have made the experiment of comparing a suitable passage of Waugh's fiction with another extract from this grave biography of Campion; not with the aim of showing that novelists are naturally equipped to write the Other Stuff, but to demonstrate that good writing is always good writing, no matter what the kind. I say, with all due respect to him, that Mr Williams is wrong. The highest kind of writing is not poetry; not the novel; not stage plays or television scripts. Any of these things may of course be the highest kind of writing at the time of composition; but that is just the point. The highest kind of writing must always be the task immediately in hand – an epic, a history, a report, a letter to a friend. All have their claims on the sincerity and skill of the writer.

It is time, I see, for closing remarks. Do you want recommendations and precepts? I will give you three. First, find models that you admire, and study them deeply and persistently. In the few comments I have made on my last illustration, I have tried to show what technical study of a model might yield. It will require much of you; not only your native perception, but an ability to formulate at least some elementary linguistic notions. You will thus learn about the structure of language while you are pondering the strategies of prose. My second recommendation is that you should try to understand critically the choices you make as you write. Writing is a continual process of choosing. If you cannot account for and justify every choice that you make, use the waste-paper basket. My third precept is less technical than moral. I would have you take a conscious pride in our language. Respect our English tongue – it is the only rag of a flag we have to wrap ourselves in. We, its students, are also its servants; we have both the privilege and the responsibility of trying to write well, but we shall bear neither if we go about our work without joy in this language which so many have used so creatively. But enough. Not long ago I spoke of my anxiety about beginning this lecture. I can now tell you that I have no qualms at all about finding an end. I shall do something precise, unhackneyed and appropriate. I shall stop talking.

The text of a lecture delivered in February 1987, to an undergraduate audience at University College London.

9 Composition and creativeness

Creative writing, I was once informed by an educationist, 'is not a subject for university studies'. I thought I could make a guess at the kkind of argument underlying this assertion, supposing him to mean that creativeness cannot be taught, because it is bound up so variously and so intricately with the experience of life in general, with maturing judgement, with innate artistic ability, with the general capacity to manipulate symbols and arrange significant forms in significant relationships. I divined, in his rejection of 'creative writing' as an academic subject, a complex theory of art and artistry transcending the limitations of the curriculum. In fact, his objections were simpler and more drastic than I had supposed. The crucial question, he went on to tell me, was 'How do you mark it?' – that is, how do you reconcile its subjective spprawl with the necessary objectivity of a tutor firmly assigning grades and the examiner drawing up precise columns of percentages?

As it happens, it is no more difficult to evaluate a piece of creative writing, carried out under tutorial guidance, than it is to assess any other sample of work done by a student of arts and letters. If we can assess the content, style, and presentation of an essay on Dickens, we can make shift to arrive at a mark for a piece on Plum Pudding or Pop Music or Sexual Politics. If we presume the student able to judge the narrative and linguistic skills of a story by Ernest Hemingway, we might fairly presume ourselves able to judge the student's own narrative powers. If we consider that a piece of stylistic *analysis* can be assigned a mark, then we should as readily concede the possibility of grading a stylistic *synthesis*, that is, a piece of composition. Stylistics and creative writing are, indeed, the *recto* and *verso* of the same theme.

This matter of assessment, however, is beside the point. My colleague was wrong about the crucial question, which is not 'How do you mark it?', but 'How might you teach it?'. Assuming that most people are capable of writing a well-formed sentence, how do you teach them to write two well-formed and properly connected sentences, adding a third, and a fourth, and a fifth, to constitute a well-formed text? And assuming that anyone – or nearly anyone – can botch up a story, how might you teach them to narrate more effectively? Above all, how do you give them access to those inner creative resources which are also the resources of hope, of consolation, of reconciliation, of courage and survival in a crass world? These are the really interesting questions, all the more interesting because their solutions are not to be proposed in some facile recipe, but only through a long, exacting, disciplined study of language, of the making of texts, of cognition and perception, of the nature of symbolism and mimesis. Such topics certainly have a place in university studies.

As a first contribution to this vast theme, I make the following proposition: that if creativeness cannot be taught, composition certainly can, and that we may have access to creative mysteries through the study of compositional skills. The making of the simplest expository text can call for the exercise of complex imaginative powers. There is creativeness in composition; whence it is not unreasonable to assume that there is composition in creativeness, and that the apparently free play of fantasy may be governed by principles as firm as those that guide the construction of mundane expository prose.

THE LINGUISTIC REPERTOIRE

Asked what is involved in composition, we might answer that the process must involve cognition, memory, acts of choice and the operations of a kind of logic. Writers, in other words, are acquainted with the resources of their native language, retain them more or less actively in mind, can draw at will upon this mental store and can relate their options to a pattern of reasoning and exposition. Here, then, are four aspects of the compositional faculty: let us identify them as 'repertoire', 'storage', 'selection' and 'prediction', with the proviso that these terms are descriptive aids, not scientific categories.

REPERTOIRE

Repertoire can be construed in two complementary senses, as (a) the totality of available knowledge or skill, and (b) the part of such knowledge or skill that has been mastered by the individual. This distinction is important in many acquisitions and abilities. I may, for instance, refer to 'the repertoire of keyboard music', meaning everything that has been written for keyboard instruments; within which I struggle to maintain and extend 'my pianoforte repertoire', meaning the few pieces that I am able to perform with insight and confidence. The total repertoire of language (or rather, of the mother-tongue) may be defined as everything listed and codified in currently authoritative works of grammar and lexicography. This, however, involves much that is already obsolete, and also ignores much that is of too recent a date or too questionable an origin to have won the recognition and surety of academic record. The individual repertoire reflects a sense of the total resource, reflects an awareness of obsolescence and gain, but never wholly commands or exploits the lexical and grammatical stock. The user of language is inevitably confined by psychological limitations that oblige him or her to follow his or her habit – and here let us recall the etymological connection between 'habit' and 'having'. My repertoire in language is what I have, or possess, not simply through passive observation, but more especially as a result of willed acquisition, of practice, and through my awareness of the contextual implications of the words and phrases I use.

A repertoire requires syntactic alternatives appropriate to shifts of social or stylistic demand. It also demands a provision of idiomatic meshes, or 'interlocks' (the term is my own) between syntax and lexicon. Consider, for example, the terms in which a headmaster might rebuke an unsatisfactory pupil, or an employer address an unruly subordinate:

1 I have warned you over and over again.
2 You have been repeatedly admonished.

Sentence 1 expresses a degree of familiarity and closeness; sentence 2 is more distant, formal, 'colder' in manner. (A student, asked to comment on these two sentences, made the interesting observation that 2 sounds 'planned' or 'contrived', whereas 1 has an air of spontaneity.) Such impressions arise in part from the vocabulary (e.g. 'warn' versus 'admonish', 'over and over againn' versus 'repeatedly'), but not from that alone. More fully, they are a consequence of interlocks between grammar and vocabulary; in this case, between the active voice and the familiar colloquial lexicon (sentence 1), or between the passive and somewhat more formal lexical items. 'Repeatedly' is a bookish adverb, and the Latinate 'admonish' has quite grandiose stylistic pretensions. One might add, speculatively, that frequency of occurrence governs the distinctive impression made by sentence 2 – i.e. that the passive construction is less common than the active, and, correspondingly, that 'admonish' is a peripheral item of vocabulary, as opposed to the more central 'warn'. This would account for my student's feeling that 2 is 'planned'. It also suggests that the repertoire must include primary and secondary syntactic resources, together with appropriate lexical interlocks. The notion of a 'core' vocabulary (a central and indispensable body of words) is relevant here. The 'core' vocabulary, we might say, is related to a 'core' syntax; and as the vocabulary is extended, so the syntactic acquisitions must also extend.[1]

A repertoire supposes dozens of syntactic options in hundreds of semantic interlocks. In theory, all possible occurrences are available to us, as competent native speakers; in practice, we have habitual recourse to a restricted number. Thus the question arises, whether the individual repertoire can be extended? I can add to my pianoforte repertoire; can I analogously extend my holdings in language and style? The answer is yes: the repertoire may be enlarged in at least three ways. First, there may be a conscious effort to acquire and practise structures passively recognized but seldom employed actively. This calls for some critical self-monitoring. One must be aware at all times of being involved in the process of writing, and one must cultivate the ability to rehearse mentally and evaluate all the choices that composition brings in its train, from one moment to the next.

Another way depends on the imaginative power or playfulness of the individual, who may *invent* a word, a turn of phrase, a construction, in response to the challenge of a context, the pressure of an occasion that allows no time for reflection, the need to identify a fugitive insight. Such inventions are almost a matter of daily occurrence; literary artists, children and foreigners conspire to make them. I am reminded of the conference speaker who, charmingly pitting her wits against the English language, produced the sentence 'He marries Naomi a bit'.[2] This is perfectly intelligible. We recognize its affinity with constructions in which the adverbial 'a bit' accompanies a verb denoting an activity, process, or feeling ('He plays golf a bit', 'Marriage has changed her a bit', 'She likes him a bit'). Strictly speaking, 'He marries Naomi a bit' is not acceptable as Standard English, because an adverbial of degree is generally incompatible with a verb denoting an institutional or 'performative' act. To say 'he marries Naomi a bit' is comparable to saying 'The priest baptized the baby a little', or 'The judge pronounced sentence to a certain extent'. However, we might say that it carries linguistic credentials enabling us to recognize the purport of a spur-of-the-moment idiom: 'Without entering into the formal relationship of marriage, he has some of the attributes and attitudes of a husband.' Whether such invention lodges in the idiomatic repertoire, or falls away at once, having served its immediate purpose, is no doubt a matter of chance.

First, then, the repertoire is extended by practice; second, by the haphazard of invention. Third, it may grow through contact with the anonymous workings of usage in the speech-community, workings that eventually lead to change and augmentation in the literary standard. For example, in current colloquial English there is an observable tendency to blend constructions of the existential type, e.g. 'There has been a murder', with those of the passive type, e.g. 'A murder has been committed', producing a semantic/syntactic hybrid, 'There has been a murder committed'. Of this, I may observe that it is not yet in my literary repertoire (I write 'An exhibition has been arranged', but would hesitate before committing myself to 'There has been an exhibition arranged'); nevertheless, such a construction, enjoying the acceptance of current usage, might enter into my habit if I were to realize a distinctive – that is, a *contrastive* – use for it. I might, for example, perceive a contextual distinction between 'A course has been offered', with the implied meaning 'We have offered a course', and 'There has been a course offered', which could mean 'Someone else has offered a course'. It is a matter of discovering contexts in which the dubious construction defines a meaning contrastively, thus taking its place in a regular pattern of choice and no longer functioning as a mere slipshod alternative to a 'standard' or supposedly 'correct' item. In ways such as this, spoken usage is always adding to the repertoire of writing.

STORAGE

If I suggest that the items of my linguistic/stylistic repertoire are *stored* in such a way as to permit of fairly rapid mental access, I am obviously attempting to express in metaphor an intuition for which I can hardly find supportive proofs. Any discussion of psychological stock-keeping in language has to proceed through plausible and possibly heuristic images. The analogy with computers, with mechanisms of input and retrieval, is almost inevitable; but the creative mind is something more than a computational machine. Homelier comparisons may be made with simple constructive processes, such as carpentry. Take the case of the domestic handyman. As he carries out a job, he needs various tools, fastenings, materials, etc., which may accumulate in a random heap on his bench. There, they are theoretically accessible for immediate use, but if the pile is so untidy that it takes a long time to find any item, the process of construction will be inhibited, will be vulnerable to lapses of continuity and concentration, may even come to a halt because the ratio of retrieval activity to construction activity is discouragingly high. Efficient workmanship requires the proper retention and quick accessibility of materials; therefore each workman finds some principle of storing what he needs where he can find it quickly. It is not a God-given, rigidly determined scheme, but some method or combination of methods that happens to suit his working style.

What is true of carpentry, a physical process, has analogous bearings on literary composition, a mental process. Here, to be sure, the workman has ready-made and orderly packages of tools and materials in the shape of dictionaries and grammars. Dictionaries in thesaurus form, or grammars designed on 'communicative' or 'notional' principles are, in effect, schemes of storage.[3] In the course of composition, however, we may wish to consult grammar or thesaurus only as a last resort, preferring in the first instance an imaginative searching (or scanning, or mobilization) of the mental store. If I ask myself how I set about the recovery of appropriate words and phrases, various procedures suggest themselves. It is possible, for example, to search for some elusive piece of vocabulary by proposing different syntactic frames. ('To open a door we need a -----', '-----s are what we need to open doors', 'It is with -----s that doors are opened', etc.) Lexical items may be scanned in associative sets, e.g. as synonyms, antonyms and hyponyms, or as holonyms and meronyms.[4] (Thus 'key' belongs meronymically to the holonymic domain of 'security', in which it has a kind of antonymic relationship with 'lock'). Phonological features such as alliteration and rhyme may be significant aids to the retrieval of the words that elude us as we compose. Edward Sapir calls attention to 'the heuristic value of rhyme', the discovery of the 'right' word in consequence of the need to make a phonetic match; and over and over again, in literary prose, it is apparent that the impulse to give alliterative shape to a phrase or clause has led to a felicitous choice of words.[5] Even the demands of rhythm, calling for a certain number and pattern of stressed and unstressed syllables, may mobilize stored resources. We may suppose that there are basic principles of storage with many variations. There are differences between individuals, and possibly variations in the practice of one and the same individual using language in different contexts, for different purposes. The question

'How do you find the right word?' is endlessly answerable, and in the end has no ascertainable answer. A fixed mode of storage might suggest a fixed and somewhat limited repertoire, with regular choices and a rather dull, register-bound style. Official correspondence, for example, in the form of business letters, routine applications and acknowledgements, testimonials and so forth, can be rattled off in routine fashion because its repertoire of phrases is always at hand and presents no exploratory complications. The same poverty of repertoire, with consequent ease of storage, is notable in some academic writings.

SELECTION

Bound up with the question of storage is the matter of *selection*. With this, however, we come a step nearer to the concrete domain of the text. Whereas we can only make analogical guesses at the 'how' of storage, selection demonstrates the 'what'. As soon as an item is taken out of the psychological holding, to be realized in the substance of the text, it becomes accessible to investigation; because then we know not only what is chosen, but also, by inference, the companion fact of what is not chosen. The choice manifested on the page reflects a choice that is not on the page. The passive construction, for example, implies the rejection of its immediate partner, the active; for without the existence, and therefore the potential use of, the active, the passive would have no stylistic or creative significance. It often appears that the selections a writer makes are binary options, for example of active versus passive, transitive versus intransitive, declarative versus interrogative and so on. This intuition may possibly reveal something about principles of storage – say, that complementary or contrastive items are contingently stored, so that an x calls up the possibility of a y. On the other hand, this notion of binary choice may simply be a set response to common models of how the mind works when it sets up its searches. (Parlour games like 'Twenty Questions' illustrate the same response.)

A typically recurrent option involves 'branching', meaning the distribution of subordinate material in relationship to a stem or principal structure. Consider:

1 When she came there, the cupboard was bare.
2 The cupboard was bare when she came there.

The first of those examples is a distich from the well known nursery rhyme of Mother Hubbard. Stylistically, it represents a *left-branching* structure, meaning that the subordinate clause 'when she came there' occurs before, or in linear terms to the left of, the main clause 'the cupboard was bare'. The second example illustrates the *right-branching* option, the selection not made by the anonymous composer of the nursery rhyme. Here the main clause comes first, and the subordinate clause follows, to the linear right. Now it is not at all difficult to justify the choice of a left branch in the patterning of this nursery rhyme. The story of Mother Hubbard – who went to the cupboard, to fetch her poor dog a bone – is a performance for children, and performances require their moments of tension and suspense, their artful delayings of a concluding act or fact; so – she went to the cupboard – and 'when she came there . . .'? This, let me note, is not an argument for left-branching in all narrative circumstances; it happens to be appropriate, and, indeed, felicitous, in this particular context. Creative selections involve not only a knowledge of available linguistic/stylistic options, but also the evaluation of contextual demands.

Some major principles of selection may be identified in *ad hoc* terms, as 'distribution', 'focus' and 'key'. By 'distribution' I mean the ordering and processing of information in the linear development of the text; the option of left-branching or right-branching is a distributional choice. 'Focus' involves devices that shift emphasis and give particular prominence to one or other element in a sentence. The passive/active alternation is a common resort for adjusting focus:

1 All the mistakes have been corrected.
2 We have corrected all the mistakes.

The normal 'end-focus' of the declarative sentence operates to make 'corrected' the major informational item of 1, and 'mistakes' the prominent element in 2. Note also:

1 I like Couperin.
2 Mozart I almost worship.

The first of these represents the normal, or, as they say, 'unmarked' word-order, with the customary end-focus; whereas the second, with its 'fronted' Direct Object, making what grammarians call a 'marked theme', achieves a double focus, on 'Mozart' and on the verb, 'worship'.

I use the word 'key' in an attempt to identify that elusive impression often called 'tone of voice', or 'manner'. It is a way of managing the text that reflects the writer's attitude towards his topic, and, by implication, towards his audience.[6] Understatement, for example, is a way of keying the text so as to convey a tone of cool detachment, bantering amusement, even irony:

1 He is very clever.
2 He is not without talent.

The second of those sentences might possibly be taken at its face value – as when I write, in judicious assessment of a student, 'he is not without talent' (= 'he has some ability') – or it may be gently ironic, as though I were to observe of Rembrandt, 'he is not without talent'. Options of key, like other options, are taken with reference to specific contexts.

PREDICTION

Acts of prediction connect reader and writer in the twin processes of making and interpreting the text. The intelligent reader follows a text predictively, picking up procedural clues supplied by the writer, anticipating the development of the argument or narrative. The writer not only supplies the indices that lead, or in some cases deliberately mislead the reader; he may also turn out to be the bondservant of his own predictions – that is to say, once his choices have set the text in a certain direction, it is difficult for him to leave the predicted path, unless he takes the bitter option of starting all over again. It is a familiar paradox of composition that we are free to make the choices that subsequently limit our freedom.

The predictions made by the writer are of two kinds: predictions of content and predictions of language. There is an implication that the subject matter will take a particular form and there is an indication that certain linguistic features, steering the course of the text, are likely to occur. Suppose, for example, that I begin an academic essay in the following style: 'My purpose in writing this paper is twofold.' Note, first of all, that this represents a choice; I select 'My purpose in writing this paper is twofold', and reject 'I have two purposes in writing this paper'. The contextual motivation for this choice may be that I wish to imply a *single* purpose with two components, rather than two distinct purposes. The word 'twofold' virtually suggests as much, and such idioms as 'singleness of purpose' lend colour to the supposition that a purpose may allow division, but not discontinuity. This opening might thus predict, as to content, a unified theme with subdivisions that do not impair the essential unity. There may even be an implication that the proposed subdivisions, by complementing each other, confirm the wholeness of the governing theme. (For instance:

'My purpose is twofold: to explore the elements of composition, and thence to provide some access to the secrets of creativeness.')

As to its language, the statement 'My purpose . . . is twofold' predicts some sort of enumerative framework in exposition: 'My purpose is twofold . . . first(ly) . . . then (next, second[ly], consequently) etc.' So powerfully is this predictive note conveyed by the word 'twofold', that unless it is followed immediately by a citatory signal, such as an i.e. or a colon – unless, that is, the sentence is made to continue – the writer is virtually committed to further signals of enumeration. I am *theoretically* free to begin my supposed article thus:

> My purpose in writing this paper is twofold. I think composition can be imaginatively taught. Creativeness is not an impenetrable secret.

Theoretically free, but in practice bound, if only for my readers' comfort, to some form of metadiscursive commentary, that is, a guide or prospectus to the text, thus:

> My purpose in writing this paper is twofold. Firstly, I would like to argue that composition can be imaginatively taught. Secondly, I wish to suggest that creativeness is not an impenetrable secret.

The form of the text follows predictively from 'twofold'. As soon as I use that word, explicitly marked processes of enumeration, or inference or both, become all but obligatory.

CREATIVE STIMULI

This account of compositional processes suggests a working from the invisible domain of repertoire and storage towards the visible structure manifested in selections and predictive procedures. While this hypothesis may beg a number of theoretical questions, I can testify that it has proved useful in practice. There is nothing in it that is not amenable to teaching at a quite elementary level. Students *can* be taught to extend their stylistic repertoire, *can* be trained in the skills of adroit selection, *can* be shown how to plan a text so that its expository and argumentative routes are clearly and predictably set out. Such is the teaching of composition. But *creativeness*? That question remains. How does the practice of composition promote, or give access to, the workings of the creative imagination?

Creativeness in language is to some extent language-inspired. By practising the basic craft of writing, students discover, in a dozen and one detailed instances, the potential of the language to express concepts and insights, and in the exploration of that potential begin to discover their own creativeness. Difficult though it certainly is to illustrate this theme briefly and simply, we may nevertheless venture a small demonstration, based on the use of the so-called 'existential construction', in sentences such as 'There has been an accident'. Taking that sentence, let us assume, for purposes of contextual motivation, some such situation as the breaking of crockery by a careless husband/home-help/child: e.g. 'What was that noise, darling?' – 'Nothing, Mummy, there's just been a little accident.' (Meaning 'I have appreciably reduced the size of your Crown Derby dinner service.') In many contexts of that kind it appears that the existential proposition may have the status of an oblique confession; until, that is, we arrive at some such interlock as 'There has been a murder'. At first sight 'There has been a murder' would seem fairly implausible as a confessional utterance. I reel into a police station, groaning distressfully that I have murdered someone – lover, colleague, casual bystander, no matter whom, the point being that the victim is nominally or pronominally denoted. What is much less likely is that as I surrender my revolver or knife or bottle of rat-poison I will exclaim, 'Officer, there has been a murder'. The meaning 'I'd rather not name the culprit if you don't mind', coyly appropriate to the admission of mishaps with dishes, hardly extends to the confession of homicide.

Yet no sooner do I put this point than it occurs to me that one might press the unlikely meaning into the service of humour or fiction. Picture, perhaps, a cartoon: a man, huge of limb, brutal of feature, stands, axe in one hand, smoking machine carbine in the other, his clothes drenched in gore, corpses littered around him in postures of massacre, sheepishly remarking to the note-taking police sergeant, 'There's been a bit of a murder, constable' – as though he were owning up to a little mistake, a spot of bother, a minor accident on his way to the office. More seriously, imagine a story, objectively narrated, beginning with the sentence 'There has been a murder'. Because readers will more or less automatically discard the possibility of this being an oblique confession, it is some time, possibly not until the end of the story, that they are able to identify the murderer as the narrator him- or herself. ('There has been a murder . . . and now they are coming for me.') Examples such as these suggest that common usage involves uncommon possibilities that can be creatively exploited.

But of course creativeness is not stimulated wholly by language. It is stimulated also by the diversity of daily experience, as and when we are able to discard ordinary assumptions or presuppositions and look at the commonplace through the eyes of a stranger or an uncommitted observer, saying 'what if?' and 'as though'. The first step towards creative perception is to take away the support of the obvious explanation and the received account, in order to revitalize experience. Sometimes life lends a hand, with revelations so bizarre that we could hardly have trusted our own imaginations to contrive them. James Joyce calls such encounters 'epiphanies'; for lesser folk, perhaps, 'apparitions' would be the appropriate word – things that would seem unlikely if you put them into a book. Here is a minor instance out of my own experience, recalled from a time when some weeks of every year were spent nomadically, in a canal boat. It is a bleak and rainy evening in early summer, and I witness something rather odd – a man slowly trudging along the canal towpath *playing the bagpipes*, and behind him, marching resolutely, swinging her arms and raising her knees high at every step, a girl of about sixteen years of age. There is no one else, not a soul to be seen, in the drizzling twilight, and I, snugly hidden away in the cabin of my boat, am the only observer.

So what are these people doing? What is the significance of this strange action? Are the man and the girl related? How can they persist, with such concentration, such ritual solemnity, in such wretched, dispiriting weather? Do they feel no discomfort? Where are they going? Where did they come from? Because the event is detached from everyday connections, because there are no obvious explanations (e.g. that they are members of a marching band, out for a little practice), imagination may go all the more readily to work. Fictionally, I might choose to classify this event as some kind of commemorative act ('. . . and every year, without fail, on this night, in loving memory of Grandfather McTavish . . .'), and to work out my explanations – my 'story-line', as script-writers say – from that assumption. With the process of 'working out' comes the demand to identify my conjectures and insights by consulting my stored repertoire and making rapid and effective selections, so as to create textual patterns of prediction and orientation. Indeed, I have already begun to do this in my description of the event, in which I have made the man 'slowly trudge' and the girl 'march resolutely'; do not these expressions in some way suggest interpretations of character, attributions of personality?

The practice of language stimulates creativeness; questioning or playful response to experience stimulates creativeness; creative usage and creative response nourish one another interactively. All imaginative design in language follows these laws, if laws we may call them. Thus it comes about that the routine practitioner of compositional arts makes a very interesting discovery; that there are deep-seated relationships between ostensibly diverse types of composition. In particular there are affinities between the procedures of certain kinds of prose exposition – notably the literary essay so well established in English tradition – and types of fiction such as the anecdote or the short story.

A STRUCTURE IN EXPOSITION

Obviously, such a claim calls for illustration. Let us then consider some general compositional features, notably of selection and prediction, in two pieces of literary writing, the one a passage of expository prose, the other the opening of a short story. Here, to begin with, is Bertrand Russell, arguing a political-economic theme:

> I have been informed repeatedly, by persons who considered themselves hard-headed realists, that men in business normally desire to grow rich. Observation has convinced me that the persons who gave me this assurance, so far from being realists, were sentimental idealists, totally blind to the most patent facts of the world in which they live. If business men really wished to grow rich more ardently than they wish to keep others poor, the world would quickly become a paradise. Banking and currency afford an admirable example. It is obviously to the general interest of the business community as a whole to have a stable currency and security of credit. To secure these two desiderata, it is obviously necessary to have only one central bank in the world, and only one currency, which must be a paper currency so managed as to keep average prices as nearly constant as possible. Such a currency will not need to be based upon a gold reserve, but upon the credit of the world Government of which the one central bank is the financial organ. All this is so obvious that any child can see it. Yet nothing of the sort is advocated by business men. Why? Because of nationalism, that is to say, because they are more anxious to keep foreigners poor than to grow rich themselves.[7]

At first reading, this has the character of dryly reasoned argument, an impression which arises not only from the rather 'academic' turn of some constructions (for instance 'To secure these two desiderata, it is . . . necessary to have, etc.'), but also from the general planning of the argument, from proposition to example to inference to reiterated propositions. (On this, more presently.) At a second reading, however, it appears that this piece of exposition is not wholly conventional in style and method; that it is a creative variation – perhaps disingenuously creative – on the conventions of academic reasoning; that in fact it might be construed as a sub-species of fiction, in which there are characters playing ironically regarded roles.

The first sentence of the passage provides the key to this ingenious style of sub-fictional argument:

> I have been informed repeatedly, by persons who considered themselves hard-headed realists, that men in business normally desire to grow rich.

Now, in considering this opening, let us evaluate two possible selections from our interlocking repertoire of lexical and syntactic choices:

1 Some people have often told me.
2 I have been informed repeatedly by certain persons.

We noted a little earlier the 'distancing', 'ironizing' potential, in some contexts, of the passive, with its suggestion of *prepared* as opposed to *spontaneous*. The very first clause in Russell's text may be said to 'key' the piece, by conveying to the reader an authorial attitude, a detached (or apparently detached) ironic posture. This impression is confirmed by what is clearly a designed interlocking of vocabulary and syntax. Thus we read 'informed', rather than 'told'; 'repeatedly', rather than 'often'; and 'persons' rather than 'people'. 'Persons' suggests a category from which it is either impossible or of no consequence to deduce individual identity; Coleridge's 'person from Porlock' is a good example of the word's dismissive potential.

A further instance of the ironic management of language in this opening sentence is seen in the phrase 'who considered themselves hard-headed realists'. Compare these two assertions:

1 He is a realist.
2 He calls himself a realist.

The implication of 2 is clearly to cancel the assertion it makes. He calls himself a realist – but isn't. He is a self-styled realist, and self-styling is deceptive. All the more deceptive as Russell presents it, because the verb he uses in his text is not 'call' (meaning 'name'), but 'consider', implying some process of thought and judgement. 'Consider' interlocks with 'inform', not only as an ironically formal item of vocabulary, but also as a word suggesting mental activity – a suggestion that Russell is about to rebut, dismissing businessmen as 'totally blind to the most patent facts'. Thus the imputation of deceptive self-appraisal is added to that of faceless impersonality.

The sentence begins to look a good deal less 'academic' and

'objective' than we may at first have been willing to suppose. Russell does not refer openly to 'fools', much less to 'liars', but his somewhat arch contrivances of style invite us to assign to these 'persons' and 'men in business' the role of blunderers who in their self-interest have lost self-knowledge. His reading is not

1 Realistic people have often told me that businessmen usually want to get rich

which might imply 'I take their word for it', but

2 I have been informed repeatedly, by persons who considered themselves hard-headed realists, that men in business normally desire to grow rich,

implying, 'I am sceptical of what they say'.

A point of interest incidental to these two versions of the message is that the first example allows the reader to suppose that 'realistic people' and 'businessmen' could be different parties (class A reports on class B), whereas the second example – the wording of Russell's text – bears the clear implication that 'persons who consider themselves hard-headed realists' and 'men in business' share an identity (class A characterizes class A). This further colours the text with irony. If I say 'Bob says Jim is clever' it may be fairly assumed, in the absence of any clue to the contrary, that my assertion is non-ironic; but if I say 'Bob says Bob is clever', the possibility of irony, or at least of disparaging comment, must be much more apparent. Russell will go on to argue that Bob (i.e. the businessman) is not nearly as clever as he claims to be, but in the first sentence that argument is no more than a potential, lurking in a tone of voice. Russell presents himself as a kind of passive victim, the mere recipient of assurances he is hardly in a position to evaluate. This self-deprecating tone – 'I only know what people tell me' – is rather cunningly maintained in the second sentence. There, Russell does not say 'I have observed that the persons who gave me this assurance, etc', but 'Observation has convinced me that the persons who gave me this assurance, etc'. It amounts to the same thing, but in the pantomime of the text it does not signify the same kind of role-playing. Russell is 'informed' by 'certain persons'; then he is 'convinced' by 'observation' – an abstraction here allotted a certain *persona*. This stance, of one who is passively informed or convinced, prepares us for the triumphant assertion, later in the text, that 'any child can see it'.

The two opening sentences are closely linked, and form a preamble, or 'pre-topic' to the argument. The actual topic is formulated in the third sentence, 'If business men really wished to grow rich, etc'. The expository procedures of the whole paragraph may be tabled as follows:

pre-topic: I have been informed repeatedly, by persons who considered themselves hard-headed realists, that men in business normally desire to grow rich. Observation has convinced me that the persons who gave me this assurance, so far from being realists, were sentimental idealists, totally blind to the most patent facts of the world in which they live.

topic: If business men really wished to grow rich more ardently than they wish to keep others poor, the world would quickly become a paradise.

argument: Banking and currency afford an admirable example. It is obviously to the general interest of the business community as a whole to have a stable currency and security of credit. To secure these two desiderata, it is obviously necessary to have only one central bank in the world, and only one currency, which must be a paper currency so managed as to keep average prices as nearly constant as possible. Such a currency will not need to be based upon a gold reserve, but upon the credit of the world Government of which the one central bank is the financial organ.

summary: All this is so obvious that any child can see it. Yet nothing of the sort is advocated by business men. Why?

recapitulation of topic: Because of nationalism, that is to say, because they are more anxious to keep foreigners poor than to grow rich themselves.

The section I have called 'Summary' might as fittingly be called 'Recapitulation of the pre-topic', in that it resumes or echoes certain elements of vocabulary; 'men in business' is echoed in 'business men', 'hard-headed realists' is counterpointed by 'any child', 'patent' finds a parallel in 'so obvious', 'blind' is matched by 'see'. The themes of obviousness and perception are linked throughout the text, together with intensifiers of one kind or another: '*totally* blind', '*most* patent facts', '*so* obvious', '*any* child'. A minor – virtually subliminal – theme in the lexicon is represented by the phrases '*desire* to grow rich', 'wished to grow rich more *ardently*', and 'they are more *anxious*'. On the one hand ardent desire, on the other hand mere anxiety; on one side the language of love, on the other the vocabulary of neurosis. So in yet another way the pretensions of the thick-sighted and sentimental men of business are deflated.

Russell's method is more than argument; it is argument in masquerade. His exposition, in itself a conventional model of academic reasoning (of the type 'given *a*, then *b*, from which follows *c*') is couched in a little play of personae, in which the Philosopher confronts certain Persons, alias Men in Business, whose crassly self-interested manoeuvrings are exposed as a sham. In other words, the passage conveys a sense of personality and interaction which is not exactly fiction, but not too far from it. It would be easy enough to 'depersonalize' the passage in a revision beginning:

> It is frequently asserted that the purpose of business is to create wealth. This, however, is manifestly not the case. If the object of commercial activity were really to create wealth, rather than to maintain poverty, the world would soon be transformed.

This rewriting speaks for (or perhaps against) itself, demonstrating, by its significant omissions, the creativeness of Russell's technique – the creativeness of a parable in which reasoning and story-telling are conjoined. It is perhaps a deceitful manner of exposition, because it predisposes the reader to dislike certain characters in the fable, and hence to accept as valid any argument against them. After all, there may be arguments on their side. Perhaps they are sincerely concerned for the well-being of humankind. Perhaps it is not so obviously necessary, or desirable, or even possible, to have one central world bank. But cunningly prepared sympathies override our reservations, and we accept the proposition for the sake of the fable. The structure of argument blossoms creatively. Then can the converse be true – can we see in the creative elaborations of the story-teller the ordinary scaffolding of composition?

CONSTRUCTING FICTION

Let us consider the opening of a story. It is called 'Speak like a native', and this is how it starts:

A smoky frost over Nottingham; blood-orange sun weeping into the mist over Basford and Bulwell and Cinderhill; red-raw acres of brick shivering in the depressed morning light. Such a day, thought Rashid Ali Wadekar, such a day on which to be indisposed. To be *gravely* indisposed, to have quite decidedly a disorder of the alimentary tract. And then to have to venture out – in order to seek advice of a medical man – in these *damnably* inclement conditions! He crammed his fur-trimmed hat more tightly down on his head, shrugged his thin coat closer about him, and shuffled anxiously along Mansfield Road in the direction of Dr Leiver's surgery.

The surgery was in an ill-kempt Victorian house, with coloured lead-lights, scalloped barge-boards, and sad grey-green privet hedges; the doctor's patients waited in what had once been the drawing-room, among the ghosts of former lacemakers and their spouses. As Rashid made his painful way up the front garden path, past overgrown borders and overblown rose bushes, he caught sight of some of the morning's morose intake, sitting coughing in the deep bay window. They appeared to be unreasonably numerous. He entered the waiting room resolved to urge instant treatment of his own case on compassionate grounds. How fortunate, he reflected, how *providential* that his English was now in tip-top form and fully equal to such an emergency as this! With all due modesty he could claim to speak the language like a native, an absolute native.

Dr Leiver's receptionist, a woman of stolid iron-grey aspect, looked up from her work of sorting through a long file of cards.

'Ey oop, m'duck,' she said. This is a Nottingham greeting, and is as much as to say, *Salaam*.[8]

The first sentence of this passage presents us with something apparently deviant from the syntactic repertoire upon which one might generally draw in written discourse. Here is a feature not seen in argumentative prose like that of Russell: a sequence of clauses with no main verb. From this alone we might predict the kind of text we have to deal with, and we could make the prediction even if we were presented only with the first sentence and no explanatory context, for verbless clauses in parataxis suggest the conventions of the stage direction or the narrative setting.

We might make further predictions as to the content and general 'atmosphere' of the story, because of the author's play with commonplace collocations. Expressions so familiar as to be literary clichés are transmuted, e.g:

sparkling frost	becomes	smoky frost
blazing or brilliant or bright sun	becomes	blood-orange sun
yellow or golden acres	becomes	red-raw acres
acres of corn	becomes	acres of brick
waving or shimmering	becomes	shivering
cheerful morning light	becomes	depressed morning light

The reader who notes these phrasal echoes sees how the time-worn conventions of landscape description and pastoral scene-setting are parodied and perverted. This suggests that there may well be humour in the ensuing story, though humour of a somewhat lugubrious kind; for the terms in which this townscape is described hint at discomfort, ailment, even injury (e.g. 'red-raw'). Anyone making such a prediction would be quite correct. The setting of this narrative is a doctor's waiting room, full of people preoccupied with their complaints.

Observations on the syntax and vocabulary of this fictional opening point at first to a type of discourse very different from that of argument or expository rhetoric; a discourse in which important signals are conveyed through what appears to be a deviant or parodic repertoire. Nevertheless, the fiction is constructed on principles of linkage and development not at all unlike those of non-fictional exposition. The story has frames comparable with those of argumentative procedure. One of the things we must do in argument, for example, is to make explicit connections between sentences, so that the reader (or listener) may follow the unfolding design. But the story-teller is no less committed to the craft of connecting. Compare the first two sentences of Russell's argument with the first two sentences of our story:

argument: I have been informed repeatedly, by persons who considered themselves hard-headed realists, that men in business normally desire to grow rich. Observation has convinced me that the persons who gave me this assurance, so far from being realists, were sentimental idealists, totally blind to the most patent facts of the world in which they live.

story: A smoky frost over Nottingham; blood-orange sun weeping into the mist over Basford and Bulwell and Cinderhill; red-raw acres of brick shivering in the depressed morning light. Such a day, thought Rashid Ali Wadekar, such a day on which to be indisposed.

The second sentence of the argument is overtly linked to the first, principally by means of the expression 'this assurance', which refers to 'informed repeatedly . . . that men in business normally desire to grow rich'. The link is of the type known as *anaphoric*, and it is most obviously expressed by the word 'this', which has the force of what grammarians call a *deictic*, that is, a 'pointing' expression. Thus the two opening sentences of the argument are demonstrably connected. Now it may seem that the first two sentences of the story do not require, and indeed do not manifest, any such argumentative procedure. The fact is, however, that they, too, are anaphorically linked, by the expression 'such a day', which subsumes, as it were, the whole of the preceding sentence. In that phrase, the word with deictic, 'pointing', force is 'such'. We may say, then, that the phrases 'this assurance' and 'such a day' play equivalent roles in the structure of what are ostensibly very different styles of discourse.

The clear deictic link between opening sentences might be taken for a standard feature of 'reasoned' prose; we talk, after all, of 'close-knit' argument. Whether it is such a common feature of narrative framing is less readily apparent. We can say, however, that some stories open in a fashion that shadows the preamble to an argument. Take, as paradigms, the following (invented) examples:

1 We are repeatedly said to be equal under the law. This assurance comforts us.
    (A paradigm for the opening of an argument. 'This' makes the deictic–anaphoric link. The purpose of 'this assurance' is to spare the writer the trouble and the awkwardness of repeating the whole of the first sentence as the subject of the second.)

2 The rain was pouring down and I had lost my hat. It was that sort of day.
    (A paradigm for narrative opening. The deictic word is 'that'. The expression 'that sort', however, subsumes not only a piece of text but also certain implications which readers are left to supply for themselves. The unspoken comment is 'Wouldn't you just know it?'.)

3 The rain was pouring down, and I had lost my hat. What a day, I thought.

(A further paradigm for a narrative opening. The deictic is 'what'; but with the shift from 'that sort of day' to 'what a day' – to 'inner speech', or the direct reporting of a thought – we move from the implied comment to the voicing of the implication.)

This last example is the pattern reproduced in 'Speak like a native', where a sense of the speaking voice has to be very quickly established. The root joke of the story is the contrast between the Pakistani student's elaborately 'correct' if somewhat old-fashioned English, and the demotic, dialectalized speech of the Nottingham 'natives'. The voice of one native (the receptionist) is heard at the end of the preamble to the story; Rashid's own speech-patterns are established earlier, in the form of unspoken reflections. It is characteristic of his 'literary' style that he says to himself 'Such a day' rather than 'What a day'. This is one feature among others of the 'keying' of the story, leading the reader to expect parodic humour. It provides, incidentally, a minor illustration of what I mean by 'repertoire', 'storage' and 'selection'. In my repertoire, forms of selection like 'What a . . .!' and 'Such a . . .!' would seem to be contingently stored; ordinarily I would select 'What a . . .!', but if I want to create the impression of bookish or studied speech, I select 'Such a . . .!' This selection is a linguistic prediction of more bookishness to come. All this may sound like a mechanical, step-by-step process, but of course it is not; it takes place in one impulse of the creative imagination.

The points at which Rashid's subjective voice takes over from the objective voice of the narrator are clearly signalled in the text by 'reporting' verbs like 'thought' and 'reflected'. In fact, there are two brief episodes of Rashid-speech embedded in the authorial narrative:

1 Such a day, thought Rashid Ali Wadekar, such a day on which to be indisposed. To be *gravely* indisposed, to have quite decidedly a disorder of the alimentary tract. And then to have to venture out – in order to seek advice of a medical man – in these *damnably* inclement conditions!

2 How fortunate, he reflected, how *providential* that his English was now in tip-top form and fully equal to such an emergency as this! With all due modesty he could claim to speak the language like a native, an absolute native.

Certain clues, apart from the reporting verbs, indicate that this is the character's speech-style, not the author's descriptive norm. A mimicry of typical patterns of stress and intonation is suggested by the italicized words, and there is an evident characterizing intent in phrases that ape the old-fashioned, elaborate, schoolmasterly style of the college-educated Rashid – 'gravely', 'alimentary tract', 'medical man', 'tip-top form', 'fully equal to', 'with all due modesty', 'an absolute native'. This mimicry is taken almost to excess, in order to establish the character firmly before the first shock-moment of the story, the breaking-in of real 'native' speech with the receptionist's 'Ey oop, m' duck'.

It is in fact with those words that the story really begins. We can analyse this opening in terms generally equivalent to those we have used to describe a pattern of argument. The author gets into the narrative by way of a 'pre-topic' passage, establishing a setting or frame for the story; thence to a brief adumbration of the story's 'topic', or theme; and so to the onset of the 'argument', or plot. This is the suggested construction:

pre-topic:	A smoky frost over Nottingham; blood-orange sun weeping into the mist over Basford and Bulwell and Cinderhill; red-raw acres of brick shivering in the depressed morning light. . . . They appeared to be unreasonably numerous.
topic:	He entered the waiting room resolved to urge instant treatment of his own case on compassionate grounds. . . . With all due modesty he could claim to speak the language like a native, an absolute native.
argument: [plot begins]	Dr Leiver's receptionist. . . . 'Ey oop, m'duck,' she said. This is a Nottingham greeting, and is as much as to say, *Salaam*.

So the story begins, with a kind of expository progression comparable to that of a case presented in a well formed argument. In argument, we might expect at the close some recapitulation of the topic and its preliminaries – and indeed we have shown how this happens in Russell's brief critique of the businessman's economic philosophy. But such recapitulations also occur in stories. Here, for example, are some sentences from the final paragraph of 'Speak like a native'. In each case there is a verbal echo of something in what I have called the 'pre-topic' phase of the story:

The blanket was warm under his back, the pillow firm yet soft round his head and neck.
(Compare, from the opening: 'He crammed his fur-trimmed hat more tightly down on his head, shrugged his thin coat closer about him . . .')

He felt comforted and at peace. He was at last in the care of a qualified medical man.
(Compare, from the opening: 'And then to have to venture out – in order to seek advice of a medical man – in these *damnably* inclement conditions!')

It only went to show what he had always *maintained*, that if you were going to speak English at all it paid to speak it really *well*. Speak like a native, *that* was the ticket.
(Compare, from the opening: 'With all due modesty he could claim to speak the language like a native, an absolute native.')

Evidently this sample of fiction has a structure not utterly different from that of a piece of argumentative prose, whatever we may find to say about idiomatic and lexical differences, differences in what used to be known as the 'diction'. The realization that there are quite powerful similarities of method between two apparently divergent modes of discourse may encourage the student and the teacher who struggle with the seemingly intractable problems of the creative writing class. They may be encouraged to believe that if one has the wit to make an argument, one has the wit to frame a story; more than that, one has the wit to demonstrate to others the possibility of making a story; so teachers have the wit to liberate the creative capacity in themselves and their pupils.

I repeat the proposition with which I began: there is creativeness in composition and composition in creativeness. For the purpose of studying this relationship, all kinds of communication invite our attentions. To study the most commonplace writings – letters, reports, memoranda, public notices – is to gain insight into the nature of discourse, into the use of language in the management of personal relationships and interactions, into the arts of publicity and propaganda, and into many other aspects of our living and thinking. Certainly composition is a subject for university studies. It has goals and rewards in the form of an enhanced personal efficiency in what educationists like to call 'language skills'. The ultimate goal and final reward, however, is not for teachers to turn their pupils into competent publicists, copywriters, correspondents, polemicists, or tellers of tales.

It is for teacher and pupil together to discover what creativeness in language is, where it is to be sought, how its features are charted; and from their explorations of this fascinating country to bring back tokens of promise, glimpses of the spirit moving and working in the boundless principality of the word.

This is the text, somewhat modified and expanded, of a paper read at an international seminar on stylistics and pragmatics, held at the Catholic University of Tilburg (now the University of Brabant) in 1983. The proceedings of the conference were published under the title *Pragmatics and Stylistics*, ed. J. Renkema and W. van Peer (Amersfoort/Leuven: 1984).

10   Historic event, creative effort: the making of a dramatic poem

At about five o'clock in the afternoon of Wednesday, 6 April 1803, two gentlemen went into Hyde Park, in London, with the intention of exercising themselves, their horses and their dogs. They were persons of some consequence, for Britain, briefly at peace, would soon be at war again, and these were officers in the armed forces. Robert Montgomery, at the age of twenty-eight, was a Lieutenant Colonel of the 9th Regiment of Foot, a man with aristocratic family connections, who had, we are told, 'fought bravely in the service of his country'. James Macnamara, at thirty-five, was a Captain in the Royal Navy, who had distinguished himself in action at the crucial battle of Cape St Vincent, had won the friendship and patronage of Admirals Hood and Nelson, and was generally popular in the Navy at a time when to be a naval officer was to be one of Britain's élite. These two men, you might say, were pedigreed representatives of the nation's manhood.

So we find them going about their blameless business on an April afternoon, on horseback, accompanied by their friends and their dogs.[1] The dogs were of the Newfoundland breed, a strain then quite fashionable. Lord Byron was to own a Newfoundland dog called Bosun, of which he said, on its death, that it possessed 'beauty without vanity, strength without insolence, courage without ferocity, and all the virtues of man without his vices' – a pronouncement not without poetic relevance to the story we now have to tell.[2] Notwithstanding Byron's recommendation of the type, the particular dogs of our anecdote were insolent enough, or ferocious enough, or perhaps just doggy enough, to fall out with each other and begin a fight. An eyewitness suggests that the aggressor was Captain Macnamara's dog, the larger of the two, but the information is not strictly relevant to the morality of the tale, the dogs being probably the least important and certainly the most innocent actors in this tragicomedy.

What followed the dogfight is clear enough in outline, though some points of detail are muddled in the newspaper reports. Then as now, it appears, memory could play tricks on witnesses convinced of their ability to recall things lately seen or heard. Then as now, a reputable journal could report inconsistently on minor particulars. This tale of the dog that worried a dog is a typical example of the difficulty of ascertaining the facts even of very recent events. However, the central happenings are not in dispute. Dismounting to separate the growling animals, the gentlemen presently began to growl at each other in tones of courteous discourtesy. All might have ended in growling, and no harm done, had not Colonel Montgomery made an observation variously reported but generally agreed to have contained the phrase 'you know where to find me', or 'you know where to call upon me'. Now this was serious; this transformed the scene from passing caricature to inevitable tragedy. Words, after all, are only words; even words spoken in heat are only words; but Montgomery's utterance went beyond the ordinary communicative or expressive function of words. His words were a kind of act; they constituted, indeed, what modern philosophers would call 'a speech act'. They were tantamount to saying 'I challenge you to a duel'; they were so understood by Macnamara and by more than one bystander who heard them. This could not be ignored. According to the code of the day, no gentleman, and certainly no officer, could evade a challenge and expect to enjoy the continued respect of his equals and subordinates. Here was a dispute which, in the jargon of the time, needed to be 'adjusted'.

Suddenly there were people at hand, eager to make the adjustment as quickly as possible; friends and associates came on to the scene like the chorus in an opera. Watches were consulted; pistols were agreed upon, as the proper sort of weaponry; a meeting place was set, at Primrose Hill, near Chalk Farm, then on the rural edge of London, suitably remote from the prying attentions of the law and its officers, the Bow Street runners. All this was done in a remarkably short space of time; the dogs were forgotten, what mattered now was the challenge. Away then went Captain Macnamara, to fetch his case of pistols, asking his good friend Captain Barry to act as his second, and prudently supplying himself with a surgical attendant, who bore the grotesquely apposite name of Heaviside. Away, too, went Montgomery, to find *his* second, one Sir William Kerr, evidently a man of some experience in affairs of honour, having we are told, 'himself lost an arm in a rencontre in Ireland'. The Irish, incidentally, had the reputation of being enthusiastic duellists who scrupulously followed an elaborate code of quarrelsome etiquette.

A mere two hours after the original encounter, Montgomery and Macnamara repaired to Primrose Hill, to the appointed place, and there confronted each other at twelve paces – this being, one presumes, what Sheridan's comic Irishman, Sir Lucius O'Trigger, might have called 'a pretty gentleman's distance'.[3] Distances, and indeed the general form of the duel, were agreed by principals negotiating through their seconds. In this instance we know from the testimony of one of the seconds that it was agreed the men should stand twelve paces from each other, 'then level and fire as they pleased'. Let surgeon Heaviside, as reported by *The Times*, take up the story:

> The Gentlemen took their stands and fired nearly together. Colonel Montgomery fell; and not having provided any surgical assistance, the witness offered his service, but on going up to him the Colonel exclaimed 'I am shot through the heart' and immediately expired. The ball appeared to have entered between the fourth and fifth rib.[4]

A little later, Mr Heaviside was able to conduct a post-mortem, the details of which illustrate with sufficiently gruesome force the inadvisability of standing up at twelve paces to a discharge from a duelling pistol:

> The ball . . . had passed through the lobe of the lungs, and had torn the large vessels in its passage. There was a portion of the ribs on the right side driven into the lungs, and from three quarts to a gallon of blood effused into the chest. On examining the inside of the ribs, on the left side of the chest, he found many of them broken, which made him conclude that the ball had passed through the chest. He took out the ball from under the left shoulder blade, which must have made its way there between the sixth and seventh ribs.[5]

Montgomery was dead, but Macnamara had not escaped unscathed. He, too, had been struck by a pistol ball which, according to the appallingly methodical Heaviside, 'had entered the right hip and traversed the belly'. It was remarkable that he was able to make the journey back to London; even more remarkable was the testimony of a bystander that he did not fall when he took the bullet. That seems hard to believe, but the whole episode is indeed scarcely credible. The fact remains that he was able to return to town, where he was presently arrested by the Bow Street runners. He was put to bed at a hotel in Jermyn Street, which, for the time being, was to serve as his remand prison.

A coroner's inquest was held on Friday, 8 April, to determine how the deceased met his death, and if there might be grounds for a subsequent prosecution. There were many who believed that to kill a man in a duel was no less than murder, but this coroner, it seems, was not of their number. His view was that

> where two persons meet to fight without having had sufficient time to cool upon their quarrel, in the event of the death of one, the crime of murder could not be charged against the other. The present case certainly was of this description, the quarrel having begun at five o'clock, and the duel taken place two hours after.

He then expressed his opinion that the observation of the deceased 'that Captain Macnamara knew where he was to be found' could have no other meaning than a challenge; and he thought this circumstance was favourable to Captain Macnamara. He was even at pains to elicit from one witness the information that at the time of the duel Macnamara was still shaking and agitated, as though with passion; presumably this supported the contention that the dispute had not been given time to cool. Under this direction, the coroner's jury returned a verdict of manslaughter. Their view of events was not shared by the Chief Magistrate, Sir Richard Ford, with whom depositions were subsequently lodged at Bow Street. It was his intention to commit Captain Macnamara to prison, and to bring him to trial on a charge of murder. As to the first of these intentions, Mr Heaviside reported that it would be fatal to the Captain, whose wounds were grave; in consequence of which he was permitted to stay in his Jermyn Street hotel. In the meantime the seconds, Sir William Kerr and Captain Barry, had quietly left London for foreign parts, leaving Macnamara to face the indictment, on 14 April, of 'having been aiding and assisting in the murder of Colonel Montgomery'. Once again, fortune or public feeling seems to have been on Macnamara's side. A grand jury threw out the Bill of Indictment, and it was determined that Macnamara should stand trial at the Old Bailey for manslaughter.

Macnamara was accordingly brought to trial on 22 April, little more than two weeks after the absurd and fatal encounter in Hyde Park. They fetched him from his hotel at eight or nine o'clock in the morning, the coach proceeding through the streets to Newgate Prison very slowly, on account of his injuries. From prison he was taken to the Bailey where, at one o'clock there began a trial that was at once the most ordinary and extraordinary affair. For the barristers it had nothing of legal interest to offer, and was thus very ordinary; for the general public it must have had the extraordinary quality of what would now be a front-page story. Prosecuting counsel began by good-humouredly informing the jury that there was no law in the case, that the facts were not in dispute, and that all they had to do was to decide whether the accused was indeed guilty of manslaughter in accordance with the evidence he would lay before them. He then proceeded to establish his case, calling witnesses to testify to the circumstances of the quarrel, the challenge and the duel, and occasionally allowing counsel for the defence to put questions about the demeanour or tone of voice of the antagonists.

When prosecuting counsel had thus presented his evidence, Macnamara was asked if he would like to say anything in his own defence, and in response to this invitation he delivered an oddly eloquent speech, informed by a kind of anguished intensity. The circumstances of the quarrel, he said, were insignificant, the heat it had generated was of no consequence, the arrogant words could be overlooked, any personal resentment was and must be forgotten. What could not be forgotten was the challenge, framed in those fatal words 'you know where to find me'. Even that, Macnamara suggested, might have been tolerated at some less warlike time. 'Gentlemen', he told the jury, 'I am a Captain in the British Navy'. This statement he elaborated, explaining that as one whose duties involved sending others into deadly danger, he could not expect to enjoy their respect, or keep his good reputation among his colleagues, if he himself were seen to shrink from danger. His honour would be irremediably tarnished. As an officer and a gentleman he had been bound to accept the challenge. He had no personal knowledge of Colonel Montgomery and had conceived no personal resentment against him. Indeed, he had gone to Primrose Hill in the hope that some 'explanation' might be forthcoming, some reconciliation effected, that would render the duel unnecessary.

His speech was followed by an episode of solemn comedy. The testimony of the prosecution was incontrovertible, but he was permitted to call witnesses who would testify to the excellence of his character; and never can a prisoner at the bar of the Old Bailey have been attended by so many distinguished referees. The list was headed by Lord Hood and Lord Nelson, who spoke of a man in whose person military prowess and civil benevolence rapturously embraced each other. The tenor of their message, in modern terms, was that Captain Macnamara, so far from being a man of violence, was a veritable charmer. This same opinion was relayed by a succession of admirals and captains who might well have been rehearsed by defence counsel, so remarkably similar were the expressions they used; Macnamara was 'agreeable', he was 'pleasant', he was 'moderate', he was 'humane', 'liberal minded', 'gentlemanly', 'possessed of good humour and hilarity', he was all things amiable, and only under extreme provocation could he have been brought to try his hand at pistol shooting. These attestations were perhaps not without their effect on the jury, for although the judge's summing up quite clearly indicated his opinion that manslaughter was proven – indeed, his lordship hinted that Captain Macnamara was lucky not to be answering the greater charge of murder – the jurymen retired for a mere twenty minutes and came back with a verdict of 'Not guilty'. It was one of those cases, not uncommon in England, in which the jury exercises its right to ignore the bench, and in this case there was never any doubt where popular feeling lay; it lay with the Navy, under Admiral Nelson, the bulwark of British liberties at a time when Britannia really did rule the waves. So ended a piece of theatre which had made some stir in London for two April weeks in 1803, in an interval of the great European drama. The players dispersed, some of them to take part in the next act of a seemingly endless tragedy, for within a few weeks England was again at war. Admiral Nelson was to meet his death at Trafalgar, two years later; Captain Macnamara survived the war, rose to the rank of Rear Admiral, and made for himself a name which was eventually to be enrolled in that ultimate memorial, the *Dictionary of National Biography*. But the Newfoundland dogs, the irrevocable words and the scene on Primrose Hill faded from the national consciousness.

Faded, that is, until they were vividly restored, in the year 1930, by the poet Edmund Blunden – himself a man who had 'fought bravely in the service of his country', a veteran of the First World War, holder of the Military Cross, and author of what is arguably the best English account of life and suffering on the Western Front, a book of prose and verse called *Undertones of War*. Setting aside that one masterpiece, it cannot be claimed that Blunden is a writer of the first rank; here, nevertheless, was a cultivated, sensitive man and an accomplished minor poet, associated with that school, or rather that style of writing we call Georgian. The Georgians wrote gentle verse for gentle folk. They wrote of peaceful and pastoral things, of quiet souls and quiet places; of love, and apples, and moonlight, and cornfields, and girls with flowers in their hair, and sleepy villages, and rural wisdom. Nobody ever said *merde* in a Georgian poem. Then

along came T.S. Eliot and other modern storm-troopers to kill all
that stone dead. But it never did quite die; and mawkish though it
was at its worst, at its best it produced some very capable poets,
Blunden among them. His interest in Montgomery and Macnamara
arose in connection with a project he had conceived, of writing in
verse some sketches of historic trials. This collection, of which four
pieces were completed, was to bear the general title *To Themis*.[6]
Themis is a name for the goddess of justice, who was also the
mother of Prometheus, hero of a creation myth. Prometheus it
was who took clay figures of humanity and inspired them with life,
and with that in mind we may perhaps think that Blunden's title,
To Themis, is programmatic in more than one way. Not only does
it announce that justice is the topic; it also casts the poet himself
in the role of a Promethean figure whose creative powers breathe
life into inert historical clay figures. Here he is, then, bringing
life-breath and poetic fire to our duelling dolls, Montgomery and
Macnamara:

Incident in Hyde Park, 1803

The impulses of April, the rain-gems, the rose-cloud,
The frilling of flowers in the westering love-wind!
And here through the Park come gentlemen riding,
And there through the Park come gentlemen riding,
And behind the glossy horses Newfoundland dogs follow.
Says one dog to the other, 'This park, sir, is mine, sir.'
The reply is not wanting; hoarse clashing and mouthing
Arouses the masters.
Then Colonel Montgomery, of the Life Guards, dismounts.
'Whose dog is this?' The reply is not wanting,
From Captain Macnamara, Royal Navy: 'My dog.'
'Then call your dog off, or by God he'll go sprawling.'
'If my dog goes sprawling, you must knock me down after.'
'Your name?' 'Macnamara, and yours is –' 'Montgomery.'
'And why, sir, not call your dog off?' 'Sir, I chose
Not to do so, no man has dictated to me yet,
And you, I propose, will not change that.' 'This place,
For adjusting disputes, is not proper' – and the Colonel,
Back to the saddle, continues, 'If your dog
Fights my dog, I warn you, I knock your dog down.
For the rest, you are welcome to know where to find me,
Colonel Montgomery; and you will of course
Respond with the due information.' 'Be sure of it.'

Now comes the evening, green-twinkling, clear-echoing,
And out to Chalk-Farm the Colonel, the Captain,
Each with his group of believers, have driven.
   Primrose Hill on an April evening
   Even now in a fevered London
   Sings a vesper sweet; but these
   Will try another music. Hark!
These are the pistols; let us test them; quite perfect.
Montgomery, Macnamara six paces, two faces;
Montgomery, Macnamara – both speaking together
In nitre and lead, the style is incisive,
Montgomery fallen, Macnamara half-falling,
The surgeon exploring the work of the evening –
And the Newfoundland dogs stretched at home in the firelight.

The coroner's inquest; the view of one body;
And then, pale, supported, appears at Old Bailey
James Macnamara, to whom this arraignment:
   You stand charged
   That you
   With force and arms
   Did assault Robert Montgomery,
   With a certain pistol
   Of the value of ten shillings,
   Loaded with powder and a leaden bullet,

   Which the gunpowder, feloniously exploded,
   Drove into the body of Robert Montgomery,
   And gave
   One mortal wound;
   Thus you did kill and slay
   The said Robert Montgomery.

O heavy imputation! O dead that yet speaks!
O evening transparency, burst to red thunder!
Speak Macnamara. He, tremulous as a windflower,
Exactly imparts what had slaughtered the Colonel.
'Insignificant the origin of the fact now before you;
Defending our dogs, we grew warm; that was nature;
That heat of itself had not led to disaster.
From defence to defiance was the leap that destroyed.
At once he would have at my deity, Honour –
"If you are offended you know where to find me!"

On one side, I saw the wide mouths of Contempt,
Mouth to mouth working, a thousand vile gunmouths;
On the other my Honour; Gentlemen of the Jury,
I am a Captain in the British Navy.'

Then said Lord Hood: 'For Captain Macnamara,
He is a gentleman and so says the Navy.'
Then said Lord Nelson: 'I have known Macnamara
Nine years, a gentleman, beloved in the Navy,
Not to be affronted by any man, true,
Yet as I stand here before God and my country,
Macnamara has never offended, and would not,
Man, woman, child.' Then a spring-tide of admirals,
Almost Neptune in person, proclaim Macnamara
Mild, amiable, cautious, as any in the Navy;
And Mr Garrow rises, to state that if need be,
To assert the even temper and peace of his client,
He would call half the Captains in the British Navy.

Now we are shut from the duel that Honour
Must fight with the Law; no eye can perceive
The fields wherein hundreds of shadowy combats
Must decide between a ghost and a living idolon –
A ghost with his army of the terrors of bloodshed,
A half-ghost with the grand fleet of names that like sunrise
Have dazzled the race with their march on the ocean.

Twenty minutes. How say you?

                                        Not Guilty.

Then from his chair with his surgeon the Captain
Walks home to his dog, his friends' acclamations
Supplying some colour to the pale looks he had,
Less pale than Montgomery's; and Honour rides on.

I am aware, at this point, of dealing with a twice-told tale; in
particular, I am aware of having assumed two narrative roles, first
as a reporter and then as a performer. I know, furthermore, that in
reporting the story of Colonel Montgomery and Captain Macnamara,
I have in fact made a digest of several reports appearing in *The Times*
between 9 and 23 April 1803.[7] These reports are not in every detail
consistent with each other; I have felt obliged to adjudicate between
them, to select, to compress, to give prominence to some matters and
neglect others, to give expression to my perception of a developing
narrative. I have also been prompted here and there, even in the face

of my own wish to tell a round unvarnished tale, to put into the telling some comments of my own, whether in the form of explicit statement or, perhaps implicitly, in the choice of a word, the turn of a phrase, the placing of an emphasis, the tenor and focus of a personal style. I have to acknowledge here the age-old paradox that the struggle to express creates a distance from the matter which is to be expressed; that the creative effort re-designs the original fact; that we come further and further from facts in our desire to grasp and present a truth. I have reported a story, but my stance as a reporter cannot be quite neutral, however much I would like it to be so. The mere endeavour to make a text, to depart from the text of *The Times* and shape a text of my own, involves me in the manipulations of literary style, and literary style is never neutral. It always stands between the reader or listener and the world it purports to represent. It always requires an understanding of its internal conventions and codings.

This, then, has been one of my roles, the assumed role of reporter. I have told the story in my own words, and have then presented it in someone else's words, those of the poet Edmund Blunden. He, too, made the creative effort of selecting, compressing, modifying, shaping the prominences of the narrative to his own liking, conveying an interpretation in his own distinctive style. Because the poet rules in his own kingdom, you may suppose that I have no part to play in the *poetic* re-creation of this tale; that I am a mediator, and no more than that. And yet as soon as I begin to read the poem aloud I take on another creative role, that of performer. To perform the piece I must have a considerable degree of competence in the English language, not only in the sense of knowing what the words mean and how the sentences are to be construed, but far beyond that, in the greater sense of being at home with its discourse conventions. I must know what is usual and what is unusual; what is prosaic and what is poetic; what is general in the language and what belongs to some particular register or function; what must be regarded as formal or 'literary' in style and what may be allowed to be informal or colloquial. I must be acquainted with what linguists call prosodic and paralinguistic features, and what the passenger on the Piccadilly tube calls the manner of speaking and the tone of voice. I must have some idea of how English people of a certain social class sound when they are angry or haughty or conciliatory. And knowing all this, I must also be able to find what I know in the words that lie before me on the page; to retrieve from the script, as an instrumentalist retrieves from a musical score, the sounds of discourse which build up the shape of discourse which eventually represents the meaning of discourse. Or rather, my perception of the meaning through a particular performance, through the 'delivery instance',[8] as Roman Jakobson calls it. For tomorrow, or even in the next five minutes, I might give a slightly different performance, present a new delivery instance. A sensitive pianist will seldom play a sonata in quite the same way twice running; a good actor will not forever play the same Hamlet; a reader for whom a poem truly exists will rarely give two successive readings without variations in delivery that suggest yet another interpretation of the text. The performer's is also the effort of one who creates. Here, then, are three versions of creative effort: the reporter's attempt to reconstruct the story from the facts; the poet's creation of a fact that transcends the facts; and the performer's effort to realize and interpret the poetic fact by giving an acoustic presence to the text.

But let us be just, and let us, as they say, get our priorities right; let us insist that among these versions of creativeness, the poet's is the greatest. He offers us a style, a way of using language, that is more than simply expressive or ornamental; it creates a world of action and judgement. 'Incident in Hyde Park' is a text that relies on a studious cultivation of language to convey, above all, its attitudes, its *ethos*. Here we have a very stylish, or better, a highly *stylized* poem, a recital of words evoking our consciousness of other words. Anyone reading it, certainly any native British reader with a measure of literary competence, cannot fail to be struck by two elements in its language. One of these elements is irony; from first to last one has the impression of an author expounding his theme in commentary tones that range from playfulness to wounded mockery. The other element, a corollary of the first, is pastiche. No one will suppose that this is Blunden's own style, or that it represents the poetic language of his time, or even of the school of poets with which he was associated. It reads like an attempt to evoke the language of a period; it is, so to speak, a costume language, or a stylistic mask, or at all events a language designed to fit the staging of a very theatrical poem. The effect of this extraordinary 'stylizing', with its attendant implications of ironic mime, is to dismiss from the mind of a receptive reader any notion that this is merely a versified report. Clearly it is not a report. The past tense, the linguistic symptom of *reportage*, occurs in only two or three places in the poem; the narrative stance is the present, and the story is told as though it were unfolding before our very eyes, cinematographically. It seems, moreover, that what the poetic cinema shows us is not a tale of the 'real' Robert Montgomery and James Macnamara – even the newspaper reporters appear to have had some difficulty in establishing 'realities' – but of *a* Montgomery and *a* Macnamara, agonists in a peepshow with transcendent moral implications.

Blunden's handling of the material supplied by *The Times* of London suggests immediately this transformation from mundane fact to moral fable. He freely selects, ignores, or adapts details from the newspaper narratives, sometimes choosing a version and following it quite closely, sometimes picking up and combining phrases from this account or that, sometimes indulging his own power of invention. He invents, for example, Admiral Nelson's speech, though the invented words are by no means out of keeping with some actual phrases of testimony given on Macnamara's behalf by his brother officers. Faced with conflicting reports that Montgomery held his commission in the Guards (according to *The Times* for 8 April) and in the 9th Regiment of Foot (9 April, in the report on the Coroner's inquest), he prefers what is no doubt the less reliable version, probably because 'Guards' fits into a line of verse more cosily than '9th Regiment of Foot', but conceivably, too, because by assigning his Montgomery to the army's élite corps – he even makes him a colonel in the Life Guards – he would sufficiently emphasize the jealous confrontation, the war of honour between the high and mighty army and the great and glorious navy. So important is this confrontation, so central to the drama, that one might suppose from the poem that Montgomery and Macnamara were the sole actors, apart from the dogs, in the scenes in the Park and at Primrose Hill. In the poetic account there are no witnesses, no bystanders, no friends of the accused or acquaintances of the deceased, no seconds, no Captain Barry, no Sir William Kerr, no members of the lower orders, no passers-by, no other participant except Heaviside, distantly alluded to as 'the surgeon'. All those onlookers who, by bearing witness, confuse the issue, are eliminated. Alone, at the centre of things, we have 'two faces', confronting each other at 'six paces' – six, though Captain Barry's testimony gives the number as twelve. Blunden may have imagined, of course, that the two men, standing back to back, each took six strides before turning to fire. What seems more likely, however, is that where twelve paces is a dangerous distance, six is damned dangerous; and that a face seen six yards away is more expressively a face than the white countenance glimpsed at thirty-six feet.[9] What the newspaper says becomes irrelevant; it is the poet's view of things that now counts.

The most interesting digression from the original material is, in fact, a stylistic manipulation controlling what I have just called the 'view of things'. It concerns the wording of the indictment read by the clerk of the court. We are of course familiar enough with courtroom

scenes in plays and films, even if we are not habitués of the Old
Bailey, to recognize that lines 41–53 of Blunden's poem imitate
a non-poetic register, the language of judicial procedure. But let us
compare Blunden's framing of the charge with the wording reported
in *The Times*. Thus Blunden:

> You stand charged
> That you
> With force and arms
> Did assault Robert Montgomery,
> With a certain pistol
> Of the value of ten shillings,
> Loaded with powder and a leaden bullet,
>
> Which the gunpowder, feloniously exploded,
> Drove into the body of Robert Montgomery,
> And gave
> One mortal wound;
> Thus you did kill and slay
> The said Robert Montgomery.

And *The Times*:

> The Indictment stated, that he stood charged, on the Coroner's
> Inquisition, with having, on the 6th day of April, in the Parish of
> St Pancras, made an assault on Robert Montgomery; and that with
> a leaden bullet, shot from a certain pistol, he did kill and slay the
> said Robert Montgomery, by giving him a mortal wound, of which
> he died.[10]

The newspaper version reads as one might expect a juridically
formulated charge of manslaughter to read. The poetic version
appears to correspond to the legal stereotype, and indeed echoes
a phrase here and there, such as 'leaden bullet', 'kill and slay',
'give a mortal wound'. Where it almost comically departs from
its model is in the phrases 'the gunpowder, feloniously exploded',
and 'a certain pistol/Of the value of ten shillings'. It is the latter,
in particular, that must excite in us a sense of authorial irony;
for while it might be appropriate to a charge of theft, in which
the value of stolen property would be stated, it is hardly relevant
to a case of unlawful killing. Blunden is surely joking with the
formalities of the law - but the joke is ironic, and implies a serious
question, the question being, 'Is this what a man's life is worth'?
If the poem contained no other stylistic device indicative of the

author's stance of compassionate irony, this interpolation into the orthodox wording of the indictment would still serve as a powerful guide. This in itself directs us to a 'view of things'; this detail alone announces what other lines and passages in the poem variously say, murmur, declare or exclaim: that this would be funny, if it were not so tragic.

And indeed, much of the text *is* concerned with murmuring, declaring and exclaiming: with *speaking*, in various forms, through various agencies. It is essential to the fable that the poem's 'speakings' are non-human as well as human. Montgomery and Macnamara speak, as do Lord Hood and Lord Nelson, as does the Clerk of the Court, as does the Foreman of the Jury; but the dogs also speak, in the style and tone of their masters, and the very pistols speak, in a harsh colloquy that disrupts the devout singing silence, the sweet vesper, of Primrose Hill. From all these voices no reason emerges, no discursive pattern such as might reconcile us to an argument, a meaning and a fair conclusion. The poem reads like a patchwork of speakings rather than continuous discourse. And yet it constantly implies the obligation not only to speak but also to respond, an implication which is also powerfully present in the newspaper reports, which make much of the tone in which things are said, and the circumstance that one protagonist replied or did not reply to the other. Macnamara's courtroom defence contains a passage that strikingly suggests the bond of necessity in which one interlocutor holds another. 'Words', he says, 'receive their interpretation from the avowed intention of the speaker. The offence was forced upon me by *the declaration, that he invited me to be offended . . .*'. This seems tantamount to saying that if I speak, you must answer, however reluctant you may be, and however awkward the consequences. The implicit obligation is expressed in the poem in that curiously formal phrase 'the reply is not wanting', applied first to the dogs and then to the masters. Blunden's version of the masters' altercation is drawn from evidence given by various witnesses at the inquest and the trial; chiefly from the trial testimony of one Charles Smith.[11] A telling feature of the poetic text is that there are no reporting verbs, even of an ordinary kind, like 'say' and 'reply', with the result that it is remarkably easy to lose track of the turns in conversation, and to decide who is speaking. Blunden himself apparently loses track, allocating to Montgomery an assertion attributed in court to Macnamara.[12] But this scarcely matters, nor does it matter that in reciting the poem a performer will be hard put to it to distinguish between the intonations of the two men. It does not matter because our poetic contestants are virtually *doppelgänger*. The evidence for and against does not matter. Morally and circumstantially it is six of one and half a dozen of the other; they are like Tweedledum and Tweedledee who went to fight a battle, and the cause of their quarrel is hardly more absurd than the rattle which brought those celebrated siblings into conflict.

Blunden, indeed, must have blessed his poetic luck when he discovered that he had been granted for his purposes a Tweedledum and Tweedledee, an alliterating and counterpoising pair: 'Montgomery, Macnamara six paces, two faces; Montgomery, Macnamara –both speaking together.' Montgomery–Macnamara; The Army–The Navy, if you like, but Montgomery–Macnamara will serve very well as phonaesthetic tokens. These lines at the centre of the poem encapsulate a principle that runs throughout: of duality, of symmetry, of antiphonal structure. Repeatedly, expressions find their exact counterpoise, whether the matching is immediate, as in the third and fourth lines:

And here through the Park come gentlemen riding,
And there through the Park come gentlemen riding

or whether lines are more distantly equated, as in the compound nouns and compound adjectives of 1 and 24:

The impulses of April, the rain-gems, the rose-cloud

Now comes the evening, green-twinkling, clear-echoing.

This principle of symmetry in the narrative style of the poem is notably reinforced by phonetic devices. The end-chime, the *homoioteleuton*, as the rhetoricians call it, of 'evening', 'twinkling', 'echoing', 'riding', 'mouthing', 'sprawling', 'falling', is one such device. Another is alliteration, and here Blunden has in at least one place made creative use of wordings supplied by his newspaper sources. The wordings I refer to are, once more, in Macnamara's courtroom speech, which opens in a style strikingly similar to that of the corresponding speech in the poem:

The origin of the difference, as you see it in the evidence, was insignificant:- The heat of two persons, each defending an animal under his protection, was natural, and could not have led to any serious consequences. It was not the deceased's defending his own dog, or his threatening to destroy mine, that led to the fatal catastrophe: it was the defiance alone which most unhappily accompanied what was said.[13]

In this passage we see word items – 'difference', 'defending', 'deceased', 'destroy', 'defiance' – which have evidently stimulated the alliterative and other phonetic patterns of lines 59–62 in the poem:

> Defending our dogs, we grew warm, that was nature;
> That heat of itself had not led to disaster.
> From defence to defiance was the leap that destroyed.
> At once he would have at my deity, Honour.

I would draw attention to the rhythm of these lines. It is characteristic of the general narrative rhythm of the poem, and it is based on the stress-timing of English, the so-called isochronism that spaces the beats evenly in formal delivery.[14] If I were trying to teach a foreign student the basic walking tempo of English, its *andante sostenuto*, I might very well avail myself of sentences such as 'And here through the Park come gentlemen riding', or 'The surgeon exploring the work of the evening', or 'From defence to defiance was the leap that destroyed'. It is perhaps more than a walking rhythm; it is a pacing that takes the text along almost irresistibly. This striding measure is periodically interrupted, however, by other rhythms that impede the otherwise unrelenting march; by the four-line intermezzo on Primrose Hill, for example, or by the 'indictment' section, or even by short passages of authorial commentary, notably lines 54–5. The passage of versified conversation, from line 10 to line 23, also somewhat disrupts the pacing rhythm, for although Blunden has made from the original material a selection of utterances that pattern well into verse, they are not symmetrically matched, and indeed it is noticeable that they either break up the verse-line or overrun the line-end. The poem embraces in its technique speech-rhythm and verse-rhythm; furthermore, it establishes a rhythm for the narrative and rhythms for the dramatic intrusions into the narrative. There is in the poem a rhythmic principle which is more than decorative. Metre and meaning are bound up with each other; the prosody is significant.

It is most palpably, though by no means exclusively, in its use of sounds and rhythms that the poem takes its distance from the raw facts talkatively reported in the columns of *The Times*. The meticulous process of 'stylizing', as I have called it, goes on from start to finish, transforming the original material until the material itself, like the origin of the duellist's quarrel, passes into insignificance. The ordinary reader, unencumbered by the antiquarian zeal of professors, can enjoy Blunden's poem on its own terms, without being driven to consult ancient copies of national newspapers. One of our current TV advertisements, for an insurance company, carries the slogan 'We won't make a drama out of a crisis'. That may be as short a way as any of describing what Edmund Blunden did. Out of a crisis, the petty crisis of two silly dogs fighting, the personal crisis of two sane men duelling, he made a drama.

The drama goes beyond Newfoundland dogs and Napoleonic manners. It reaches other people, in other times and places, with ideas about an idea. The idea is not justice, as the general title *To Themis* might encourage us to believe; it is – fairly obviously – honour, or, if we like to be more precise, the idea of honour in manifest conflict with the idea of justice. In his summing up at the trial of James Macnamara, Mr Justice Heath dryly observed, 'it appears that the law is a stranger to those nice sentiments of honour'. Here 'nice' has the sense of 'delicate', 'precise', 'fastidious'; his lordship was speaking ironically. The judge's words are taken up in all gravity by Blunden in a line which suggests both the retiring of the jury to consider their verdict in private, and, more generally, the retiring of objective judgement from an elusively subjective matter: 'Now we are shut from the duel that Honour/Must fight with the Law.' Note the capital letters; Honour and Law are rival personalities, even rival gods; Blunden's Macnamara refers, indeed, to 'my deity, Honour' – a phrase which the historical Macnamara is not reported as using in his discourse on the right and obligation of a gentleman to defend his good name. It is the god, Honour, who rides triumphantly out of the poem in the pacing rhythm – tum-ti-ti-tum – of the final phrase, 'Honour rides on'. (Honour still 'rides', we may notice, though by now Captain Macnamara merely 'walks'.)

It is not difficult to read in all this an opinion of Honour as shrewd and sceptical as that expressed by Falstaff in the play of *Henry IV* – 'Can honour set to a leg? no: or an arm? no: or take away the grief of a wound? no. Honour hath no skill in surgery, then? no. What is honour? a word. . . . Who hath it? he that died a' Wednesday'. 'He that died a' Wednesday',[15] meaning any poor, forgotten Tom, Dick or Harry; meaning Colonel Montgomery; meaning, it is surely not unreasonable to suggest, all those comrades of Edmund Blunden, all those brave young officers and men who died or were hideously wounded, physically and mentally, in the carnage of the Somme and Passchendaele, and Loos, and Ypres, in a conflict which started when a Serbian student, motivated by honourable ideals, took a pistol shot at an Archduke. I would suggest that 'Incident in Hyde Park', this poem ostensibly about a duel, is a way of looking at the greater conflicts of men, at war, and the sentiments of war, and the hollowness of those sentiments, truly idols, if by that word 'idolon' we mean an unsubstantial image, a phantasm. But this is only my re-creation of what Blunden created from what he read in an old newspaper. There is in these matters a chain of consequences which I am almost tempted to describe as a chain of necessity; it pleases me, at all events, to think that somewhere under the soil of England there may lie the remains of one who possessed beauty without vanity and strength without insolence, the bones of a dog who began a tussle that caused the quarrel that led to the duel that furnished the reports that informed the poet who wrote the poem that pleased the professor who now perceives the necessity of coming to a full stop.

The text of a lecture delivered at the Centre Universitaire de Luxembourg in March 1989 at a seminar, the central theme of which was the interpretation and performance of dramatic texts.

11 English: a global resource?

Hae tibi erunt artes . . .

Once upon a time, between a brewery and a slaughterhouse there stood a certain primary school, or rather – for this was once upon a very long time – an elementary school. It was called Thwaite Street. Sometimes at night, in that vagrancy of the mind that comes just before sleep, I return to Thwaite Street. I see its grimed Edwardian Gothic brickwork; I see the fisticuffed playground; I see the governmental cream and brown of corridors that smelt dismally of paint and polish and moist plimsolls; I hear the gusty gramophone that marched us into our classrooms, sometimes to the tune of the British Grenadiers, sometimes, incongruously, to the strains of 'The Stars and Stripes for Ever'; but most of all I see and hear Miss Kirby. Miss Kirby had not been to college – but to say that is as pointless as it would be to say that Attila the Hun lacked formal qualifications. Like him, she was good at her job. Like him, she went about it with a conviction not unaugmented by violence. She was less than five feet tall, and she packed a ringing right hook. We took her very seriously.

Every Monday when little Miss Kirby bustled into her class, she would have the monitors give out the atlases, and bid us open them at the double page where Mercator's projection displayed a world dominated by the colour red. As she moved among us with colonizing knuckles, we became cheerfully interested in that colour. We followed her as she traced from meridian to happy meridian the global glories of red: from the pacific isolation of New Zealand westward to the hump of Australia, and north west to India with the elephant face, and on again via spatterings of little red islands to Africa patched and plotted with red, and westward still to North America, that cockadoodle continent, where Canada, crowing over the merely apple-green States, announced still the triumph of red, of the British Empire, on which sun never set, over which the flag always flew, in which one language ruled unceasingly over a babble of diverse tongues.

Were Miss Kirby alive now, it would not at all surprise her to be told that upwards of 300,000,000 people today have English as their native tongue, and that a further 400,000,000 make regular use of it as a second or auxiliary language.[1] It might of course surprise and even offend her to learn that those gum-chewing and gangsterish Americans are now largely responsible for the geopolitical success of English. In her Thwaite Street days, she would certainly have preferred to think of our English as a providential ordinance, a privilege imposed on the lucky natives wherever conquest and colonization brought first the British flag, then the British merchant, then the British administrator. A global resource indeed, she would have said, the resource of civilization. Such were the conventional, generally unquestioned and unsurprised views of her time. It is for us, in our own time, to be surprised that remarkably few members of the world-wide community of English speakers now show much resentment or resistance towards the language thus unconditionally visited upon them. The English language may be held suspect in Quebec, and perhaps not unreservedly adored in Cardiff, but its standing remains quite high in, for example, Calcutta. All things considered, this is remarkable.

To tell this tale requires a skilled historian, which I am not; but still I would like to remark on some of the odd ways in which our language has got about the world. Let me then make use of three representative puppets, whom I shall call the Merchant, the Educator and the Pioneer. Each of these types has carried English abroad as a resource. But there have been different reasons for carrying it; different ways in which it has been received and perceived by those to whom it has been carried; and different ways in which the resources of the English language have served the needs of the carrier.

The Merchant's way with English was to allow a little of it to those with whom he came into trading contact; enough to promote the transaction of business, but not enough to give the other fellow genuine access to what was, in the circumstances, the dialect of power. The literary prototype of 'the other fellow' appears in *Robinson Crusoe*, in Defoe's portrayal of the character whose name is generally mispresented, in folk usage, as 'Man Friday'– as though 'Man' were a humane honorific, comparable with Saint, or Sir, or King. Nowhere in the book does Crusoe refer to 'Man Friday'; he calls his companion either Friday, plain and simple, or 'my man Friday', in which usage 'man' means servant.[2] Crusoe is kind to his servant; he gives him Bible readings and theology lessons and tries to convince him that eating people is inexpedient; but he never does anything to improve Friday's grammar, so that to the end the poor fellow thinks that 'me' is a subject pronoun and is convinced that the plural of 'man' is 'mans'. There is an underlying assumption that Friday's capacities are too frail for Standard English; and an even darker, unspoken implication that it would not be appropriate to his place to encourage him to learn it.

Crusoe refers to Friday's 'broken English'; nowadays we might call it 'pidgin' though in fact the speech that Defoe imputes to Friday is 'pidgin' only in its incidental reflection of the master–man relationship; a pidgin language is not simply a ramshackle dialect with a go-as-you-please grammar and a few bits and bobs of baby-talk. It is the product of two languages in contact, and the result of the contact is something new, something with its own rules, its own structures, its own creative principles of growth in vocabulary and idiom. Pidgin languages are as a rule born out of mercantile or logistic requirements; we commonly find them in coastal areas, in archipelagoes, in frontier regions, in theatres of war, in centres of commercial activity such as plantations; but in some cases they acquire a social base of such breadth and strength that they become the mother language, the first language of a community, in which case they are called 'creoles'.

Of the hundreds of pidgin languages which exist round the world, many are English-based, though it is far from being the case that the pidgin partnership, so to speak, always includes English. There are forms based on Portuguese, on Spanish, on French, on Dutch, on Arabic; there are some based on African languages in contact, for example, in the copperbelt area of Zambia. But the English-based varieties are certainly quite numerous, and generally illustrate both the vulnerability and the viability of this form of language. Bamboo English, a barter language which came into being during the Korean war, exemplifies the vulnerability of its kind; it died out after the soldiers went home. Others, however, like Krio, a first language in Sierra Leone, or Jamaican creole, with over two million speakers, or the Fijian Beach-la-Mar (formerly called Sandalwood English) or the Tok Pisin of Papua New Guinea, used by something like a million people, are, it would seem, quite robustly viable.[3]

Even a casual study of the vocabulary and idiom of the Pidgin English will turn up much that is charming and suggestive of great ingenuity and playful creative power. Who could be less than captivated by the rendering of 'feather' as 'grass belong bird', or 'piano' as 'fella bokus you faitim he cry'? In the lexicon of pidgin it often seems that the naïve perception, the innocent imagination come into their own, redeeming the mere 'business language' with the possibility of poetry. Here is a piece of classic text translated into Tok Pisin:[4]

Dispela em i gutnius bilong Jisas Kraist, Pikinini bilong God.

Perhaps not too much ingenuity is required to recognize that as the opening of St Mark's gospel, 'The beginning of the gospel of Jesus Christ, Son of God'. It goes on:

Long graun i no gat man, maus bilong wanpela man i singaut, i spik 'Redim rot bilong Bigpela'[5]

This is perhaps a little more difficult and calls for a glossary. 'Long graun i no gat man' means 'wilderness', 'maus bilong wanpela man i singaut' means 'the voice' ('maus') of 'one man who cries out' ('wanpela man i singaut'). Thus 'the voice of one crying out in the wilderness'. 'Bigpela', 'Big Fellow', signifies 'the Lord', and 'rot bilong Bigpela', 'the road that belongs to Big Fellow' is 'the way of the Lord'; thus 'redim rot bilong Bigpela', 'Prepare ye the way of the Lord'. The ingenuity of it is wholly admirable. I think however, that my favourite phrase in Tok Pisin must be one taken from *Rotsefti Long Niugini*, 'The New Guinea Highway Code', where the colourless official phrase 'In the event of an accident' is translated with virile candour as *Sapos yu kisim bagarap*.[6] There you may glimpse the sort of expression that real-life Crusoes have taught your actual Fridays.

Nearly seventy years ago Otto Jespersen prophesied that what he called 'these makeshift languages' must die out because of their technical inadequacy; the implication being that their speakers would turn away from them in dissatisfaction and resort to the language on which the makeshift was primarily based.[7] The presence of English, for example, would tend to drive out the use of pidgin. In this, I think, Jespersen was mistaken. The makeshift languages *are* at risk, but their deaths, when they occur, are social deaths, the result of the fragmentation of a community or the removal of the motives, commercial and otherwise, that have brought them into being. There is no particular evidence that their speakers chafe at their lexical and grammatical defects. Friday will happily go on talking Fridayese, until Crusoe decides that Friday might be put to work keeping the accounts and running the office of his brand new goatskin umbrella factory. Then the picture begins to change a little.

Here the Educator, our second representative figure, comes into the imperial story. His role is to supply the language curriculum that will develop what our modern jargon calls 'the infrastructure' – or more briefly, to train clerks. I think it fair to say that colonial education in India and Africa from about the middle of the nineteenth century onwards aimed chiefly at the making of minor functionaries and useful subordinates. Take the primary case, the case of India. In the year 1835, we find Thomas Babington Macaulay, later to be Lord Macaulay, presiding over a body called the Indian Committee for Public Instruction. Macaulay was at the time in the employ of the East India Company at a salary of £10,000 a year, an enormous sum for those days. In his capacity as president of the said committee, Macaulay urged the desirability of creating – and here I quote – 'a class who may be interpreters between us and the millions whom we govern – a class of persons, Indians in blood and colour, but English in taste, in morals and in intellect'.[8]

That repellently cool pronouncement heralds the onset of a century of colleges and diplomas and degrees, and the emergence of a type of educated, gifted, ambitious Indian, whose particular fluency in English has often been the object of parody, because of its strenuous mixture of formal literary language and enthusiastic colloquialism, in the endeavour to be 'absolutely and unequivocally top-notch'. However, all that the parody does, in the end, is to reflect a serious and purposeful way of speaking. There is a splendid account of the Indian way in a recent novel by Upanamayu Chatterjee, called *English, August*, and significantly subtitled 'An Indian Story'. In this passage, Srivastav, a District Officer in the Indian Administrative Service, reflects on the necessity of learning English, and of preserving English, even in post-imperial India:

> The English we speak is not the English we read in English books, and, anyway, those are two different things. Our English should be just a vehicle of communication, other people find it funny, but how we speak shouldn't matter as long as we get the idea across. My own English is quite funny too, but then I had to learn it on my own. . . . In Azamganj, where I come from, I studied in a Hindi-medium school. Now people with no experience of these schools say that that's a good thing, because we should throw English out of India. Rubbish, I say, many other things are far more important. I *know*, bhai. . . . When I went to college in Lucknow I felt completely stupid. So I began to read English on my own. I had to, because English was compulsory for the Civil Services exam. So I read Shakespeare and Wordsworth and people like that, very difficult. It's still important to know English, it gives

one . . . confidence. . . . That a young man in Azamganj should find it essential to study something as unnecessary as *Hamlet*, that is absurd, no, but also inevitable, and just as inevitably, if we behave ourselves, in three generations it will fade.[9]

'Where's your Lord Macaulay now?' one might say. Srivastav would happily jettison English literary culture, which he finds absurdly irrelevant to the needs and problems of India, but he will not so happily surrender the resource of the English language. Many Indians today would agree with him. In a country riven by ethnic and religious conflicts, often bound up with emotional commitment to this language or that, English stands neutral; and since each of the sixteen official languages of the constitution presents some difficulty, major or minor, to speakers of the remaining fifteen, you might as well learn English. As Srivastav puts it, it gives one confidence.[10]

It is one of history's gentle ironies that during the 1920s and 1930s the medium of political subversion in India, the errand-bearing servant of the growing Nationalist movement, was not Urdu or Hindi or Bengali or Punjabi or Gujerati or Mahrati, but English. Lord Macaulay's boys, you could say, got the message. It makes one think of that moment in *The Tempest*, when Caliban rounds on Prospero and says 'You taught me language, and my profit on't is, I know how to curse'. English, however, has survived in India as a resource that transcends cursing, and even transcends its immense administrative convenience. For the educated Indian it has a psychological value as a medium through which certain kinds of experience are habitually apprehended. Anyone who has watched the films of Satyajit Ray will know what I mean by this. His middle-class Calcuttans shift back and forth, sometimes in mid-sentence, between their native Bengali, in which, obviously, their most intimate thoughts are communicated, and their carefully acquired English, in which, it seems, they often negotiate and discuss matters of public import. Take this happy bilingualism a little further and you come to a stage of linguistic resourcefulness in which the emotions and the processes of thought – the inner rhetoric, so to speak – are Indian, but the language in which they are realized is English. This describes the work of the very talented Indian novelists, and their numbers are growing, who now write in English. There is no better comment on their talent than what Salman Rushdie has humorously said of it: 'The Empire strikes back.' I must add here that the same thing could be said, with equal justice and for comparable reasons, about writers in Africa, in states that were once under British rule.

When the British went to India, they took their language to another people, who shaped it as a resource; when they went to places like North America and Australasia, they took it as their own resource, to another land. I am making the distinction rather simply, with the intention, as you will doubtless gather, of introducing my third puppet, the Pioneer. Of this type, the most outstanding representative is clearly the American, and it is in the end the American experience that has established English as a world language. Two hundred years ago, Noah Webster was fervently convinced that what I have just called 'the American experience' would create a language quite unlike the parent tongue. 'Several circumstances', he wrote,

> 'render a future separation of the American tongue from the English necessary and unavoidable. Numerous local causes, such as a new country, new associations of people, new combinations of ideas in arts and science, and some intercourse with tribes wholly unknown in Europe, will introduce new words into the American tongue. These causes will produce, in course of time, a language in North America, as different from the future language of England, as the modern Dutch, Danish, and Swedish are from German, or from one another.'[11]

Things have not quite turned out as Webster anticipated, or indeed hoped. Despite the fact that we say 'pavement' and they say 'sidewalk', or that we say 'over the road' and they say 'across the street', British and American can still make shift to understand each other without benefit of a Hugo's word and phrase book. Nevertheless, Webster's delineation of those 'numerous local causes' is accurate, if we add to them something he may not have anticipated: the stream of European immigrants entering America from the 1840s onwards – German, Polish, Irish, Italian, Jewish, the 'huddled masses yearning to breathe free', who were to breathe freely on the American language in the most un-Websterian ways.

It is appropriate in this instance that I should cite a lexicographer, because if you try to talk about the history of American English, you will find yourself discussing its words, word by word, and idiom by idiom, helplessly committed to anecdote and hearsay and neighbourhood talk. This is because the history is not metropolitan; it is essentially regional, and if you want to find out how America speaks, you must have a sense not only of how it goes in New York and Los Angeles, but also of how it goes in Dime Box, Texas and Punxutawney, Pennsylvania. Well, I will not attempt to theorize; I will only indicate some categories under which America's words might be referred to her history, colonial and post-colonial. There are words from mother English which have simply been transplanted; there are English words which have taken on new references; there are words which have passed out of English usage altogether, but which still mean something in the United States; there are words belonging wholly to the American experience and resulting from contact with other languages and cultures; words brought into being by the necessity of naming objects, inventions, social phenomena; and words Americans have created for themselves in the characteristic you-got-it-we-name-it of their linguistic inventiveness. In all this there are decades of commentary, and I have perhaps five minutes; then let me take three words at random: one a standard item, one from regional dialect, one a piece of jocular slang. To begin with, the word 'brook'; to be sure, a very ordinary word, and so there is nothing very remarkable, we might think, about the title, *West Running Brook*, of a volume of poems by the New Englander Robert Frost. Nothing remarkable, except that the word of itself strongly suggests the speech of New England. It is certainly no longer exclusive to that area, but still the dialect maps and surveys like those of Hans Kurath, and more recently, Frederick Cassidy, will tell us that it is established preponderantly in the North East.[12] Elsewhere in the eastern United States, we find 'creek', 'run', as in the Battle of Bull Run, 'branch', as in 'bourbon and branch water', and occasionally, 'kill', a word of Dutch origin which appears in names like Catskill. My point here is that 'brook', the common mother-country word for a small watercourse, keeps its tenure in the region first settled from the mother country.

A somewhat different fate befell the sixteenth-century word 'civet cat', which students of the always necessary Shakespeare will recognize as referring to quadrupeds of the species *viverra civeta*, from the products of whose anal pouches, believe it or not, the perfumes of Araby were distilled. When the word crosses the Atlantic and turns up in the Ozarks, and in territories mainly west of the Mississippi – the pioneering West – it refers to a very different sort of perfumery. It denotes either the polecat or the skunk, *mephitica mephitica*, and in that meaning undergoes wonderful mutations, becoming 'civvy cat', 'ciffy cat', 'chivy cat', 'civic cat' and 'civic kitty'. These forms are now attested by a few speakers who were asked about local names for this smelly animal. The word 'skunk' itself is an Algonquin word which came into English quite shortly after the first settlements, and suggests the process of interchange or pidginization that must have then gone on at the frontiers of settler experience. 'Skunk' has become the standard word; the word which the pioneers subsequently took with them in their westward expansion, the word which faintly recalls the England of Elizabeth, is now used only in dialect, and in its country of origin is used not at all, except perhaps by zoologists and Shakespeare commentators.

My third example arises out of a question put by field investigators gathering material for the *Dictionary of American Regional English*. Asked 'What do you open up and hold over your head when it rains?', respondents in Maine, Rhode Island, New Jersey, New York State and sundry other places well east of the Mississippi river answered 'bumbershoot', or in some cases 'bumpershoot', 'bumptershoot', 'bumbleshoot', 'brumbershoot' and 'blundershoot' – a jocular blend, it seems, of 'bumbrella' and 'parachute'. Now it happens that far, far west of the Mississippi, on the north-west coast of America, in the city of Seattle, the word 'bumbershoot' joyously and exclusively denotes a yearly festival or hootenanny, balloon-bedecked and ballyhooed, of culture, cookery and clowning. When I was there some years ago, correspondence in the local newspaper indicated that Seattlers were uncertain about the origin of the word 'bumbershoot' but there was some support for the notion that it was a British word. I have since done enough ferreting to be fairly certain that it never was a British English word. It is a Yankee word, in the strict sense of Yankee; but Maine and Rhode Island are a long way from Seattle – so far, perhaps, that they might as well be British. What we see here is a word migrating to a new context and a new usage within the continental United States, echoing that earlier process by which English words made the Atlantic migration to fresh existences in the New World. Anyone who tries to read the American lexicon not for casual amusement but with the eye and intention of an interpreter must notice how, repeatedly, the words will cluster to a theme. The theme is the drift westward, the migration into possibility, the yellow brick road that has led at last to Sam Goldwyn and Satchmo and the Surfers and Superman and Silicon Valley and the Space Age.

If I had a hundred examples, I suppose they could do no more than glance at the prodigal diversity, the vigorous creativeness of which the Americans themselves are consciously proud. That pride is not untouched by anxiety about the current state of the language. The authoritarian concern that generally afflicts middle-class Americans when they feel their language is at risk was seen in the 1960s when Webster III – the third edition of *Webster's New International Dictionary*, a reference book of almost scriptural status – was widely denounced, outside academic circles, for its concessions to permissiveness in grammar and usage. Since then, American linguistic defensiveness has discerned another kind of threat in the expansion of the Hispanic population, particularly in the southern and western states. This has led to sometimes heated debate on the subject of bilingualism in schools; and the debate on bilingualism extends to even more anxious argument on the subject of bidialectalism, particularly with regard to the English spoken by inner-city blacks, and the social and educational problems presented by divided usage in a seemingly divided urban society. But still we are talking of what H.L. Mencken uncompromisingly called The American Language, a language which, perhaps to the occasional annoyance of the quiet Canadians, speaks its confidences at large and out loud. The common perception was put to me at the time of the Iranian hostage crisis by a gentleman in Florida, who told me 'we got this great language, and that's why we're so good'. Not far down the highway, a huge signboard exhorted the passing motorist to NUKE THE AYATOLLAH.

The link between language and self-esteem can be explored in the usage of another kind of pioneer, the kind who some two hundred years ago made the first European settlements in Australia. Some people, of course, quit these islands for southern latitudes whether they wanted to or not. Others arrived in the country as legitimate immigrants. In colonial rhyming slang, 'immigrant' is 'jimmygrant'; and with a bit of journalistic jingling, 'jimmygrant' turns to 'pommygrant', spelt 'pomegranate' – whence 'pommy' and 'pom'. (Mere word-play – no reference to blushing complexions.) 'Pommy' dates from 1913. Nearly a century earlier, in the 1820s, vernacular Australians – meaning, by and large, the descendants of the convict settlers – called themselves 'currency', after the paper money printed in the colony; new arrivals from Britain were called 'sterling'. These usages evidently implied no comparisons of value; in fact, the expressions 'currency lad' and 'currency lass' became popular and entered into common usage and sentimental balladry. It sounds confident enough, if a little self-conscious, and indeed one might hesitate to attribute want of confidence to a country that has accommodated Captain Bligh and Dennis Lillee.[13] On these matters, however, we may learn much from *The Australian National Dictionary*, which is edited by Dr W.S. Ramson. In a preliminary account of his labours, Dr Ramson draws attention to some characteristic, even diagnostic, Australian usages.[14] The word 'colonial', for example, is an oddly two-faced item. Dr Ramson quotes a passage from a novel in which a character who is obliged to admit that he has heard of Marcel Proust exclaims, 'For Christ's sake, I may be a colonial but I'm not a bloody moron!'. This suggests the internal conflict of one who might like it to appear that he cares little enough for the name and fame of Marcel Proust, but who is at the same time oppressed by the shouldering shadow of Europe with its literature and art. The dilemma produces a state of mind for which the Australians themselves have coined the phrase 'culture cringe'.

If 'colonial' is one diagnostic word in the Australian lexicon, another, and a very important one, is 'mate', and the conceptual term 'mateship'. The ethos of 'mateship' is discussed at some length in Lawrence's novel, *Kangaroo*. It was the sort of thing that appealed to him, embodying, no doubt, the dark mystery of maleness. However, Dr Ramson, who knows what he is talking about, explains that '*mateship* is never really the bond between equal partners, as implied in a primary sense of *mate*, but an ideal'. He also quotes from the *Sydney Bulletin*: 'When they call you mate in the N.S.W. Labor Party, it is like getting a kiss from the Mafia.' Ramson is critically alert, it seems, to the inherent sentimentality of 'mate', and to the increasing tendency among Australians to make ironic fun of this revered notion. Nevertheless, Australian 'mate' expresses something different from 'friend' or 'buddy' – just as, for that matter, American 'mom' connotes something not wholly present in 'mummy' or in Northern English 'mam'. In the separate territories of English, the same word does not necessarily carry the same value.

Australian English implies a character that is by turns laconic, aggressive, idealistic, sentimental and often shrewdly and crudely humorous. Until quite recently, what the average Briton knew about it might have been conveniently summed up in the words 'sheila', 'cobber' and 'fair dinkum' – somewhat old-fashioned Australianisms, and all of them, incidentally, British in origin. But it is becoming much more familiar. I am struck by the extent to which Australian words have entered, in some cases re-entered British English, at least to the extent of being listed in our dictionaries. On my desk I have the *New Collins Concise Dictionary*. In it, I find the word 'ocker', and also the noun and verb 'chunder'. A 'chunder' is the same thing as a 'technicolor yawn' – a picturesque idiom not listed in the lexicon; it refers to what happens in the car-port when you have had too many tubes of the Amber Nectar. My dictionary lists 'shoot through' and also 'blow through', both meaning to depart precipitately: *abiit, erumpit, evadit, excessit* – 'he blew through'. I find 'bludge', meaning 'to scrounge' – but that again is a word of British origin – and a remarkable number of meanings for the colour word 'blue'. It can mean, it seems, a person with red hair. It can mean an argument or a fight; it can mean an error; in the form 'a bluey' it can denote, in an earlier sense, a swagman's bundle, and in a more recent meaning, a summons – I conjecture, from the colour of the paper. How current these various usages are I have no way of knowing. Collins may have included them in the dictionary to promote its sale in Australia; or perhaps to enable British viewers to follow the text of *Neighbours*;[15] but whatever the reason I find it of some significance that these words are included in a popular general-purpose dictionary, designed mainly for the British market and claiming to provide – I quote – 'a balanced, up-to-date survey of contemporary English'.

What the dictionary represents is a claim to centrality, fusion, integration; to the presentation of a world of English as a whole, one community of linguistic resources. By contrast, anyone setting out to observe the spreadd of English and its diversities of usage must have a sense of disintegration. It seems as though there is no longer one English language, but that there are several Englishes. There are national Englishes, like those I have been discussing, each informed by a distinctive culture. There are technical dialects, such as the language of airport controllers, the language of maritime pilotage, called 'Seaspeak', computer talk, space jargon.[16] In scientific and scholarly communications, English has become so important that our continental colleagues are obliged to become fluent at least in writing it, whatever their academic subjects might be. Then we must consider that English is the first language of travel and tourism; and also claims a prominent place in entertainment and pop culture, as the Eurovision Song Contest annually reminds us. Look, too, at how English leaves its fashionable contaminations in other languages everywhere. It is no longer restricted to a few Anglicisms like 'pudding' in French, or 'baby' in Swedish; even distant, stiffly-syllabled Japanese is smartly sprinkled with chic English loan-words like 'birudingu' (building), 'hoteru', (hotel), 'baipasu' (bypass), 'aisukurimu' (ice cream), 'baku-miraa' (rear-view mirror), and, amazingly, 'man-shon' (condominium). Our language is everywhere in the world – staring out of street signs, shouting from hoardings, winking in lights, honking from tannoys, and its omnipresence now is attributable not so much to the combined endeavours of the Merchant, the Educator and the Pioneer, as to the irresistible partnership of the Inventor and the Designer. Designer English is – hooray and alas – a reality. English goes with the new technology, with fashion, with business, with life in the fast lane.

But is it disintegrating? Has it presumed too far, and begun to die? This is a common anxiety and also a very old one. The seventeenth-century grammarian, Alexander Gil, at one time schoolmaster to young John Milton, was convinced that English was going to Hell in a handcart. Being precluded, for obvious reasons, from blaming the Yanks, the trade unions, the comprehensive schools or the BBC, he blamed Geoffrey Chaucer, then comfortably in his grave for more than two hundred years. Chaucer, it seems, had by his practice promoted the vicious habit of using French words – degenerate, hard-mouthed, altogether un-English vocables like 'justice', 'mercy', 'virtue', 'compassion'. You will find his grievance in the preface to his *Logonomania Anglicana*, and the spirit of it is quite familiar; if Disgusted of Tunbridge Wells were to write in scholastic Latin, he or she would sound exactly like Alexander Gil.[17] The denunciatory attitude, the implications of corruption from without and treachery from within recur in later ages, when, however, the role of villain is frequently taken over by the Americans. Thus the Fowlers, in their classic text *The King's English*, having warned all Englishmen that 'a very firm stand ought to be made against *placate, transpire,* and *antagonize*', proceed to level a charge at another treacherous author, the last writer one would expect to find in the dock:

> There is a real danger of our literature's being americanized, and that not merely in details of vocabulary, but in its general tone. Mr Rudyard Kipling is a very great writer, and a patriotic; his influence is probably the strongest that there is at present in the land; but he and his school are americanizing us. His style exhibits a sort of remorseless and scientific efficiency in the choice of epithets and other words that suggests the application of coloured photography to description; the camera is superseding the human hand.[18]

Mr Kipling evidently makes an *exceedingly* good Kodak.[19] This is at least an original objection to American English. Usually it is denounced for its wordiness; here it is stigmatized as *efficient*. How ill-bred of the Americans, the Fowlers seem to be saying, how mechanical and vulgar of them to get at our mother-tongue and start using it *efficiently*.

Well, but whose language is it, anyway? Whose tongue are we talking about? The Fowlers clearly thought – and my Miss Kirby would have agreed with them – that English was theirs by birthright, and used by other people at best on terms of government licence. It is no longer possible to think like that. Here in the last quarter of the twentieth century we must at length acknowledge the claims of other people on the English language, claims as proud and defensive as our own, claims to linguistic autonomy. The conventional wisdom allows two courts of authoritative appeal, British English and American English, but a world-wide tendency working within the conventional wisdom points towards the future establishment of local centres of authority: Nigerian English, Indian English, Jamaican English, and so on, each with its own standard of practice.[20] 'Friday's child', it has been truly said, 'has far to go'. That prospect even brings into question the validity of a good old phrase, 'the mother tongue'; for we may ask not only, 'whose tongue are we talking about?', but also 'whose mothers are we talking about?'. One of the most accomplished novelists writing in English today is Anita Desai, child of a Bengali father and a German mother. English is her elected language, perhaps, but not her mother tongue. To take a homelier example, English is not the mother tongue of that highly successful businessman Robert Maxwell, although Mr Maxwell might be described as a major shareholder in English Language Incorporated.[21] English is now used as a preferred language by all sorts of people whose mothers crooned exotic lullabies. We have to accept that this language is ours, but not ours alone; that if it is a resource, it is not a resource controlled by a donor, used on the donor's conditions, to the donor's liking. Things may happen in English without the consent of true Britons, or efficient Americans either, for that matter.

Obsessive fear for the fate of the language is in part the fear of change, which is always interpreted – sometimes quite voluptuously – as change for the worse. It is also in part a troubled sense that diversity is dangerous and variety potentially vicious - a perception apparent in the centuries-old folk-etymology that readily associates 'babble' with 'Babel', or profusion with confusion. I first began to teach nearly forty years ago, at a time when not very many people were fully conscious of, or prepared to accept, the decline of Britain as a world power. In those days, the only variety of English taken at all seriously by most of our academic scholars was the standard, principally the literary standard, of metropolitan England and its institutions. The study of the English language meant, in the main, the study of how that standard had come into being; and from textbooks and lecturers the student gained the impression that it had pretty well come into being by the eighteenth century. The rest was epilogue, or qualified for merely peripheral comment.

That attitudes have now greatly changed, has been due more than a little to the acceptance that Britain's power in the world has indeed declined, and a corresponding realization that the English language is a stable economic asset, one of the few remaining to us. This has begotten the major industry of teaching English to foreigners, and has transformed a once reclusive, leather-patched tribe of philologists into smart-suited British Council salesmen, ready at the ring of a phone to go jetting down to Rio with a well-tried lecture on conversational functions of the modal auxiliaries, or devices of textual cohesion in tourist brochures. Variety has become more than the spice of life; it is our daily bread, the very staff of life. The study and teaching of English as a diversity of resources has taken impulse from the growth of other studies; from linguistics, obviously, but also from sociology, social anthropology, communication theory and computer science. As a result of this impetus, the British, who in my youth had the continental reputation of ignorantly neglecting their own language along with nearly everyone else's are actually held in high international regard among Anglists. We have some eminence in a number of fields: in textology, in discourse analysis, in the study of language varieties, as well as in the traditional disciplines of lexicography and grammar. Lexicography is a field in which we are learning, or re-learning, to excel. Not only are more and more good dictionaries being published – both for general and special purposes – but the art and methods of the lexicographer are currently being transformed by the technology of the computer. As for grammar, I will only mention, as the signal event of this decade, the publication, in 1985, of *A Comprehensive Grammar of the English Language*, a monumental work, the crowning achievement of Sir Randolph Quirk and those associated with him in the Survey of English Usage based at University College London. This great grammar both examines and munificently displays the resources of the English language.[22]

I have been keeping this word 'resource' before you, in tactful repetitions, and dutifully, as one doing his homework or fulfilling a promise. I will now confess that the phrase 'a global resource' is none of my making, but I suppose, a typical piece of current occupational jargon. I am happy to think that the English language is a global resource, but you may have divined, as a kind of sub-text of my address, that I am not absolutely sure how the word 'resource' is to be understood. Are we talking of a natural resource, like a forest or a coalfield; of an artifical resource, like machinery or furniture; or a spiritual resource, like imagination, or humour or music? Language presents analogies with all of these. As a basic property of the human being, it is a natural resource. In its adaptation to specific functions, whatever they may be, of keeping records, pleading cases, devising instructions and so forth, it is an artificial resource. And it is a spiritual, or, if you will, a heuristic resource, fortifying heart and soul, not only when it enters into the forms of poetry and great literature, but also when any of us, by the blessing of the moment, find words for the elusive thought, the ephemeral feeling, and in doing so experience that strange, stock-still euphoria, a spellbound hilarity, which is the symptom of discovery, of recognition, of knowledge, of self-appeasement. It is clearly the business of a teacher of English to examine language as a natural resource, and as far as possible to promote the artifice of language by studying and demonstrating its varied functions. We try by all means to be of use in the world, and to accept, as worthy and honourable, routine tasks of the kind that intellectual pride easily disdains. Yet I would be betraying my own temperament and, I think, the duties of my office if I did not put before everything else the spirituality of language as a personal resource, and if I did not hope by teaching or example or sheer luck to share that resource with others. For on that personal conviction everything depends. Without it there is no true understanding of language; without it there is no true attainment of skill in language; without it, indeed, there is no contribution to a real 'global resource', there is only a vulgar, slick species of merchandising. Forgive me if I am a little solemn; it is quite unlike me; but in a lecture like this a pinch of *gravitas* may perhaps help to bring out the flavour.

At the beginning of my lecture I flouted convention, and, indeed, academic etiquette; since it is usual on these occasions for the new professor to pay historical tribute to previous occupants of his chair. My chair, however, has no previous occupant, for although Nottingham has had, in the person of Kenneth Cameron, a distinguished Professor of English Language, I am the University's first Professor of Modern English Language. Naturally, I hope to justify the University's confidence in me as a promising old man, but I have no historical tradition to appeal to; for which reason I began by invoking dear Miss Kirby. It is arguable, after all, that for every hopeful lad and lass the first and most influential Professor of Modern English is the class teacher in the primary school. If Miss Kirby were here now – and perhaps she is mistily present – I should like to say to her a few words in valediction. I should like to tell her, please miss, one of your boys has become a professor. And you, Miss Kirby, would reply, 'Well, it took him long enough, such a daydreamer, always crossing his pen-nib and spattering ink on his shirt'. For which, miss, I suffered often and grievously. But I bear you no grudge, because I owe you much; not for your draconic disciplines or the penitential thoroughness of your teaching, but rather for something you offered as a concession to your own weakness as well as ours – your Friday afternoon readings from Stevenson and Kipling. Then, indeed, you showed us a meridian beyond the brewery and the slaughterhouse; then you let us glimpse the art of language to beguile and console and cajole and with its beauty and sudden merriment catch at the indrawn breath. The one thing you did in relaxation from your ferocious curriculum was your most valuable act as a teacher. There is a lesson in that somewhere. But all this was once upon a very long time, Miss Kirby. Time passes, indeed it does, and there is much left to do. So, dear ghost, let us close the old atlas; and take out our pens and best jotters; and wipe our noses; and get to work.

The text of my Inaugural Lecture as Professor of Modern English Language, given at the University of Nottingham, November 1988.

Appendix A

3: THE DIFFICULTY OF EXPLAINING

Abbreviations

Chambers Concise 20th Century Dictionary   Cham
The New Collins Concise Dictionary of the English Language   Coll
The New Penguin English Dictionary   NewPen
The Longman Dictionary of Contemporary English   Longman
Webster's New World Dictionary, 2nd College Edition   Webster
Collins COBUILD English Language Dictionary   COBUILD
Reader's Digest Universal Dictionary   Univ
The Shorter Oxford English Dictionary   SOX

RAIN CHECK

Cham

– *U.S.* a ticket for future use given to spectators when a game or a sports meeting is cancelled or stopped because of bad weather. (*take a raincheck (on)*) (*coll.* orig. *U.S.*) to promise to accept an invitation at a later date.

Coll

– *n U.S.* **1** a ticket stub for a baseball game that allows readmission on a future date if the event is cancelled because of rain. **2** *take a raincheck* to accept or request the postponement of an offer.

NewPen

NO ENTRY

Longman

n. informal esp. *AmE* an act of not accepting something when it is offered with the condition that one may claim it later: *I don't want a cigar now, thank you, but I'll take a rain check on it.*

Webster

1. The stub of a ticket to a ball game or other outdoor event, entitling the holder to be admitted at a future date if the event is rained out. **2.** an offer to renew or defer an unaccepted invitation.

COBUILD

If you say that you will *take a rain check* on an offer or a suggestion, you mean that you do not want to accept it straight away, but you might accept it later: an informal expression, used mainly in American English.

Univ

n. U.S. A ticket stub for an outdoor sports event entitling the holder to admission at a future date if the original event is rained off. – *take a rain check* To postpone acceptance of an offer on the understanding that the offer may be taken up later.

SOX

[In the *Addenda*]
rain-check (or **-cheque**) *orig. U.S.* a ticket given to spectators at a baseball match providing for admission at a later date if the game is interrupted by rain; also *transf.* and *fig.*

ARCH (adj)

Cham

adj cunning, waggish, roguish, shrewd. [OE *aerce- erce-* through L from Gr *archi- archos*, chief]

Coll

adj. [1 'chief' etc] 2 knowing or superior; coyly playful; *an arch look* [cl6 independent use of ARCH-] . . . [ult. < Gk *arkhi* < *arkhein* to rule]

NewPen

[1 prenominal arch-] 2a cleverly sly and alert b playfully saucy [ME *arche-, arch-* fr. OE *arce-* and OFr *arche*, &c]

Longman

adj. making fun of people in a clever or playful way: *an arch smile –* **ly**, *adv 'I know what you're thinking!' said the old lady archly.*

Webster

[1 prenominal] 2 clever, crafty 3 gaily mischievous, pert [an *arch* look] [Etym. as usual]

COBUILD

An **arch** look or expression is mischievous and cunning EG *She giggled and gave me an arch look* **archly** EG *She caught his eye and smiled archly.* A tone of voice that is **arch** suggests that you think you are more important or clever than anyone else EG *His tone of voice tends to be rather arch* [Marginally suggests synonymic relationship with 'superior', antonymic with 'humble']

Univ

[1 prenom.] 2 Mischievous, roguish: *an arch glance* [Etym. as usual]

SOX

a (sb) 1547 [The prefix ARCH- used independently as adj. [1 prenom] 2 [from association with *wag, knave*, etc. and hence with *fellow, face* etc.]. Clever, cunning, waggish. Now usu. of women and children: Slyly saucy, pleasantly mischievous 1662 [Etym. as usual]

FOLD IN

Cham

to mix in carefully and gradually (*cook*)

Coll

(*tr*) to mix (a whisked mixture) with other ingredients by gently turning one part over the other with a spoon.

NewPen

[sub **fold**]
to gently incorporate (a food ingredient) into a mixture without stirring or beating – usu. + *in*

Longman

phr.v. [T] **1** (**fold** sthg <----> **in**) to mix (something eatable) into a mixture that is to be cooked, by turning over gently with a spoon: *Fold in two eggs and then cook gently for thirty minutes* (also **fold into** as phr.vb)

Webster

Cooking to blend (an ingredient) into a mixture, using gentle, cutting strokes.

COBUILD

1 in cooking, when you **fold** a substance **into** another substance, or when you **fold** it **in**, you put the first substance into the second substance very gently and mix the two together EG *Fold the flour into the butter using a metal spoon* . . . *Beat the egg whites until stiff and* **fold** in 2 oz. sugar. [Grammatical notes marginally, + citation of *add* as superordinate term]

Univ

[sub **fold**, not cited as phr.vb]

In cooking, to mix in (an ingredient) by slowly and gently turning one part over the other.

SOX

NO REFERENCE TO THIS MEANING

[The *Longman Dictionary of Phrasal Verbs* has:
3. (in cooking) to add (materials) carefully to (other materials) usu. with a spoon . . . *Fold the beaten egg in(to) the flour*]

REGALE

Cham

v.t. to feast: to treat to (with *with*) [Fr. *régaler* – It. *regalare*, perh. *-gala* a piece of finery]

Coll

vb (*tr* usually followed by *with*) **1** to give delight or amusement to: *he regaled them with stories* **2** to provide with abundant food or drink – *n* **3 a** feast **b** a delicacy of food or drink. [Etym. as above]

NewPen

1 to entertain sumptuously **2** to give pleasure or amusement to < *-d us with stories of her exploits* [Fr. *régaler* fr. MF, fr *régale*, feast, fr. *ré* + *gale*, pleasure, merrymaking – more at GALLANT]

Longman

v **regale** sbdy **with** sthg. *phr.v* [T] to entertain with: *He regaled us with stories of his youth.*

Webster

vt – **galed'** – **gal'ing** [Fr. regaler < the *n*] **1** To entertain by providing a splendid feast **2** To delight with something pleasing and amusing. – *vi* – to feast – *n* [Fr *régal*, earlier *régale* < *ré* (see RE-) + OFr *gale*, joy, pleasure (see GALLANT)

COBUILD

– **regales**, **regaling**, **regaled**. If you **regale** someone with stories, jokes, etc., you tell them a lot of stories or jokes, even if they do not want you to EG *I used to have a dentist who regaled me with extraordinary stories*. [Supplies marginal note on syntax]

Univ

v. – **galed**, – **galing**, – **gales** – *tr*. **1** To delight or entertain; give pleasure to; *regaled us with folk songs*. **2** To entertain sumptuously with food and drink; provide a feast for. – *intr*. To feast – see synonyms at **amuse**

SOX

v. 1656 [– Fr. *régaler* fr. *ré*- RE + OFr *gale*, pleasure, joy: see GALE sub2, GALLANT] **1** *trans*. To entertain or feast (a person etc) in a choice manner **b** Of things: To furnish (one) with a choice feast or refreshment 1721 **2** to gratify or delight (the mind) by some pleasing influence or occupation; to entertain (a person) in a highly agreeable manner 1671 **b** to affect with a pleasurable sensation 1703 **3** to gratify, please, delight, by a gift, deference, etc (*rare*) 1671 **4** *refl* To entertain or recreate (oneself) with food, drink, or amusement 1719 **5** *intr* to feast; const. *on, upon, with* 1678
[Citations follow]

ENTROPY

Cham

(phys) n. a measure of unavailable energy, energy still existing but lost for the purpose of doing work because it exists as the internal motion of molecules; a measure of the disorder of a system; a measure of heat content, regarded as increased in a reversible change by the ratio of heat taken into an absolute temperature. [Gr *en*, in. *tropē*, turning, intended to represent 'transformation content']

Coll

n. pl – *pies* **1a** thermodynamic quantity that changes in a reversible process by an amount equal to the heat absorbed or emitted divided by the thermodynamic temperature. It is measured in joules per kelvin. **2** lack of pattern or organisation, disorder. [c19 < EN + TROPE]

NewPen

n. **1** a measure of the unavailable energy in a closed thermodynamic system **2** a measure of the amount of information in a message that is based on the logarithm of the number of possible equivalent messages. **3** the degradation of the matter and energy in the universe to an ultimate state of inert uniformity. [G. *entropie* fr. Gk *en* + *tropein* to turn, change – more at TROPE]

Longman

n. [U] **1** a measure of the sameness between the temperature of something which heats and of something which is being heated: *Entropy increases as the heat becomes the same all through a system.* **2** the tendency of heat and other forms of ENERGY in the universe to spread out evenly and gradually disappear.

Webster

n [G. arbitrary use (by R.J.E. *Clausius* 1822–88, Ger. physicist) of Gr. *entropē*, a turning toward, as if < *en(ergie)*, ENERGY + Gr *tropē* a turning: see TROPE] **1** a thermodynamic measure of the amount of energy unavailable for useful work in a system undergoing change **2** a measure of the degree of disorder in a substance or a system: entropy always increases and available energy diminishes in a closed system, as the universe. **3** in information theory, a measure of the information content of a message evaluated as to its uncertainty.

COBUILD

is, in formal English, a state of disorder, confusion, and disorganization. [Indicates synonymy with 'chaos'; notes 'non-count' noun]

Univ

n. **1** A measure of the capacity of a system to undergo spontaneous change, thermodynamically specified by the relationship $dS + dQ/T$, where dS is an infinitesimal change in the measure for a system absorbing an infinitesimal quantity of heat dQ at thermodynamic temperature T. **2** The tendency of the energy in a closed system, including that of the universe itself, to become less available to do work with the passage of time. **3** a measure of the randomness, disorder, or chaos in a system specified in statistical mechanics by the relationship $S + k \ln P + c$, where S is the value of the measure for a system in a given state, P is the probability of occurrence of that state, k is the Boltzmann constant, and c is an arbitrary constant. [German *Entropie*: Greek *en*, in, + *tropē*, a turning, change]

SOX

1868 [— G. *entropie* (Clausius, 1865) f. Gr. έν EN + τροπή, transformation; see Y2] *Physics* The name given to one of the quantitative elements which determine the thermodynamic condition of a portion of matter.

[There follows a fairly long quotation from Clausius]

Appendix B

10: HISTORIC EVENT, CREATIVE EFFORT

Extracts from *The Times*, 9–23 April 1803, reporting the inquest on Colonel Robert Montgomery and the trial of Captain James Macnamara, RN.

Reporting the Coroner's Inquest (April 8; reported April 9)

Testimony of Lord Burgharsh

The first words he heard were uttered by Colonel M. who said, "Well Sir, and I will repeat what I have said, if your dog attacks mine, I will knock him down." To this Captain Macnamara replied, "Well, Sir, but I conceive the language you hold is arrogant, and not to be pardoned." Colonel M. said, "this is not a proper place to argue the matter; if you feel yourself injured, and wish for satisfaction, you know where to find me." Capt. M. replied "not for what has happened, but if you were to insult me, I would take notice of it as soon as any man." Colonel M. said "No, Sir, I wish to seek no quarrel, but I adhere to what I originally said, 'if your dog was to attack mine, I would knock him down.'" Capt. M again repeated, "it was arrogant language, and that he would as soon meet Col. M. as any other man." Col. M. again observed, "he desired no quarrel with him." Capt. M. then rode on, but shortly turned round, and repeated "that he would as soon fight as any man", at the same time shaking a stick at Col. Montgomery which he held in his hand.

Testimony of William Sloane (a friend of Col. Montgomery)

When Col. Montgomery's dog was attacked, Col. M. jumped off his horse to rescue him. Col. M called out to Capt. Macnamara to take off his dog. Capt. M. replied, "Have you the arrogance to say that I am to take away my dog." I heard the expression of arrogance made use of several times by Capt. M. Lord Burgharsh joined us at this time. Col. Montgomery expressed a disinclination to quarrel, but said "if Capt. Macnamara felt himself hurt, he knew where to find him." Both parties proceeded towards Piccadilly, Col. M. and his friends being a little before. I conceived the matter was ended.

Testimony of James Macnamara (nephew of the Captain)

I do not know the deceased. I was riding on horseback on Wednesday afternoon, about four o'clock, in company with Capt. Barry and Capt. Macnamara. Capt. M. and Col. Montgomery each had a Newfoundland dog following him, which on meeting each other began fighting. Colonel M. got off his horse in a great passion, and swore he would knock Capt. Macnamara's dog down. Capt. M called to him and said "You will please to recollect it is my dog." Col. M. said "I do not care if it is your dog, I will knock him down." He repeated this several times. Capt. Macnamara then said, "You shall knock me down first." Col. M. replied, "that shall be as it may happen", at the same time observing, "why don't you get on your horse and take away your dog?" Captain M. said, he was not accustomed to be spoken to in that way, to which Col. M. replied, that if he had offended him, he knew where to call upon him (the deceased had previously given his address). Captain Macnamara said, "I shall do that without asking for your permission."

Testimony of Stephen Sloane (brother to William)

Colonel M. looked round, and upon seeing his dog, which was quite a young Newfoundland one, engaged fighting with another of the same kind, but larger and stronger, he got off his horse to part them; Colonel M. observing at the same time that he would knock the other dog down if he flew upon his dog. Captain Macnamara then rode up, and said, if Colonel M. knocked his dog down he must knock him down also. I have forgotten what was exactly Colonel Montgomery's answer, but I think it was, that the Park was too public for the adjustment of a dispute. He then gave Capt. M. his name, not his card. Captain Macnamara, then, in a violent passion, told his name, and that he was in the Royal Navy. Capt. M. observed it was arrogant to desire him to call off his dog. Col. M. observed, Captain Macnamara could not suppose he intended any insult to him, either by what he had said or done; and he concluded by saying, that if Captain Macnamara's dog did again commit any violence, he would do what was in his power to defend his own dog.

Reporting the trial (April 22; reported April 23)

The Indictment

The Indictment stated, that he stood charged, on the Coroner's Inquisition, with having, on the 6th day of April, in the Parish of St Pancras, made an assault on Robert Montgomery; and that with a leaden bullet, shot from a certain pistol, he did kill and slay the said Robert Montgomery, by giving him a mortal wound, of which he died.

Testimony of Lord Burgharsh

I heard this expression – "Your dog attacked mine". I heard Captain Macnamara say – "Your desiring me to call off my dog was arrogance, and not such language as should be used to a Gentleman" or "by a Gentleman", I do not recollect which. Colonel Montgomery said "If you feel yourself injured, you know where to find me; do you feel yourself injured?" Capt. Macnamara answered "Not by what has already passed; but if you say any thing which is an affront, I will take it up as soon as any man in England."

Testimony of William Sloane

Colonel Montgomery turned round and separated the dogs. He then called out, "Whose dog is this". Capt. Macnamara answered, "It is my dog." The other then said "If you don't call your dog off, I will knock him down." Capt. M. replied – "Have you the arrogance to say you will knock my dog down?" Col. Montgomery said – "I certainly shall, if he falls on my dog again." . . . The Prisoner said "I am Captain Macnamara, of the Royal Navy." Col. Montgomery said – "It is not my intention to quarrel with you; but if your dog falls on mine, I will knock him down."

Testimony of Stephen Sloane

. . . I saw the dogs fighting; the Colonel's dog was underneath. He went and separated them, and said, "I will knock that dog down." Capt. Macnamara rode up and said "If you knock my dog down you must knock me down first." Col. Montgomery then made some observation. He said a public place like that was not proper for the adjustment of any dispute. "My name" said he, "is Col. Montgomery, and you know where to find me." The other replied, "My name is Capt. Macnamara of the Royal Navy". Col. Montgomery observed that if he conceived any offence he knew where to find him; the other said he did not find himself offended by what had passed; but that if Col. Montgomery did say anything which was intended to offend him, he would take it up as readily as any man.

Testimony of Charles Smith (not called at the Inquest)

The Col. separated the dogs, and said he would knock down that dog which attacked his. Captain Macnamara rode up and said – "if you do, you must take the consequences, or knock me down too." The Col. then said – "Why did you not call your dog off?" Capt. M. replied – "No: I did not chuse [*sic*] to do so; and I will not be dictated to by you or any other man." Col. Montgomery then got off his horse; and said – 'Well, Sir, if your dog fights mine, I repeat to you, that I will knock him down. You shall be very welcome to know where to find me. As a Gentleman you might have called your dog off." The Prisoner replied – "No, Sir, I did not choose to call off my dog, I chose to let them fight; and I tell you again, I will not be dictated to by you or any other man. I ought to know where to find you, for what you have already said."

From Captain Macnamara's speech in his own defence

The origin of the difference, as you see it in the evidence, was insignificant:– The heat of two persons, each defending an animal under his protection, was natural, and would not have led to any serious consequences. It was not the deceased's defending his own dog, or his threatening to destroy mine, that led to the fatal catastrophe: it was the defiance alone, which most unhappily accompanied what was said: words receive their interpretation from the avowed intention of the speaker. The offence was forced upon me by the declaration, that he invited me to be offended, and challenged me to vindicate the offence by calling upon him for satisfaction. "If you are offended with what has passed, you know where to find me."

From the summing-up by Mr Justice Heath

. . . the crime of manslaughter consists in slaying a man on sudden provocation; fortunately for the Prisoner – very fortunately for the Prisoner, we are not to examine the extent of that provocation; yet there was a very considerable time between the quarrel and the time of fighting a duel . . . it appears that the law is a stranger to those nice sentiments of honour.

Notes

1 Standards and stuff

1 The terms 'perfective' and 'progressive' are discussed in Randolph Quirk, Sidney Greenbaum, Geoffrey Leech and Jan Svartvik, *A Comprehensive Grammar of the English Language* (London: Longman, 1985) 4.17–40.

2 *The Shorter Oxford Dictionary*, 3rd edn (Oxford: Oxford University Press, 1972; repr. 1984).

3 In the early days of the Corporation, under the ordinance of Lord Reith, BBC radio announcers were indeed obliged to put on dinner jacket and black tie to read the evening news.

4 For a dramatic representation of the necessary distinction between pronunciation and other constituents of 'good' English, see the famous scene in Shaw's *Pygmalion*, Act II, in which Eliza Doolittle, the Cockney flower-girl, is taken to a tea-party, where she delivers a racy East-End discourse in impeccable West-End accents; after this, Professor Higgins, her mentor, begins to realize that there is more to language than phonetics, and more to usage than pronunciation.

5 A perhaps more immediate reason for the Fowlers to name their book *The King's English* was that the title echoed that of an earlier book on usage, *The Queen's English*, published in 1864 by Dean Alford.

6 H.W. and F.G. Fowler, *The King's English* (Oxford: Oxford University Press, 1906; repr. 1979) p. 76.

7 H.W. and F.G. Fowler, op. cit., pp. 58–9.

8 Lord Chesterfield, *Letters*, ed. Bonamy Dobree, 6 vols (London: Eyre & Spottiswoode, 1932) letter 123.

9 A slightly earlier instance of 'standard' in this socio-literary sense is Swift's ironic usage in the Introduction to his *Polite Conversations* (1737/8): 'the Discourse of the Company was all degenerated into the smart sayings of their own Invention, and not of the old true Standard.'

10 John Trevisa published in 1387 his translation of Ranulph Higden's *Polychronicon*. Higden's history of the universe ended at the year 1327. Further instalments, also in Latin, were supplied by others, until Trevisa came along with his English version, from which this quotation is taken. (The spelling is, of course, modernized.) Trevisa's work is published in the Rolls Series, 9 vols (London: 1865–86).

11 H.C. Wyld, *A History of Modern Colloquial English* (Oxford: Oxford

University Press, 1936) p. 18.

12 See A.C. Baugh, *A History of the English Language*, 2nd edn, revised (London: Routledge & Kegan Paul, 1957) p. 309. In the dedication to his *Troilus and Cressida*, Dryden complains, 'how barbarously we yet write and speak, your Lordship knows, and I am sufficiently sensible in my own English. For I am often put to a stand, in considering whether what I write be the idiom of the tongue, or false grammar'.

13 Examples of formal remnants of case in English are the genitive singular inflection of the noun – e.g. 'king'/'king's', and the variations of 'subject' and 'object' pronouns, e.g. 'who'/'whom'. Such instances apart, English has lost 'case' as a morphological category. The semantic notion of 'case', however, remains, as something lurking under the surface of discourse. This has led some linguists to propose a 'case grammar', mapping semantic role-relationships – the 'who-does-what-with-which-to-whom'. See, for example, J.M. Anderson, *The Grammar of Case. Towards a Localistic Theory* (London: Cambridge University Press, 1971).

14 H.W. and F.G. Fowler, op. cit., p. 128.

15 Otto Jespersen, *On Some Disputed Points in English Grammar*, SPE Tract 25 (Oxford: Clarendon Press, 1926).

16 H.W. Fowler, *On -Ing: Professor Jespersen and 'the instinctive grammatical moraliser'*, SPE Tract 26 (Oxford: Clarendon Press, 1927) p. 193. Revisions in the 1931 edition of *The King's English* (included in subsequent reprints) enabled Fowler to accommodate Jespersen's criticisms while staunchly reaffirming his own preference. 'It is not a matter to be decided by appeal to historical grammar', he declared – thereby discounting Jespersen's principal resource. 'All these constructions (i.e. gerund, participle, 'fused participle') may have separate legitimate descent, yet in the interest of clear thought and expression it may be better for one of them to be abandoned.' Yet Fowler never quite succeeds, other than by intimidatory assertion, in showing that constructions such as 'We were uneasy about him going' and 'If you will pardon me saying so' are threats to 'clear thought and expression'. He finds the fused participle 'ugly', and that, for him, is probably the heart of the matter; but aesthetic objections should not be disguised as pleas for clarity or logic. It is an uncomfortable and thankless business to criticize a man who made such large and invaluable contributions to the study of English usage, but the fact is that in this instance we find him clinging, somewhat disingenuously, to an untenable position.

17 For Johnson on 'make money', see James Boswell, *Life of Johnson*, ed. R.W. Chapman, The World's Classics (Oxford: 1953), 23 September 1777: 'Don't you see (said he) the impropriety of it? To *make* money is to coin it; you should say *get* money.' To which Boswell wisely adds, 'The phrase, however, is, I think, pretty current'. Lady Holland's dislike of 'gentlemanly' is reported by Lord Macaulay (see Sir G.O. Trevelyan, *Life and Letters of Lord Macaulay* (1876)). Dean Alford (in *The Queen's English* (1864) quotes Coleridge on 'monied': 'I imagine other participles being formed by this analogy, and men being said to be pennied, shillinged, or pounded.' On 'amoral', etc., see H.W. and F.G. Fowler, op. cit.

18 Swift had a particular detestation of 'mob' (or 'Mobb', in his spelling),
    which he attacked on more than one occasion; for instance, in the
    Introduction to his *Polite Conversation*, where he ironically affects
    admiration for

> some Abbreviations exquisitely refined; as, *Pozz* for *Positive*, *Mobb*
> for *Mobile*; *Phizz* for *Physiognomy*; *Rep* for *Reputation*; *Plenipo* for
> *Plenipotentiary*; *Incog* for *Incognito*; *Hypps*, or *Hippo*, for *Hypochon-*
> *driacks*; *Bam* for *Bamboozle*; and *Bamboozle* for *God knows what*;
> whereby much time is saved, and the high Road to Conversation cut
> short by many a Mile.

Forty years on, George Campbell comments, in his *Philosophy of
Rhetoric*, on the fate of such abbreviations:

> I scarcely know any that have established themselves, save *mob* for
> *mobile*. And this it hath effected at last, notwithstanding the unrelenting
> zeal with which it was persecuted by Dean Swift, wherever he met with
> it. But as the word in question hath gotten use, the supreme arbitress
> of language, on its side, there would be as much obstinacy in rejecting
> it at present, as there was perhaps folly at first in ushering it upon the
> public stage.
>
> (Campbell, *Philosophy of Rhetoric* (1776) vol. 1, pp. 428–9)

19 The construction of 'convince' with an infinitive clause is noted in the
    3rd edition of Ernest Gowers's *The Complete Plain Words* ed. Sidney
    Greenbaum and Janet Whitcut (London: HMSO, 1986) where the reader
    is advised, 'Do not use *convince* like *persuade*. You may convince people
    of a fact, or convince them that you are right, but you cannot correctly
    convince them to do something.' In their *Longman Guide to English
    Usage* (London: Longman, 1989) Greenbaum and Whitcut say: 'Careful
    writers avoid the use of **convince** with an infinitive verb to mean "persuade
    into a course of action", as in *He convinced them to leave the country*.' The
    expressions 'you cannot *correctly*' and '*careful* writers avoid' indicate the
    stance of consultative authority commenting on a deviant practice. The
    same editors (in *Plain Words* and in the *Longman Guide*) dismiss as
    categorically wrong the use of 'refute' in the sense of 'deny', 'repudiate',
    'contradict'. As far as I am aware, the 'aberrant' usages of 'convince' and
    'refute' were current before 1986, but it takes time for these things to get
    into the textbooks. 'Cohort' and 'compatriot' (together with 'ex-patriot')
    still await the glossarists' notice.

20 'Hopefully': these and other strictures on 'this bastard adverb' are cited
    in William and Mary Morris, *Harper Dictionary of Contemporary Usage*
    (New York: Harper, 1975) pp. 311–12.

21 For a discussion of disjuncts in general, and 'content disjuncts' in
    particular, see Randolph Quirk *et al.*, op. cit., 8.121–33.

22 The second edition of Gowers's *The Complete Plain Words* ed. Sir Bruce
    Fraser (London: HMSO, 1973; repr. 1977) notes, under the entry on
    'hopefully': '*Regretfully* is already sometimes used to mean *I regret to
    say*. But this is rather perverse, because *regrettably* is already available
    for this meaning.'

2 Usage, users and the used

1 Anatomy and medical science generally provide many examples of technical terms with a figurative basis, though usually the metaphor is no longer perceived as 'live': eg. 'duodenum', 'thyroid', 'cortex', 'ventricle'.

2 H.W. Fowler, *Modern English Usage* 2nd edn, revised by Sir Ernest Gowers (Oxford: Oxford University Press, 1968).

3 Morphemes are units of linguistic form, meaningful in themselves, as words or as particles smaller than words. A word consists of one or more morphemes. 'Pack', for example, is a word consisting of one morpheme. 'Pre-pack' has two morphemes, 'pack' itself, and the prefix 'pre', with the meaning 'previously', 'beforehand'. 'Prepacked' has three morphemes, 'pre', 'pack', and the suffix-*ed*, signifying 'past time' or 'completed event'. Prefixes and suffixes – so-called 'bound morphemes', because they never stand alone as words – contribute a great deal to what is here called the 'abstractedness' of language.

4 Between 1541 and the date of the first performance of *King Lear* (c. 1606) is an interval of some sixty-five years – long enough, it might seem to modern observers, for a word to have got into common circulation; but the modern observer has the advantage of modern communications – radio, film, television, newspapers, etc. – which put words into circulation with great rapidity and soon exhaust the appeal of their freshness or strangeness. By the time a word gets into our dictionaries it is no longer 'new' – and that may happen in five years or less. In Shakespeare's day a word could still be perceived as 'new' fifty years after its entry into the language.

5 See, for example, Randolph Quirk *et al.*, *A Comprehensive Grammar of the English Language* (London: Longman, 1985) Appendix I.57–70.

6 *Daily Telegraph* (2 May 1985).

7 After the lecture some members of the audience suggested the 'treading water' reading of 'nimble footwork'. I feel obliged to record their response, but do not agree with it – hence my parenthetical comment.

8 At the time of the lecture the President of the USA was Mr Reagan – a man eminently capable of discovering the 'ship of state' metaphor; but I would expect no less of his successor, Mr Bush.

9 In reference to the fact that when a dinghy is hard-driven under sail there is often enough water in the boat to make it hard for helmsman and crew to keep their feet dry. Since this lecture was given, the meaning of 'syndrome' has become even wider and vaguer, denoting not merely an 'unfortunate characteristic', but virtually *any* characteristic or behavioural idiosyncrasy – e.g. 'the early-to-bed syndrome', 'the keep Britain tidy syndrome'. At this stage of dilution, 'syndrome' signifies nothing more specific than 'frame of mind' or 'way of doing things'.

10 *Daily Telegraph* (14 November 1985).

11 The 'Cyprus spy trial' in 1985 concerned a group of RAF servicemen, stationed on the island of Cyprus, who had been stealing and selling secret documents.

12 *The Times* (7 November 1985).

13 ibid.

14 ibid., (14 November 1985).

15 *Daily Telegraph* (20 November 1985).

3 The difficulty of explaining: a word or two about dictionaries

1 Hyponyms: hyponyms are groups of words associated under a super-ordinate concept, or 'hyperonym'. Thus the hyperonym 'furniture' includes among its hyponyms 'table', 'chair', 'bed', 'couch', 'cupboard', etc.

2 This, for my Greek audience, was of course an unnecessary explanation; the example was kept from the original talk.

3 The dictionary I had immediately in mind was the *Reader's Digest Universal Dictionary*. I find, however, that other dictionaries also cite this etymology, some quoting the French *couleur de puce*, 'flea coloured'. I have yet to meet anyone who could accurately assess the colour of a flea; it would seem in any case too minute a sample to be of use in describing fairly large areas of colour, e.g. in fabrics.

4 'Take aback' is a nautical term; a vessel is said to be 'taken aback' if, in sailing to windward, it is made to head directly into the wind, and so comes to an abrupt standstill, because the wind now blows against the sails from in front, instead of filling them.

5 'Feedback', in mechanics and electronics, means the conversion of output – e.g. of sound – into input, so that energy is recycled. (In public address systems a powerful feedback, resulting from the proximity of the microphone to the loudspeakers, can produce alarming squeals and yawps.) 'Forlorn hope' is the anglicized form of the Dutch *verloren hoop*, the 'lost troop', this being the vanguard company, or 'storm troop', put out ahead of the main battle line. The expression was taken into English military usage in the sixteenth century.

6 For a full text of the extracts taken from various dictionaries, see Appendix A.

7 The most recent (1989) edition of the *Oxford English Dictionary* cites two spellings, 'rain check' and 'rain cheque', and for the latter quotes a sentence from Raymond Chandler's *The Big Sleep* – without noting, however, that Chandler's usage is humorous and parodic, mocking the social pretensions of an affluent and snobbish family.

8 It was almost unbelievably rash of me to mock the notion that 'entropy' might signify delapidation or mere untidiness of a domestic sort. It is used in just that sense by John Updike (an irreproachable stylist) in *The Witches of Eastwick* (Harmondsworth: Penguin, 1985, p. 216): 'The women returned hellos, and in the Armenians' hardware store tried, like everybody else, to describe with finger sketches in the air, the particular thingummy needed to repair a decaying home, to combat entropy.'

4 Our true intent: or, what's the point of punctuation?

1 Some account of restrictive and non-restrictive clauses should be found in any good grammar of English; see in particular Randolph Quirk *et al.*, *A Comprehensive Grammar of the English Language* (London: Longman, 1985) 17.3–4.

2 William Wordsworth, *The Prelude, A Parallel Text*, ed. J.C. Maxwell (Harmondsworth: Penguin, 1971). For the passages cited, see pp. 320,

321 and Maxwell's editorial comment on p. 25.

3 As a matter of incidental interest, the word 'point' is also used by Tudor musicians to denote a short theme – a musical sentence. The history of punctuation is in fact somewhat complicated by its relationship, in the Middle Ages, with the development of musical notation, and in particular in the 'pointing' of the text for the benefit of singers. Our exclamation and question marks originated in the need to mark vocal inflections. Texts for singing could be further 'pointed' by means of a mark called the *virgule* (a 'little rod', represented thus: /), which indicated a light pause. This mark can be found in early printed books, but later gave place to the comma, which thus acquired the joint value of a syntactic marker and a pause marker. See note 8 below.

4 The translation here quoted is that of H. Caplan, in the Loeb Classical Library edition (London: Loeb Classical Library, 1954).

5 Demetrius, *On Style,* ed. and trans. W. Rhys Roberts (London: Loeb Classical Library, 1927; repr. 1965) p. 303n.

6 Aristotle, *The 'Art' of Rhetoric,* trans. J.H. Freese (London: Loeb Classical Library, 1926; repr. 1947) p. 375.

7 George Puttenham, *The Arte of English Poesie* (1589), ed. Gladys D. Willcock and Alice Walker (Cambridge: Cambridge University Press, 1936) p. 76.

8 Seventeenth-century directions for the use of the comma and the semi-colon draw attention to the 'delivery style'. Ben Jonson *(English Grammar,* 1636) observes that 'A semi-colon is a distinction of an imperfect sentence wherein with somewhat a longer breath, the sentence following is included'. Thomas Hodges's *English Primrose* (1644) recommends 'At a comma, stop a little . . . at a semi-colon, somewhat more'. Remarks of this kind suggest that probably by the end of the sixteenth century the semi-colon (in conjunction with the colon and the comma) had already acquired a dual value: a) in connection with the articulation of the argument – the 'syntactic analysis'; and b) in connection with the recital of the text – the 'delivery style'. The evidence generally suggests that while colon and comma have a long tradition as articulators which subsequently developed the auxiliary role of pause-markers, the semi-colon originated as a pause-marker to which some articulatory significance could then be attributed.

9 The suggested emendations of Capell and Knight are recorded in the notes to H.W. Furness's edition of the play, in *A New Variorum Edition of Shakespeare* (London: 1895).

10 Harold F. Brooks, ed., *A Midsummer Night's Dream,* The Arden Shakespeare (London: Routledge, 1988) Appendix IV.

11 In classical rhetoric, the *captatio benevolentiae,* 'capturing of good will' was the process of mollifying a prospective audience, whether by flattery or self-deprecation or the promise of good things to come. This is precisely what Quince is trying to do.

5 The possibilities of paraphrase

1 Quoted from 'The genie in the bottle', an essay by Richard Wilbur prefacing a selection of his poems in the collection *Mid-Century American Poets,* ed. John Ciardi (New York: Twayne Publishers Inc., 1950) p. 6.

2 'Competence' is a technical term in general linguistics, particularly in the 'generative' model associated with Noam Chomsky and his followers, who argue that human beings have a specific competence to create language and a cognitive power to analyse its operations. The notion of 'literary competence' is broadly analogous to this. It implies an innate control of the symbolic forms and procedures fundamental to the making of literature.

3 An acquaintance who was a schoolboy at Christ's Hospital during the 1940s has informed me that in those days the word 'crotty', in school slang, was a noun meaning a foolish or inept person. (The present-day equivalent would be, I suppose, 'wimp', or possibly 'nerd'.) His explanation, that the word derived from the name of a Mr Crotty, a clergyman, who had delivered to the boys a sermon of appalling banality, has the ring of folk-myth – eponymy raised on onomatopoiea, so to speak. But my telephone directory tells me that the name Crotty does indeed exist; and I am further informed, by Patrick Hanks and Flavia Hodges, in their *A Dictionary of Surnames* (Oxford: Oxford University Press, 1988) that the name is of Celtic origin and is 'a by-name for a hunchback'.

6 On parody: a discourse with interludes

1 This piece of nonsense began with someone telling me that while Rome was falling the grammarians of Toulouse were debating whether the pronoun *ego* could have a vocative case. I lack both the means and the energy to check this information, but I liked the idea of pedantry having its ruthless way even in the most appalling crisis. The 'poem', or 'recital' – whatever it is – is something of an insider joke. Outsiders may have to be told, for example, that Grice's Maxim of Quality is one of the collaborative principles of effective conversation propounded by the American linguist and philosopher H.P. Grice. The Maxim of Quality enjoins the conversationalist never wittingly to deceive a conversational partner, or to say anything untrue or for which there exists insufficient evidence. See H.P. Grice, 'Logic and conversation', in P. Cole and J. Morgan, eds, *Syntax and Semantics 3: Speech Acts* (New York: Academic Press, 1975).

2 George Formby Jr (I find I must explain) was an English comedian in the 'north country' tradition, who made his name and fame in films during the 1930s, always playing the role of the good-natured idiot whose cheerfulness and innocence carries him through to the happiness of winning the race, foiling the adversary, getting the girl, etc. Formby's trademarks were his grin – he had teeth like great white tiles – and his ukulele, to the accompaniment of which he would from time to time sing roguish ditties with titles like 'Limehouse Laundry Blues'. ('Oh, Mr Wu! He's got a naughty eye that flickers/You oughta see it flicker when, he's pressing – silk pyjamas.')

Formby's catch-phrase, 'Can you hear me, mother?' was for a time an indispensable element in the idiomatic repertoire of all witty lads and lasses. It was a thirties phrase – like the sneering cry of 'Mr Christian!' which characterized Charles Laughton's performance of Captain Bligh in the film of *Mutiny on the Bounty*, and Greta Garbo's 'I want to be alone'

– an utterance often ascribed to Garbo herself, but actually spoken in the course of one of her film roles.

3 This Hopkins parody has travelled a little. I first used it in a lecture to the Poetics and Linguistics Association, and later included it in my book *The Language of Humour* (London: Longman, 1985), where its echoes of Hopkinsian phrases are more fully discussed. (See pp. 82–5 of that work.)

4 For a D.H. Lawrence parody, see my 'Bert Lawrence Gets The Bug', in *The Language of Humour*, pp. 85–6.

5 Samples of Twain in parodic action against Fenimore Cooper can be found in Robert Paul Falk, ed., *The Antic Muse: American Writers in Parody* (New York: Grove, 1975).

6 See Aristotle, *Poetics*, trans W. Hamilton Fyfe (London: Loeb Classical Library; repr. 1965) pp. 99–101.

7 For some *Raven* parodies, see Falk, op. cit. Leacock had the brilliant idea of spoofing the Homeric ship-and-hero catalogue with a versified list of railway locomotives and their drivers. See his essay 'Homer and humbug', reprinted in *The Penguin Stephen Leacock* (Harmondsworth: Penguin, 1981) pp. 36–41. His *Oroastus, a Greek Tragedy* (ibid., pp. 226–40) is one of the funniest of classical spoofs.

8 Browning's poem begins:

> Where the quiet-coloured end of evening smiles
>   Miles on miles
> On the solitary pastures where our sheep
>   Half-asleep
> Tinkle homeward thro' the twilight, stray or stop
>   As they crop –
> Was the site once of a city great and gay
>   (So they say)

9 For 'letter and diagram', see my *The Language of Humour*, pp. 87–99.

10 See J.C. Squire, *Collected Parodies* (London: Hodder & Stoughton, n.d.); also *Apes and Peacocks: an Anthology of Parodies* (London: Jenkins, 1929).

7 The meanings of metadiscourse

1 A very full treatment of the topics and terminology of metadiscourse is Avon Crismore's *Talking with Readers* (New York: Twayne, 1990).

2 For these examples I am indebted to R.A. Carter, Paul Simpson, Willie van Peer, Christopher S. Butler, J. Lachlan Mackenzie and Mike Hannay.

3 Bertrand Russell's essay 'In praise of idleness' introduces the volume of the same name (London: George Allen & Unwin, 1935; repr. Unwin Paperbacks, 1976).

4 I have invented (or adapted to my particular purpose) all of the terms in my brief account of 'lexical metadiscourse', with the exception of 'hedge' and 'emphatic' – for which see Crismore, op. cit.

5 Passages from stories by Mary Renault, Conan Doyle and E.M. Forster are here quoted from *Treasury of Great Short Stories* (London: Octopus Books, 1984) pp. 39, 307, 495.

6 'Naming of Parts' (and also 'Judging of Distances') in Henry Reed, *A Map of Verona* (London: Jonathan Cape, 1946).

8 On writing well

1 *M. Manilii Astronomicon, Liber Primus*, ed. A.E. Housman (London: Grant Richards, 1903). Introduction, pp. xvii–xviii.
2 'Simply cannot' is perhaps an overstatement; there is in fact nothing to stop us from saying 'his wish for discovering truth', other than the consensus of usage, which persuades us that we 'simply cannot' say it.
3 *Praeterea multo magis, ut vulgo dicitur viva vox afficit: nam licet acriora sint, quae legas, altius tamen in animo sedent, quae pronuntiatio, vultus, gestus dicentis adfigit*. Pliny the Younger, *Epistolae* II, 3.
4 Evelyn Waugh, *Edmund Campion* (Oxford: Oxford University Press, 1980) pp. 104–5.

9 Composition and creativeness

1 On 'core' vocabulary and other interesting matters, see R.A. Carter, *Vocabulary* (London: Allen & Unwin, 1987).
2 The 'conference speaker' was in fact one of the participants in the Tilburg seminar; if memory serves me aright, it was Professor Mieke Bal, now of the University of Amsterdam, who was responsible for this ingenious lexico-syntactic invention.
3 For an example of such a grammar, see G. Leech and J. Svartvik, *A Communicative Grammar of English* (London: Longman, 1975).
4 'Synonym' and 'antonym' are presumably well known terms. A 'hyponym' is a member of a set of words denoting particular instances of a general type, or 'hyperonym'. Thus, 'tree' is the hyperonym, or superordinate term, in the set that includes the hyponyms 'oak', 'ash' and 'elm'. A 'holonym' is a word denoting the total concept, structure, etc., of which the components or associated ideas are 'meronyms'. 'Tree' stands as holonym to the meronyms 'root', 'trunk', 'branch'; in a somewhat looser way, 'winter' is a holonym with meronyms in 'frost', 'snow', 'darkness'.
5 Sapir's essay on 'The heuristic value of rhyme' is to be found in D.G. Mandelbaum, ed., *Selected Writings in Language, Culture and Personality* (Berkeley, CA: University of California Press, 1949).
6 The term 'key' has been used by Michael Halliday to denote attitudinal properties of intonation, or what is more popularly known as 'tone of voice'. What is suggested in the present context is that 'key' may be grammatical as well as intonational. See M.A.K. Halliday, *A Course in Spoken English: Intonation* (Oxford: Oxford University Press, 1970).
7 Bertrand Russell, 'The modern Midas', in *In Praise of Idleness* (London: Unwin Paperbacks, 1976; first published 1935).
8 This is the opening of my 'Speak like a native', a short story published in the literary journal *Stand*, 18, no. 1 (1976).

10 Historic event, creative effort: the making of a dramatic poem

1 In *The Times* of 8 April 1803, Colonel Montgomery is described as having been driving a curricle. In subsequent reports, both the principals are represented as being on horseback.

2 Byron composed these lines for a memorial tablet to be erected at Newstead, near the site of the altar in the ruined abbey. Visitors today may still see in the grounds a memorial to Bosun, furnished with a long and tedious inscription in verse, much inferior in literary quality to the brief and eloquent prose eulogy.

3 See Sheridan, *The Rivals*, Act V, Scene iii. The timid Bob Acres wants to fight his duel at a prudent forty yards, but Sir Lucius, having measured out five paces, declares 'There now, that is a pretty distance, a pretty gentleman's distance'.

4 From the report on the inquest, *The Times* (9 April 1803).

5 ibid.

6 *Halfway House. A Miscellany of New Poems* (London: Cobden-Sanderson, 1932) pp. 27–41.

7 For relevant extracts from the inquest proceedings and from the trial of Macnamara, see Appendix B.

8 On 'delivery instance', see Roman Jakobson in Thomas A. Sebeok, ed, *Style in Language* (Cambridge MA: MIT Press, 1960) pp. 364–5.

9 There were, it seems, various conventions for setting the distances from which duellists were to fire. 'Six paces' could refer to the actual distance between the antagonists, or it could mean that each man was to take six paces before turning to fire. Alternatively, the seconds could pace out the ground and place their men ready to take aim. In another form of duel, the opponents walked towards a rope barrier (or some other form of marker), firing at will; having discharged his shot, the duellist was obliged to continue walking towards the central mark until his enemy had also fired.

10 See the report on the trial in *The Times* (23 April 1803).

11 ibid.

12 The trial report (testimony of Charles Smith, *The Times*, 23 April 1803) explicitly assigns to Macnamara the words 'No Sir, I did not choose to call off my dog, I chose to let them fight; and I tell you again, I will not be dictated to by you or any other man'. This is the basis for words in the poem apparently assigned to Montgomery. The turns in the dialogue apparently run as follows:

> *Montgomery*: Whose dog is this?
> *Macnamara*: My dog.
> *Montgomery*: Then call your dog off, or by God he'll go sprawling.
> *Macnamara*: If my dog goes sprawling, you must knock me down after.
> *Montgomery*: Your name?
> *Macnamara*: Macnamara, and yours is –
> *Montgomery*: Montgomery.
> *Macnamara*: And why, sir, not call your dog off?
> *Montgomery*: Sir, I chose not to do so, no man has dictated to me yet, and you, I propose, will not change that.

13 From the trial report, *The Times* (23 April 1803).
14 M.A.K. Halliday, *A Course in Spoken English: Intonation*, (Oxford: University Press, 1970) pp. 1–3, describes the rhythm of spoken English in terms of the 'foot', containing one salient ('strong') syllable, to which one or more 'weak' syllables may be added. Of this basic unit, Halliday states that 'the time taken by each foot is more or less the same' – that is, the intervals between strong beats are approximately equal. The qualification 'more or less' should be noted; speech-rhythms are not metronomically determined.
15 Shakespeare, *Henry IV, Part I*, Act V, Scene i.

11 English: a global resource?

1 Estimates of the number of people at present using English as their native language or as a second language vary somewhat. I have taken my figures from Bernard Comrie, ed., *The World's Major Languages* (London: Croom Helm, 1988).
2 In fact, Crusoe uses 'man' in the much the same way that later imperialists, in Africa and the East, would use 'boy'.
3 On pidgins and creoles, see Loreto Todd, *Pidgins and Creoles* (London: Routledge & Kegan Paul, 1974); also her *Modern Englishes: pidgins and creoles* (Oxford: Blackwell, 1984).
4 Tok Pisin = 'talk pidgin'; in phonetic transcript, 'tɔk 'pɪʃɪn or 'tɔk 'pɪʒɪn. The letter *s* implies a sound like the *sh* in 'po*sh*', or possibly like the sound of French *g* in 'page'.
5 From *Nupela Testamen Long Tok Pisin* (Canberra: British and Foreign Bible Society, 1969).
6 Literally, 'Suppose you catch him bugger-up'.
7 Otto Jespersen, *Language, Its Nature, Development and Origin* (London: Allen & Unwin, 1922) chapter 12, 'Pidgin and Congeners'. Jespersen's general point is that a pidgin is not really a mixture of 'ordinary' languages, but a makeshift form (of English, French, etc.), destined to change and die out as the users' mastery of the cultural parent language increases.
8 Macaulay, *Minute on Indian Education*, 2 February 1835. (See *Macaulay, Prose and Poetry*, selected by G.M. Young (London: Rupert Hart-Davis, 1982) pp. 719–30.) With reference to his 'class of persons . . . English in taste', Macaulay adds:

> To that class we may leave it to refine the vernacular dialects of the country, to enrich those dialects with terms of science borrowed from Western nomenclature, and to render them by degrees fit vehicles for conveying knowledge for the great mass of the population.

9 Upanamayu Chatterjee, *English, August* (London: Faber & Faber, 1988) pp. 59–60
10 In my lecture I stated that the 'official' languages of India were fourteen, according to the provisions of the constitution. My pupil Mr Partha Misra corrected me afterwards, informing me that they are now sixteen.
11 From his *Letter to Pickering* (1817).

12 See Hans Kurath, *A Word Geography of the Eastern United States* (Ann Arbor: University of Michigan Press, 1949); and Frederick G. Cassidy, *Dictionary of American Regional English*, vol. 1 (Cambridge, MA: Harvard University Press, 1985).

13 William Bligh, infamous Captain of the *Bounty*, was not a native Australian, but as Governor of New South Wales may be said to have been 'accommodated' by the country – his commanding temperament certainly called for accommodation. Dennis Lillee – should anyone need to be told this – is the name of one of the world's great fast bowlers.

14 *The Australian National Dictionary* was awaiting publication when I wrote my lecture. My information on the history of Australian usages comes from Dr Ramson's paper '*The Australian National Dictionary*: a foretaste', in Robert Burchfield, ed., *Studies in Lexicography* (Oxford: Clarendon Press, 1987).

15 This may call for a gloss before very long. Therefore – *Neighbours*: an enormously popular TV serial, of the 'soap opera' sort, made in Australia and dealing with suburban life there.

16 For a description of Seaspeak, see Randolph Quirk, *Words at Work: Lectures on Textual Structure* (London: Longman, 1988).

17 Alexander Gil, *Logonomania Anglicana* (1621), ed. Jiriczek (Strasbourg, 1903).

18 H.W. and F.G. Fowler, *The King's English* (Oxford: Oxford University Press, 1906; repr. 1979) p. 34.

19 The allusion is to a slogan (now discarded) from a TV advertisement: 'Mr Kipling makes *exceedingly* good cakes.'

20 On this subject see, for example, B. Kachru, ed., *The Other Tongue: English Across Cultures* (Urbana: University of Illinois Press, 1982); also B. Kachru, *The Indianization of the English Language in India* (New Delhi and New York: Oxford University Press, 1983).

21 Some of my hearers appeared to be puzzled at this point; which obliges me to explain that Mr Maxwell – publisher, newspaper proprietor, chairman of football clubs, holder of the Military Cross, the bluff 'Captain Bob' of journalistic satire, an Englishman if ever there was one – was born and brought up in Czechoslovakia.

22 The *CGEL* is a 'corpus' grammar; that is, its descriptions are based on a body of actually occurring spoken or written material, the Survey of English Usage, housed at University College London.

Index